CONTENTS

KU-128-480

iii

ACKNOWLEDGEMENTS

My thanks to a number of people for commenting on early drafts of various parts of the book, in particular Brian Simon, Emeritus Professor of Education at the University of Leicester School of Education; Terry Mahoney, Tutor Organiser for the WEA in the East Midlands with responsibility for School Governor Training in Leicestershire; various senior and well-placed officials in education who must remain nameless; and Terry Allcott and all of my colleagues at the Centre for Multicultural Education in the Leicestershire Education Advisory and Inspection Service who have provided advice, intellectual stimulation and comradeship. I would also like to thank Doug Holly of the University of Leicester School of Education – his friendship, general support and inspiration over the 18 year period I spent at the School of Education has been much appreciated. I am grateful to Stephanie Boyd, my editor at Cambridge University Press, who skilfully steered me and the book through the educational upheavals of the late 1980s (the publication of the National Curriculum Consultative Document and the passing of the Education Reform Act). I have no secretary to thank – I simply express my gratitude to Hossein Faradi and his staff at Datanest, Leicester, for supplying me with the marvellous Atari ST and for general patience and assistance whenever I had a problem. Last, but not least, I would like to thank my wife, Wendy Fleming, for her advice, support and understanding during the compilation of the book.

BARRY DUFOUR

Note: I should point out that the views expressed in the parts of the book written by me are entirely my own and do not necessarily represent viewpoints and policies promoted by Leicestershire or Dorset LEA.

PREFACE

This book is about the wide range of broad curricular areas that have developed in secondary schools (and to some extent in primary schools and further education colleges) during the 1970s and 1980s. I have adopted the collective term 'the new social curriculum' to describe them. They are 'new' in the sense that their appearance in the secondary school curriculum is recent compared with traditional subjects which have been on school timetables for the larger part of this century. They are 'social' in that they all attempt to inform and educate pupils in relation to certain social institutions, social attitudes and social behaviour but, like other subjects, they concern themselves with developing knowledge, skills and attitudes, so they are very much a legitimate part of the curriculum.

It is only recently that these new subjects, perspectives or areas of study have been referred to as 'cross-curricular themes'; this has been the case since the National Curriculum 5–16 Consultation Document was published in 1987. The DES and HMI had to devise a name and a place for subjects like Health Education which otherwise might be squeezed out of the curriculum (along with all the other new areas) in order to accommodate 'the essential subjects': 'It is proposed that such subjects or themes should be taught through the foundation subjects, so that they can be accommodated within the curriculum but without crowding out the essential subjects' (*The National Curriculum 5–16: A Consultation Document*, July 1987, HMSO). In other words, necessity is the mother of invention: the invention of the concept of cross-curricular themes grew out of political, administrative and educational expedience.

These political and educational problems continued to exert pressure and were to influence the emerging form and substance of the cross-curricular themes. During 1989, the National Curriculum Council was developing its ideas on the Whole Curriculum and in particular trying to formulate guidance and implementation strategies on the cross-curricular themes. It produced an Interim Report in April which was submitted to the then Secretary of State,

Mr Kenneth Baker. This report, which would have provided early indications for the teaching profession of the nature of the themes, was withheld, partly because it lacked practical guidance and partly because the DES was concerned about possible dilution or threats to the traditional subjects of the National Curriculum ('Civil Servants anger NCC by blocking report', *Times Educational Supplement*, 29.9.89). Clues to the key content of this report were contained in the National Curriculum Council (NCC) newsletter, *NCC News*, in June 1989, and further preliminary guidance was offered in the NCC Circular No 6 (*The National Curriculum and Whole Curriculum Planning: Preliminary Guidance*) in October 1989. The themes had now become 'cross-curricular issues' which were subdivided into three categories:

● *cross-curricular dimensions*   Personal and Social Development (Personal and Social Education in the secondary schools), Cultural Diversity (Education for Life in a Multicultural Society), Equal Opportunities (Gender quality). There is also reference to developing positive attitudes towards people with disabilities. These dimensions will be interwoven into the formal and informal curriculum.

● *cross-curricular skills*   communication skills such as oracy (skills in speech), literacy, numeracy and graphicacy; skills associated with problem-solving; and study skills. These are to be promoted throughout all or most of the curriculum.

● *cross-curricular themes*   Economic and Industrial Understanding, Careers Education and Guidance, Environmental Education, Health Education, Citizenship (individual, family, community, national, European and international, including legal and political dimensions). These are less pervasive than dimensions and have strong components of knowledge and understanding as well as skills.

Throughout this book, we use the generic terms, 'themes', to refer to the themes, dimensions and skills. There is a particular emphasis on themes and dimensions in the chapters we have included in the book but teaching and learning skills are given an important role within each chapter because all the contributors explore active learning methods and problem-solving, while also featuring a wide range of classroom resources which support general study skills.

Although cross-curricular, the themes do have a closer and more natural association with the social subjects in the curriculum than with, for example, the science subjects, even though this is not exclusively the case. The social subjects include: the traditional foundation subjects such as History, Geography and Religious Education; the new social subjects, namely the social sciences comprising Sociology, Politics, Economics, Psychology and Anthropology; and various integrated approaches such as Humanities and Social Studies. Teachers and other educationists involved in the social subjects have been at the forefront in promoting the new social curriculum subjects or cross-curricular themes, often as part of, or as an offshoot from, their own courses and sometimes in preference to those courses.

This book – for teachers, parents and governors – seeks to place the themes in a social as well as an educational context. Most of the themes have been responsive to, or have grown out of, major social movements within Britain and elsewhere since the 1960s. These include the world-wide peace movement; the promotion of women's rights and equal opportunities; the anti-racist movement (including multiculturalism); the human rights movement; the world development movement to secure greater justice for the third world countries (and to narrow the North–South divide between the rich and poor nations); and the 'green' movement which, with increasing urgency, has been tackling and making people aware of the global environmental and ecological crisis. The central core of the book is educational and consists of accounts of the various cross-curricular themes by acknowledged specialists. Each contribution includes a discussion of the background, the key issues and debates in the teaching of the subject, examples of good practice in schools (and colleges, where appropriate) and a guide to key resources for teachers and pupils. The place of the themes in the National Curriculum and within the additional non-statutory curriculum is also discussed.

My own view is that the themes have a great deal to contribute across the curriculum, but they are also important as subjects that can be taught in their own right. If space can be found on the timetable, they should be offered as options in the Fourth or Fifth Years or as part of a general integrated or modular programme of Humanities.

Now that governors and parents have a more defined role to play in decisions on the curriculum, they will find this book especially timely. We have tried to make the book clear and jargon-free to make it accessible to the general reader, as well as to teachers and educationists. Where technical terms are used, they are explained in the text or in the glossary. The book will also be helpful in other ways. Some of the themes, such as Anti-racist Education and Peace Education, have been controversial and treated in a sensational manner by the popular press, whereas the accounts here attempt to be balanced and comprehensive.

We have not included all of the cross-curricular themes that might find a place in the new post-Education Reform Act curriculum such as Careers Education and Guidance. Careers Education and Guidance is not a study or subject in the same way as the other ones dealt with in this book and it already forms part of Pre-vocational Education and Personal and Social Education. However, it is a vital area for young people and must find a place in the curriculum. Aspects of citizenship such as global, international and political dimensions are included in all chapters.

Finally, I hope that hard-pressed teachers (who have not previously found the time to familiarise themselves with many of the new initiatives now required in schools) will find this book a useful guide.   *BARRY DUFOUR*

NOTES ON CONTRIBUTORS

Chris Brown was, until recently, Principal Lecturer in Education at the West Midlands College of Higher Education. He is now a freelance writer, lecturer and trainer and Associate Tutor of Wolverhampton Polytechnic. He is co-editor of the journal, *The Social Science Teacher* and author of *Understanding Society* (John Murray, 1979) and a joint editor of *Social Education: Principles and Practice* (Falmer, 1986).

Hilary Burrage is Senior Lecturer in Health and Social Studies at Wirral Metropolitan College and a Tutor for the Open University M.A. in Education (Gender and Education Unit). She began teaching in 1972, but has also worked for two years at the University of Liverpool on doctoral research concerning young people's fertility. She was Honorary Secretary of the Association for the Teaching of Social Sciences from 1985 to 1988. She has published articles on education, Sociology and Health issues in academic and professional journals.

Mike Clarke is In-service Advisory Teacher for Media Education for Essex. He has been involved in Media Education since 1977, mainly in Leicestershire where he ran the Diploma in Media Studies in Education course at Leicester University School of Education, and helped to establish a GCSE Media Studies course. His publications include: *Teaching Popular Television* (Heinemann, 1987) and *Talking Pictures: An Introduction to Media Studies* (Mary Glasgow Publications, 1981).

Barry Dufour is County Inspector for Humanities for Dorset. From 1970 to 1989, Barry Dufour has held a joint appointment with the University of Leicester School of Education and with the Leicestershire LEA. At the university, he ran courses on Multicultural Education and Race Relations but his main role was to prepare graduates to teach the Social Sciences and Humanities in schools. His

LEA work initially involved part-time teaching at an innovative comprehensive school, Countesthorpe College, of which he was a founder-member but, more recently, he has been working with the advisory service in in-service education for teachers. His publications for teachers include *The New Social Studies* (written with Denis Lawton) and *New Movements in the Social Sciences and Humanities*. He has also written books for school pupils, such as *The World of Pop and Rock*. He is a Vice-President of the Association for the Teaching of the Social Sciences, and a Fellow of the Royal Anthropological Institute. He has lectured in the USA and has been involved in educational projects in West Africa.

David Hicks was Director of the Centre for Peace Studies at St Martin's College, Lancaster, and National Co-ordinator for the World Studies 8–13 Project from 1980 to 1989. He has run workshops in Australia, Canada and Italy and has written extensively in the fields of Peace Education and World Studies. His publications include: *Minorities* (Heinemann, 1981), *Teaching World Studies*, co-editor (Longman, 1982) and *World Studies 8–13: A Teacher's Handbook*, co-author (Oliver and Boyd, 1985).

John Huckle is Head of Geography at Bedford College of Higher Education. He edited *Geographical Education: Reflection and Action* (Oxford University Press, 1983) and his recent publications include a contribution to *Teaching Geography for a Better World*, edited by J. Fien and R. Gerber (Oliver and Boyd, 1988) and a module of the World Wide Fund for Nature's *Global Environmental Education Programme*.

Ian Jamieson is Professor of Education at the University of Bath School of Education. Previously he was Head of Sociology, then Reader in Business and Management at Ealing College of Higher Education. He was Evaluator and then Research Director of the Schools Council Industry Project (SCIP). He edits the *British Journal of Education and Work*. His publications include: *Schools and Industry*, co-author (Methuen), *Mirrors of Work* (Falmer, 1988), *Industry in Education*, editor (Longman), and numerous articles in the education–industry field.

Graham Pike is a Research Fellow at the Centre for Global Education, University of York. Previously, he was Deputy Director of the Council for Education in World Citizenship. His publications include: *World Studies Resource Guide* (CEWC, 1984), *Earthrights: Education as if the Planet Really Mattered* with Sue Greig and David Selby (WWF/Kogan Page, 1987), *Global Teacher, Global Learner*, with David Selby (Hodder and Stoughton, 1988), *Human Rights: an Activity File*, with David Selby (Mary Glasgow Publications, 1988).

David Selby is Director of the Centre for Global Education at the University of York. Previously, he was Head of the Humanities Faculty at Groby Community College in Leicestershire. He has written numerous articles in the field of Global Education and his latest publications include: *Human Rights* (Cambridge University Press, 1987), *Earthrights: Education as if the Planet Really Mattered*, with Sue Greig and Graham Pike (WWF/Kogan Page, 1987), *Global Teacher, Global Learner*, with Graham Pike (Hodder & Stoughton, 1988), *Human Rights: an Activity File*, with Graham Pike (Mary Glasgow Publications, 1988).

Duncan Smith runs the Centre for Management in Education in the Hereford and Worcester LEA. From 1978 to 1987 he was a member of the School Curriculum Industry Partnership, and from 1984 to 1987, the Research Director. From 1985 to 1987, he was based at the University of Warwick, Centre for Education and Industry (with responsibility for the Research and Evaluation programme of SCIP). He has written and edited several books on education and industry themes and his latest publications include: *Exploring Trade Unions: Curriculum Principles and Practice*, with R. Wootton (Longman, for SCDC, 1988), and a volume which he has edited, *Industry in the Primary School Curriculum: Principles and Practice* (Falmer, 1988).

Janie Whyld has published many articles on sexual relationships and anti-sexist work with boys, which she developed while teaching Liberal Studies in a technical college. She edited *Sexism in the Secondary Curriculum* (Harper & Row, 1983). At the Accredited Training Centre for Buckinghamshire and Hertfordshire she organised staff development courses. She also runs workshops on sexism and racism awareness, and assertiveness-training for teachers, trade unions and community groups in her capacity as a freelance consultant.

INTRODUCTION

The relative and changing status of different forms of school knowledge is raised as a key issue at the beginning of Chapter 1. It is suggested that no intrinsic reason exists for the differential designation of 'subject' and 'cross-curricular theme', and that political and social forces have been at play as much as any educational influences. The initial priority given by the government to some areas, such as Pre-vocational and Vocational Education, as opposed to others, is explained against a background of political, economic and educational changes associated with the 'Thatcher' administration since 1979. The thrust of these changes has placed the needs of 'the market' and of industry and commerce to the fore in the formulation of social policy including educational policy. Most of the themes are seen as growing out of major social movements and campaigns from the grassroots, rather than arising from government initiatives, and they have stimulated the interest of teachers and young people. The general features of these movements are analysed, with a concluding observation that the cross-curricular themes represent issues and needs of vital relevance to young people at school and to all of us.

Given the pre-eminence of government efforts to link schools with the world of work, this is the first area to be reviewed. Ian Jamieson considers the rise of the 'new vocationalism' (Chapter 2), especially since 1979, in relation to changing economic policies and in relation to the view that economic perform-ance is associated with educational performance. The result of this has been that schools and the curriculum have been drawn more closely into the world of industry, technology and commerce. He reviews the main projects and initia-tives – TVEI, CPVE, BTEC and more – in school and post-school schemes. He also discusses critically the major issues in the new vocationalism, including some of its basic assumptions about the value and efficacy of narrowly-conceived skills-based programmes.

Skills and active-learning are also key elements in Personal and Social

Education (Chapter 3). While acknowledging the importance of PSE, Chris Brown has reservations about the lack of input from the Social Sciences in these courses. He suggests that using ideas from the Social Sciences could offer a more conceptual treatment and an understanding of social structures in society, as opposed to the individualistic philosophy often promoted in PSE which assumes that most problems in life can be solved by the improvement of personal skills. Neither is he surprised by HMI criticism of poor organisation and lack of rigour in much PSE work. Although he presents a highly critical account of many features of PSE, he goes on to present a detailed review of examples of good practice represented in well-planned courses.

Hilary Burrage (Chapter 4) alerts us to the peculiar situation of Health Education which is becoming an important area for society and school. This area is often fuelled by health promotion campaigns on such topics as AIDS and drug or alcohol abuse but there are few educational experts in the LEAs or in the Health Education Authority to advise on good integrated practices in schools, even though Health Education is high on the National Curriculum Council agenda for permeation as a cross-curricular theme.

There has been much critical reaction to the mass media which has been blamed for many ills in our society. However, as Mike Clarke demonstrates, the development of Media Education in schools (Chapter 5) was not necessarily motivated by this pessimistic view. It draws on a wider educational programme incorporating many traditions. He looks at the range of teaching methods and new resources influenced by these different approaches which are now being employed in schools, and he raises a number of points about the uncertain future of Media Education, related to initial and in-service training, the National Curriculum, and the problems of support for these initiatives in schools.

In spite of a concerted campaign from the Conservative Right against Peace Education, with accusations of bias and indoctrination, none of these criticisms has been substantiated by HMI or anyone else. David Hicks traces the rise of Peace Education (Chapter 6) to a long twentieth-century tradition of interest in international understanding and citizenship. The research and curriculum development activities proliferated in the 1980s, turning it into an important area of expertise with its own substantial body of principles, good practice and resources for teaching. These are outlined here, along with the appropriate skills, attitudes and knowledge which should be explored. As with most other themes, at the heart of Peace Education lies the emphasis on active student-centred learning and a focus on issues.

In her account of Gender Education, sexism and equal opportunities issues (Chapter 7), Janie Whyld suggests that the public are much more aware of this broad area. It suffers, however, from a low priority in schools, FE colleges and in teacher education, both in terms of attempts to raise awareness and in terms of commitments to implement change in behaviour and institutional practice. She discusses how sexism occurs in schools and colleges (in courses, inter-personal relations and institutional organisation) and then she proceeds to describe strategies for dealing with it, in the classroom and at the level of staff development.

As a major social issue for schools and society, Multicultural and Anti-racist Education (Chapter 8) is linked closely with Gender Education. Racism, like sexism, forms a central feature of British society. Institutions at all levels – government, trade unions, religious organisations, LEAs and schools – have all addressed themselves to racism and have published official pronouncements which support equal opportunities in a culturally diverse society. Most declare their opposition to racism and subscribe to policies to combat it. Since the 1950s, the educational system has been involved in policy development in response to the needs of a multi-ethnic society, although this has occurred with varying degrees of enlightenment. This history is briefly reviewed. In order to be fully applied, the complex field of Multicultural and Anti-racist Education requires awareness and action across a number of areas – racism and discrimi-nation, ethnic minority experience, language, curriculum and schooling, woven together into whole school policies. The bulk of the chapter comprises an analysis of these areas with examples of good practice.

Graham Pike notes that Global Education (Chapter 9), like other forms of education featured in this book, cannot fit easily into a subject-bound, content-oriented curriculum. Although part of his chapter is about Develop-ment Education, he surveys the aims and interdependent 'irreducible' elements of the global perspective within a socio-political and educational context. He argues that pupil-centred and active-learning strategies are equally as important as the content of this wide area, but he does not neglect a consideration of content. The chapter includes a discussion of key debates about the nature of World Studies and Global Education, much of this in response to critical attack from the political Right but some of it in relation to the National Curriculum.

The environmental crisis, the stark pronouncements of recent authoritative reports and the rise of the environmental movement are the starting points for John Huckle's analysis of Environmental Education (Chapter 10). The ideo-logical differences within the movement are reflected in various interpretations of Environmental Education in schools, with the more politically aware and holistic version appearing as an integral part of Global Education. Environ-mental Education has real potential as a cross-curricular theme and John Huckle provides a detailed list of components within a number of subject areas. It has already made an impact though, through the more broadly-based and enlightened GCSE Geography syllabuses. The increasing problems with the environment are likely to encourage the expansion of a more dynamic form of Environmental Education for all pupils.

Duncan Smith reports on a growing interest among teachers in Trade Union Education (Chapter 11). This has been associated with the formidable increase in Pre-vocational and Vocational Education in the 1980s. Trade unionists are attempting to establish a more centre-stage position in these developments, alongside representatives from industry, commerce and education. The Schools Council Industry Project (which became the School Curriculum Industry Partnership) was one of the few projects which incorporated this broad partnership. It is more common for a management view to set the agenda, neglecting the view of the labour force as represented by the trade unions. Duncan Smith considers the implications for schooling of two perspectives on the role of trade unions – the consensus model and the conflict model. In terms of work with pupils, though, he recommends a wide range of emphases, including the consideration of workplace issues, industrial action, socio-economic issues, equal opportunities, the impact of new technology, and approaches through a number of subjects and routes such as work experience, Enterprise Education and work shadowing.

In spite of the UK's commitment in 1948 to disseminate the content to schools and colleges of the UN Declaration of Human Rights, David Selby suggests there has been only minimal systematic activity, until recently, on Human Rights Education in schools and colleges (Chapter 12). Now, a variety of non-governmental organisations and networks of teachers and other educators are co-operating to support work in this field, often in harmony with initiatives in teaching about international understanding, peace, citizenship and World Studies, all of which were given justification by Recommendations from UNESCO (1974) and the Council of Europe (1985). A wide range of resources are now available which are reviewed in this chapter alongside a discussion of key concepts and teaching strategies for the classroom. Again, as with all contributions to this book, the process of learning, based on a co-operative dialogue between teacher and pupil/student, is considered to be as important as the content of the work.

In the final chapter (Chapter 13), the cross-curricular themes are analysed in the context of the National Curriculum. The general background and development of the National Curriculum is explored, followed by a detailed discussion of the various possible methods of implementation for each of the themes. The special problems and opportunities for the 14–16 curriculum are considered in relation to the need to rationalise provision at this level while also ensuring that various elements of entitlement to a broad and balanced curriculum are protected. The last part of the chapter considers the particular contribution that various people and sectors of the education system can make to the effective and successful implementation of the themes. It is suggested that teachers with expertise in the Social Sciences and Humanities can play a positive role, that the initial training of teachers will be important and that LEA advisers and inspectors will have a crucial role in providing INSET. Lastly, it is argued, much will depend on the way that parents and governors interpret their powers – it is confidently expected that they will occupy a collaborative role working with teachers and headteachers to develop good practice.

BARRY DUFOUR

1

THE NEW

SOCIAL CURRICULUM:

THE POLITICAL, ECONOMIC AND SOCIAL CONTEXT FOR EDUCATIONAL CHANGE

Barry Dufour

Curriculum, Subjects and Themes

'Education' and 'curriculum' have not been defined in any previous Education Act, although the Education Reform Act, 1988, which is about both, does depart from this tradition by providing a definition of the curriculum along with a prescriptive list of subjects that must, subsequently, be taught. It is likely that because 'education' and 'curriculum' are tied in with aims and objectives and therefore values, ideologies and philosophies, the lack of definition is a positive attraction for politicians who wish to allow for flexibility or who hope to keep their aims and intentions covert. However, a broad and useful working definition of 'curriculum', which is largely about process and leaves the aims and philosophies aside, not unsurprisingly originates from the DES:

> . . . the curriculum in its full sense comprises all the opportunities for learning provided by a school. It includes the formal programme of lessons in the timetable: the so-called 'extra-curricular' and 'out-of school' activities deliberately promoted or supported by the school, and the climate of relationships, attitudes, styles of behaviour and the general quality of life established in the school community as a whole.
>
> (DES, 1980)

The 'social curriculum' refers to aspects of the school curriculum which focus on human society, social groups, social institutions and human relationships. This area has expanded dramatically since the mid-1960s, especially in the form of social science subjects such as Sociology, and through integrated approaches such as Humanities or Social Studies. (Philip and Priest, 1965; Lawton and

Dufour, 1973; Dufour, 1982; Holly, 1986). In addition, many new areas of study, now known as the cross-curricular themes, have developed during the 1970s and 1980s. These often formed part of social science subjects or of History and Geography, sometimes they appeared within integrated approaches and sometimes stood alone. These new perspectives, subjects, themes or areas of study – the terms are not intrinsically important but they are strategically important – can be referred to collectively as 'the new social curriculum'.

Eleven areas of study are dealt with in the subsequent chapters: Pre-vocational and Vocational Education, Personal and Social Education, Health Education, Media Education, Peace Education, Gender Education, Multicultural and Anti-racist Education, Global Education, Environmental Education, Trade Union Education, and Human Rights Education. In the future, other perspectives or themes could be added because one of the essential points that can be made about these themes, and about knowledge in general, is that they are dynamic, constantly changing and influenced by social, political, economic and ideological forces. This is certainly true of all school subjects and the school curriculum in general as the work of Bernstein, Young and many others demonstrates (Bernstein, 1971; Young, 1971; Apple, 1979; Gilbert, 1984). As Bernstein says:

> How a society selects, classifies, distributes, transmits and evaluates the educational knowledge it considers to be public, reflects both the distribution of power and the principles of social control.   (Bernstein, 1971)

Or, as Young suggests:

> Education has been based on an absolutist conception of a set of distinct forms of knowledge which correspond closely to the traditional areas of the academic curriculum and thus justify rather than examine, what are no more than socio-historical constructs of a particular time. (Young, 1971)

This debate is pertinent to the themes analysed in this book for several reasons, but especially in relation to the educational decade from 1979 to 1989 which witnessed the Conservative Government of Mrs Thatcher institute a radical programme of educational change culminating in the passing of the Education Reform Act in 1988 and its implementation in the 1990s. The curriculum proposals in the Act include a selective list of mandatory subjects to be taught. There is no philosophical discussion in the Act or in related papers, such as the consultation document (DES, 1987), which justifies the particular selection. Furthermore, there has been little official guidance on the identification and justification for the areas of study – called 'cross-curricular themes' (a term adopted by DES and HMI) – that form part of the government-defined National Curriculum or additional subject curriculum. Up until 1989, educationists had to rely on contacts and informants within the DES, HMI and the new National Curriculum Council in order to discover which themes were to be featured and whether some would be merged or subsumed within others or discarded.

Even more crucial, is the lack of definition or justification of what constitutes a 'subject' or a 'theme'. Whatever the case, in terms of the control and relative status of different forms of knowledge, the public and legal requirement to teach certain 'subjects' contained in the 1988 Act compared with the 'private' or 'non-public' deliberations on the 'themes' at the National Curriculum Council during the early part of 1989, clearly signals the importance and merit of the 'subjects' in contrast with the 'themes'. Goodson looks at the history of a number of 'subjects' and explores the general issues surrounding the legitimation of growing areas of knowledge as subjects. Some of the key factors in the process involve the extent and nature of professional and educational interest groups, the vested power and influence from the academic establishment in the universities, and 'climates of opinion' (Goodson, 1983).

In the case of the debate about the National Curriculum and the themes discussed in this book, it would seem that two other factors are equally as relevant:
1   Government support, to the extent of sponsorship or legislation
2   pressure group activity associated with major social movements and social forces.

For example, TVEI, an idea thought up by a small group of senior government ministers in 1982 (Sir Keith Joseph, Norman Tebbit, Lord Young), has become a central feature of educational provision along with the numerous other pre-vocational and vocational initiatives. These might be called 'top–down' initiatives.

'Bottom–up' initiatives from grassroots pressure groups or wide-scale social movements have also influenced subjects, topics and themes in the school curriculum although the precise relationship between them has still to be researched; at present this can only be the subject of speculation.

The Themes: Similarities and Differences

Each of the themes discussed in this book has its own unique position in the school curriculum. Some of them, such as Multicultural Education, have become 'whole-school' issues and therefore should affect all aspects of the life of a school including the curriculum. The same is true of Gender Education and its wider manifestation, Equal Opportunities. Some of the perspectives gained a foothold as 'studies', especially at the 14–16 age level (as CSE and GCE courses and later as GCSE courses). Examples of these include Media Studies, Peace Studies and World Studies. Their popularity has been growing, reaching down into the 11–14 age group and sometimes into the primary school. Other areas, such as Personal and Social Education (PSE), have become widespread for all ages, including, more recently, primary school levels. Although PSE enjoys wide provision at the 14–16 age range, it is non-examinable which adds to its uncertain status. Health Education has also been afflicted by a similar ambiguity, partly because it too is non-examined or non-assessed and casually slotted into parts of the curriculum – into Biology, or into Home Economics or PSE. Ecological and environmental issues have for a long time been a constituent part of many Geography and general Environmental Studies or World Studies courses. General civil rights issues have been covered in courses on Human Rights or Trade Unions although these themes have been somewhat neglected in schools: this situation is slowly changing now with the appearance of good teaching and learning materials. The most pervasive cross-curricular perspective has been Pre-vocational Education which, under many guises and acronyms such as TVEI, has spread through secondary schools and colleges in England and Wales.

All of the cross-curricular perspectives have much in common. They have all developed their own educational theories, conceptual structures, content, rationales, teaching methods and curriculum resources, along with a range of professional curriculum organisations and other forms of representation and expertise. They deserve to be taken seriously. But in spite of this, many of the themes or subjects have something else in common – they have been at the centre of intense debate and opposition from members of the Thatcher government, the media and sometimes the educational community. Many teachers, parents, governors and the public in general have found it difficult to acquaint themselves with these subjects, partly because there has often been more rhetoric than reality in the claims and counter-claims of popular discourse, and partly because each subject has become a specialist area with its own substantial literature, expertise and jargon. And although many teachers themselves have been cool towards some of the themes it has not always been as a result of deep conservatism and lack of interest. Initial and in-service programmes for teachers on the cross-curricular themes have been few and far between, so that teachers have often been unable to make informed judgements about the themes and unable to promote good practice in their schools and colleges. But the opposition towards many of the themes and the acceptance or popularity of others can be better understood when education, and not just the curriculum, is placed in a historical, political, economic and social context.

The Political and Economic Background: The 1960s and 1970s

There are several key features in the economic and political landscape as it relates to education from the 1960s to the 1980s, which form an essential part of a map for our understanding of this period and possibly for the 1990s. The 1960s

experienced a dramatic growth in educational investment and provision supported by a prevailing belief in the power of education to fulfil a number of
individual, social and economic ends – namely, to assist the development of
individuals to their full potential, to achieve equality of opportunity in society
and to make a positive impact on general economic growth.

Conversely, the 1970s were characterised by severe economic problems such
as inflation and zero growth. The oil crisis of 1973, when the price of oil
quadrupled, had a major effect on the world economy. In Britain, the economic
problems became associated with an increasing pessimism and a loss of faith in
the fruits and benefits of ever-increasing State expenditure on education –
especially with regard to its impact on economic growth. Criticism of education
was coming from several parts of the political spectrum, especially from the
Conservative Right (through the publication of the Black Papers and other
right-wing critiques of education) whose views were regularly receiving sympathetic coverage in the popular press (Cox and Dyson, 1969, 1970; Boyson, 1975;
for press coverage, CCCS, 1981). But it was the speech of a Labour Party Prime
Minister, Mr Callaghan, at Ruskin College, Oxford, in 1976, which acted as a
focus and watershed for educational debate thereafter. His speech reflected
concern about standards and about a curriculum that failed to link with the
needs of the economy and the world of work. Much of this concern had been
expressed by industrialists, many of whom were quite clear where the problem
lay. As Brian Simon observes:

> ... the immediacy – indeed suddenness – of the crisis that shook this
> country, together with others, forced a search for a scapegoat. Industrial-
> ists, whose confidence was shaken, turned on the schools. These, it was
> claimed, were failing to produce young people with the skills required by
> industry. It was not industry or industrialists that were at fault; still less
> the economic and financial system as a whole. It was the schools – and, it
> followed, the teachers and the local authorities responsible for local
> systems, so a widespread attack, and critique, was mounted.
>
> (Simon, 1988)

Sections of the Labour Party and the Conservative Party seemed to be in
agreement that preparation for life, especially in the form of Pre-vocational
Education and school–industry links, would provide part of an answer to the
economic problems. The other 'answers', it was to be discovered, would be
provided by Mrs Thatcher and the Conservative Party in the 1980s, but it is
notable that the genesis of these later policies are located in the 1970s, including
the roots of the major 1980s initiatives and funding for Pre-vocational Education.

The Conservative Right had also made a number of other criticisms of
education, claiming that standards were low, that teaching methods were slack

5

and lacked rigour, that the curriculum should revert to a sharper concentration on 'basics', and that discipline in schools should be tightened. Much of the argument centred on the debate between traditional and progressive education, although these concepts were often ill-defined or caricatured. The backlash against 'liberal' notions of education, with rallying cries from a 'Back-to-Basics' movement, was a feature of Western Europe and the USA as well as the UK (Husen, 1979; Shor, 1986). The genesis of a prescribed basic National Curriculum and a rigorous system of national testing for the 1990s can be perceived here.

The 1980s: The 'Thatcher Project'

Husen may not have been surprised at what happened in the UK in the year his book was being published: in 1979, the Conservative Party critique of education gained a powerful ascendancy with the election of a Conservative government and with Mrs Thatcher as Prime Minister. She had been a Minister of Education in the 1970s and had provided continuity for the Conservative Party view of education from the 1970s into the 1980s (in alliance with right-wing educationists and policy makers). Many of the Black Paper perspectives and the recommendations of other right-wing thinkers became policy during the 1980s, culminating in the passing of the Education Reform Act on 29 July 1988 – the most radical piece of educational legislation since the Education Act, 1944. (The curriculum component of the Act is discussed in more detail in Chapter 13.)

By observing policy development and drawing on speeches, interviews and other statements from the Prime Minister and her colleagues since, many political commentators and educationists, of all political persuasions, have outlined the elements of what has been called 'Thatcherism', or 'the Thatcher Project' by some analysts. There are many political and economic overviews of the essence of 'Thatcherism' (for example, Minogue and Biddiss, 1987; Jessop, Bonnett, Bromley and Ling, 1988; Hall, 1988), but very few scholarly and detailed critiques of the last decade from educationists. Recently, however, several educationists, educational historians and educational sociologists have published their critiques (for example Chitty, 1989).

'Thatcherism' amounts to a concerted attempt to change the ideological climate and economic structure of Britain, with the intention to break the 'post-war consensus' – on the Welfare State (health, social security, education, housing and all other sectors), on the commitment to full employment, and on détente in the realm of defence. The commitment to a market economy and an enterprise society is at the core of the project. It involves a rejection of Keynesian economics and a determination to break up and privatise the collectivist public and social institutions: the nationalised industries are being 'sold off' and most sectors of the Welfare State are being partly privatised. 'Popular capitalism' is being promoted through the sale of council houses, through the extension of home-ownership and share-ownership and through the encouragement of consumerism. At the same time, paradoxically, drawing on the power bestowed by three successive election victories in 1979, 1983 and 1987, 'Thatcherism' has increasingly centralised the power of the State.

'Thatcherism' in Education

The same forces have been at work in education. All sectors of education have endured financial cuts, from the universities through to the primary schools, and all of them have been subject to increasing government direction on how to spend their money or how to raise it. The universities, for example, have had pressure placed on them, through limited funding, to reduce their reliance on public financing and to encourage them to seek greater levels of private funding via entrepreneurial initiatives. The esteem of the state comprehensive school system has been called into question through the Assisted Places Scheme, set up by the Education Act, 1980, to provide public money to send a selected number of state school pupils to private schools, with the implication that all state comprehensive schools are intrinsically inferior to all private schools.

The autonomy, power and influence of teachers and the LEAs have been increasingly eroded through a variety of measures, in terms of their relationship with central government and with regard to their relationship with their schools. With the introduction of the Teachers' Pay and Conditions Act, 1987, teachers have had their negotiating rights withdrawn and a non-negotiated contract imposed on them by the government. LEAs have been subject to increasingly government-directed financial controls and to an increase in government prioritisation of INSET expenditure. Teachers and the LEAs have experienced a reduction in influence on their own schools because the Education Acts of 1980 and 1986 extended the power of parents and governors. The Education Reform Act, 1988, enhanced this even further by delegating certain financial, management and curricular responsibilities to the governors, and it gave parents more choice in the selection of schools for their children, termed 'open enrolment' in the Act.

In a general way, the 1988 Act incorporates most of the political, economic, ideological and educational thinking of the Conservative Government and combines unprecedented devolution in certain spheres, especially in matters of economics, with an equally unprecedented extension of state power. The devolution operates by requiring educational institutions themselves (rather than the LEA) to stand on their own feet and to be responsible for good house management and prudent financial control. Parents are free to choose the most suitable school for their children. Parents can also decide, through a ballot,

7

whether the school their children attend should 'opt out' and acquire grant-maintained status. All of this is directly in the tradition of market choice, entrepreneurial initiative and popular consumerism, all hallmarks of 'Thatcherite' economic policy and very much in line with the Thatcher populist appeal.

Conversely, the 'Thatcherite' commitment to a 'free' economy, has gone hand in hand with the creation of a strongly centralised state. Under the 1988 Act, vast new powers accrue to the Secretary of State for Education. It is not appropriate here to discuss these complex and detailed features of the Act but some readers might like to consult the Act itself (HMSO, 1988), or refer to a concise guide to the Act (Maclure, 1988), or read an illuminating critique of it (Simon, 1988). Probably the most important and historically significant part of the Act, although occupying only a few pages of the 284-page document, is the first section, which announces the imposition of a centrally-directed National Curriculum and assessment programme on all LEA primary and secondary schools. As Aldrich observes, the list of ten subjects (eleven, if Religious Education is included) is virtually identical to the 1904 Board of Education syllabus (Lawton and Chitty, 1988). The new subjects and new areas of specialism, such as the cross-curricular themes, which have evolved since the beginning of the century, are absent from the itemised list in the Act. These new subjects and themes have been at the centre of intense lobbying by various academic and professional subject associations. Many have been scrutinised by National Curriculum Council officers and working parties who are responsible for making recommendations on their form, content and implementation. (They are discussed in more detail in Chapter 13 of this book.) What seems to cause grave concern amongst many educationists – amidst doubts about the survival of many of these subjects and themes in the future school curriculum – is that the attitudes and 'climate of opinion' within the Conservative government since 1979 have often been openly hostile to many of these subjects. Senior members of the government have derided some of them, including Mrs Thatcher who aimed a rebuke at Anti-racism by saying 'children who need to be able to count and multiply are learning Anti-racist Mathematics – what ever that might be' (Pimm, 1988). And many influential members of the Conservative Right have consistently ridiculed Peace Education, Anti-racist Education, World Studies, Gender Education and many other themes (Scruton, 1985; O'Keefe, 1986).

It would not be unfair to deduce from this a certain animus towards, not only many of the social subjects and themes, but also towards many of the social movements and the social ideologies and reform programmes which they possibly represent. However, it needs to be demonstrated that the social movements are a major feature of modern life and that young people need an opportunity to study the issues they represent, in the classroom, taking due account of the requirement in the 1986 Act for a balanced presentation.

Social Movements

One of the most important changes in the social and political structure in the post-war world has been the rise of social movements associated with particular social issues and social forces linked to the promotion of equality and justice. These movements and the issues they represent are now part of the political agenda in most Western countries and in Eastern and Third World countries. They include:

- the peace movement
- the women's movement
- the movement for racial equality
- the environmental movement
- the movement for human rights and civil liberties
- the movement for development and justice for the Third World
- the health movement

Most of them gained impetus in the liberating and optimistic decade of the 1960s. By the 1980s they had established themselves not only in the political and social structure of the UK, but also in the education system, to varying degrees, as specialist areas of the curriculum. The involvement of teachers in these movements could partly explain their introduction into the curriculum. The issues represented in the movements touch many aspects of daily life, directly or indirectly, through institutional and ideological arrangements.

They have a number of features in common:

(a)   They all represent a broad spectrum of political opinions across party lines and, even though some appear to be associated with 'liberal' or radical positions, they are not necessarily linked with particular parties. They are represented and promoted through a wide range of pressure groups and organisations, ranging, in the UK, from the charities to the overtly political and 'agitprop' lobbies, although the distinction is not easily maintained.

(b)   Over time, most have moved from the margin and closer to the mainstream of political decision-making about the nature of our society. No political party in Britain can ignore the issues and perspectives they represent, which are about basic human rights and the state of the planet. The broad debates are an irreversible part of the agenda of established politics and, in one case, a political party, the Green Party, has been formed, in 1986, to campaign on one of the main issues – the environment. All are world-wide and still gaining momentum.

(c)   All are characterised, to some degree, by a politics-from-below. They typically operate through pressure groups and grassroots organisations and part of their function is to influence local and central government, although some major areas of concern such as the environment have ministerial representation

9

while others have quangos such as the Commission for Racial Equality or the Equal Opportunities Commission. All embody and promote a range of moral and social values which are liberal, humanitarian and co-operative and tending towards a concern for greater equality and justice.

(d) Membership and involvement in these movements embrace all sections of society. The professional classes, such as teachers, are well represented.

(e) Many of the movements engage the interest, commitment and participation of young people of school age and older. This last point is crucial for an understanding of the importance of the cross-curricular themes.

Young People, the Curriculum and Society

Young people are not all racists or football hooligans! Large numbers of them are interested and involved in the social movements because they care about others and the future of the planet. In November 1988, an all-party 'Commission on Citizenship' was announced, chaired by the Speaker of the House of Commons. It was set up because of 'a concern that in the United Kingdom no formal mechanism currently exists to recognise the contribution that people are currently making to the community as active citizens, in and beyond school' (*New Statesman & Society*, 25.11.88). The idea came from Community Service Volunteers, and at the launch it was suggested that examining boards might give awards to schoolchildren for 'active citizenship'. Apparently, badges were mentioned. It seemed to be defining citizenship as a matter of volunteering rather than of political rights. Many young people at the launch were not happy about this. They did not do voluntary work so they could earn badges and recognition – they did it because they believed in it and wanted to play their part in being concerned about others, about their society and about the state of the planet as a whole. This attitude was well-illustrated when thousands of people, young and old, responded to the haunting television pictures of the Ethiopian famine during late 1984 and 1985. 'Band Aid' mobilised human emotions and resources and galvanised people from all backgrounds to action. Countless numbers of young people participated in or watched the world broadcast of the 'Live Aid' concert on 13 July 1985. By the time the television satellites had been switched off, £50 million had been pledged to Band Aid's Ethiopian Fund. People of all ages had donated money, so it was not just a youth event. But what did involve young people in particular were the thousands of fund-raising events they organised in their schools, their youth clubs and local community halls. Even more pertinent to the subject of this book was the flow of school classroom projects on Ethiopia and related subjects – on development and the Third World, race, women, the environment, health, peace and human rights: all linked with the major social movements discussed above (Dufour, 1986). Rather than have this kind of work just as a response to significant events – no bad strategy in itself – all pupils should have the opportunity to learn about these particular cross-curricular themes as a planned and legitimate part of their curriculum, with due consideration for balanced treatment as required in the 1986 Act.

Other cross-curricular issues also have a vital role to play in the education of young people. Pre-vocational Education, for example, will certainly survive and flourish because all schools are now engaged in it in some form or other and the government will continue to give it priority. It may also persist because it offers the hope of employment opportunities to many young people, even if, as Finn suggests, it may also be a smokescreen for the absence of real jobs for large numbers of young people (Finn, 1987). Furthermore, educationists will need to be vigilant to ensure that a pattern does not develop whereby working class children follow the pre-vocational route while academic tracking becomes the stronghold of the middle class, thus contributing to differential opportunity in British society. Hopefully, education about trade unions may find an enhanced role in Pre-vocational Education and in other subjects as well as in its more regular site in the School Curriculum Industry Partnership (SCIP).

Media Education deserves a more extensive role than being simply tagged on to English (DES, 1988). The media play an increasingly central part in our lives and it may be that television, for example, begins to rival school in its impact on young people. The DES argued in 1983 that Media Education could be an ingredient in all subjects – perhaps this formulation should be followed.

Finally, Personal and Social Education should continue as a wide spread provision in the school curriculum. It has many possibilities because of its flexibility. It is a convenient site for educating young people about drugs, AIDS, alcohol and any other health or social issue that comes along in future but it can also contribute to a broad general education.

All of the cross-curricular themes impinge on the lives of young people and are directly relevant to the world in which they are growing up. They all relate to the individual, to society and to the future of the planet. As a matter of entitlement, all school pupils should have the opportunity to encounter the issues and subject-matter at the heart of the cross-curricular themes. And, while the status and context of different forms of knowledge will continue to be influenced by political and ideological considerations, political partiality should not be allowed to influence the final choice and status of particular subjects and cross-curricular themes for the school curriculum. The only question that should be asked is an educational one – how can all the subjects and themes fit into the curriculum? Some answers are provided in the final chapter of this book and in the specialist contributions below. In the end, the only institutions which can make these decisions must be the schools themselves but it is hoped that teachers, governors and parents (with guidance and support from the LEA) will take proper account of the needs and interests of pupils.

References and Further Resources

M. W. Apple, *Ideology and Curriculum* (Routledge and Kegan Paul, 1979)

B. Bernstein, in M. F. D. Young (ed.), *Knowledge and Control* (Collier–Macmillan, 1971)

R. Boyson, *The Crisis in Education* (Woburn Press, 1975)

C. B. Cox and A. E. Dyson (eds.), 'Black Paper 2: The Crisis in Education', *Critical Quarterly Society* (1969, 1970)

CCCS, *Unpopular Education* (Hutchinson, 1981)
Contains a detailed analysis of the educational coverage in the *Daily Mail* and *Daily Mirror* from 1975–1977. (CCCS are the initials of the Centre for Contemporary Cultural Studies based at Birmingham University)

C. Chitty, *Towards a New Education System: The Victory of the New Right 1976–88?* (Falmer, 1989)

DES, *A View of the Curriculum* (HMSO, 1980)

DES, *Popular TV and Schoolchildren* (HMSO, 1983)

DES, *The National Curriculum 5–16: A Consultation Document* (HMSO, 1987)

DES, *English for Ages 5 to 11* (HMSO, 1988)

B. Dufour (ed.), *New Movements in the Social Sciences and Humanities* (Maurice Temple Smith/Gower, 1982)

B. Dufour, in 'Teaching and Learning about Youth' in *The Social Science Teacher*, vol. 15, no. 3 (1986) (Special Edition on Young People)

D. Finn, *Training Without Jobs* (Macmillan, 1987)

R. Gilbert, *The Impotent Image: Reflections of Ideology in the Secondary School Curriculum* (Falmer, 1984)

I. Goodson, *School Subjects and Curriculum Change* (Croom Helm, 1983)

S. Hall, *The Hard Road to Renewal* (Verso, 1988)

HMSO, *The Education Reform Act 1988* (HMSO, 1988)

D. Holly (ed.), *Humanism in Adversity: Teachers' Experience of Integrated Humanities in the 1980s* (Falmer, 1986)

T. Husen, *The School in Question* (Oxford University Press, 1979)

B. Jessop, K. Bonnett, S. Bromley, T. Ling, *Thatcherism* (Polity Press, 1988)

D. Lawton and C. Chitty (eds.), 'The National Curriculum' in *Bedford Way Papers 33* (Institute of Education, University of London, 1988)

D. Lawton and B. Dufour, *The New Social Studies* (Heinemann Educational Books, 1973)

S. Maclure, *Education Re-formed: A Guide to the Education Reform Act, 1988* (Hodder and Stoughton, 1988)

K. Minogue and M. Biddiss, *Thatcherism: Personality and Politics* (Macmillan, 1987)

D. O'Keefe, *The Wayward Curriculum* (Short Run Press, 1986)

W. Philip and K. Priest, *Social Science and Social Studies in Secondary Schools* (Longman, 1965)

D. Pimm (ed.), *Mathematics, Teachers and Children* (Hodder and Stoughton/Open University Press, 1988)

R. Scruton, *World Studies: Education or Indoctrination?* (Institute for European Defence and Strategic Studies, 1985)

I. Shor, *Culture Wars: School and Society in the Conservative Restoration 1969–1984* (Routledge and Kegan Paul, 1986)

B. Simon, *Bending the Rules: The Baker 'Reform' of Education* (Lawrence and Wishart, 1988)

M. F. D. Young (ed.), *Knowledge and Control* (Collier–Macmillan, 1971)

Key Teacher Resources

J. Haviland (ed.), *Take Care, Mr Baker! (A Selection from the Advice on Education which the Government Collected but Decided not to Publish)* (Fourth Estate, 1988)
An edited collection of the 20,000 submissions sent to the government in response to Mr Baker's consultation papers which outlined most of the ideas later set out in the Act. There are no systematic public comments on these by the government and none of the submissions were ever published. They are now stored in the House of Commons library. This is an opportunity to read some and to gauge public opinion.

B. Jessop, K. Bonnett, S. Bromley and T. Ling, *Thatcherism* (Polity Press, 1988)
A view from the Left.

S. Maclure, *Education Re-formed (A Guide to the Education Reform Act, 1988)* (Hodder and Stoughton, 1988)
An invaluable summary of the Act written by the editor of *The Times Educational Supplement*. His comments and background analysis are illuminating.

K. Minogue and M. Biddiss (eds.), *Thatcherism (Personality and Politics)* (Macmillan, 1987)
A view from the Right.

B. Simon, *Bending the Rules (The Baker 'Reform' of Education)* (Lawrence and Wishart, 1988)
A carefully researched and powerful critique of the Act, exploring its ideological antecedents and intentions.

H. Young, *One of Us* (Macmillan, 1989)
A balanced and important biography of Margaret Thatcher and her period as Prime Minister.

2

PRE-VOCATIONAL AND

VOCATIONAL EDUCATION:

THE NEW VOCATIONALISM, ECONOMIC UNDERSTANDING AND THE WORLD OF WORK

Ian Jamieson

Origins

Vocationalism is not a new phenomenon in the education system of Britain, even though it is now at the centre of the debate about the nature and purpose of education in our society. The original use of the term vocation was to denote a 'calling' for the liberal professions (e.g. teaching, medicine and the law). The education offered in Britain's grammar schools in the post-war period was vocational for those middle class children who were destined to enter the traditional professions. It is only since the word vocational has become associated with occupations engaged in manufacturing industry and commerce that we talk of a separation of the world of schooling from the world of employment.

The process of separation between school and work is a complex one and cannot be discussed here in any detail. There were two main influences. The first is related to the nature of Britain's industrialisation. In the nineteenth century the Industrial Revolution created, at least in its initial stages, conditions of considerable squalor and degradation for the workforce – witness the power of that phrase 'the dark satanic mills' which is with us still. These conditions dissuaded those in charge of the nascent education system from drawing too closely to the industrial world. The second main influence concerns those very people who had power and influence over the education system. They were drawn from those strata in British society which had little in common with the world of industry – although rather more with commerce (Rubenstein, 1988). They represented 'old money' rather than 'new money'. Their influence was such that they managed to successfully insulate schools from direct associations with the new industrial order (Perkin, 1972).

One of the distinguishing features of education in the nineteenth century is that it was strongly differentiated both by social class and gender. This differentiation continued strongly into the twentieth century in the recognition that children were destined for very different occupations. The Education Act 1944 represented a public recognition of the fact that not only were children different one from another, but that economy and society were also differentiated. The curriculum of the grammar school followed that of the public schools with its emphasis on the manipulation of abstract knowledge and literary culture. Its sights were set on the higher reaches of the white-collar world and the professions. The technical schools, although largely stillborn, were to have a curriculum appropriate for the technician class, so important for Britain's manufacturing base. Finally, the secondary modern schools were to have a curriculum which was thought appropriate for the mass working class of an advanced industrial society.

The education offered in the schools of the tripartite system might be called vocational in the sense that it was thought to be fitted to the likely occupations of the incumbents. The fit however was a loose one; there was little direct association between the curriculum and the demands of the likely occupations. The most appropriate term for this loose coupling is one that only made its appearance in the latter part of the 1970s – i.e. Pre-vocational Education, that is education which prepares the basis for a more specific occupational education and training.

What changes did the move towards comprehensive education make in the 1960s? The comprehensive school movement was largely driven by the political demands for equality of opportunity. Equality of opportunity was translated into access to those well paid jobs in the middle and upper orders of society. The arguments were both political and economic. The economic argument was explained in terms of the meritocracy – the education system must make sure that it was allowing everybody with talent to rise into these important and demanding occupations. In curriculum terms this meant that the pre-vocational curriculum of the liberal professions dominated, whilst an education that might have been more suited to the technicians, clerks and the factory workers languished. To have offered such an education in the 1960s might not have been in keeping with the 'grammar schools for all' philosophy espoused by the then Prime Minister, Mr Wilson.

The Modern Period

In the 1970s the debate about the school curriculum moved onto the political agenda. The 'secret garden' of the curriculum for so long tended only by the professionals was opened up. The Prime Minister of the day, Mr Callaghan, is often credited with this act through his Ruskin speech of 1976 which launched the 'Great Debate' about education. In fact Mr Callaghan was only reflecting a debate which had started some years previously. There were several strands to the ensuing discussions. Firstly, it was argued that educational standards were falling (or at least were not high enough). Secondly, education was too remote from the needs of the economy. The performance of the economy was the major underlying reason for the scrutiny of the content of education. As Reeder (1981) has shown, at almost every historical period when the industrial economy has slumped, the performance of the education system has come in for close attention with calls for it to move closer to the needs of industry and the economy.

Britain has had a declining economy since the middle of the last century. One of the most striking of all historical observations is that 'in the course of little more than a century Britain had fallen from the top to almost the bottom of the leading group of industrial nations' (Feinstein, 1988). The economic policies of 'Thatcherism' embraced monetarism in their attempt to control inflation and this objective displaced the traditional economic policy objective of full employment which had been followed by all governments since the end of the Second World War. In addition to policies to combat inflation, 'Thatcherism' pursued a ferocious assault on the 'supply side' problems of the economy, by regulating aspects of production rather than demand (for example, through tax advantages to enterprises, in order to improve productivity). The two main features of the supply side strategy were an attack on trade union distortions of the market and the stress on the primacy of market forces, e.g. the privatisation programme. Whatever the merits of these policies, and we should note that it is widely believed that Britian's relative standing in terms of growth of real GDP and productivity has improved considerably since 1979 (Crafts, 1988), the initial effects on British manufacturing industry were severe. Very large numbers of manufacturing companies and jobs disappeared. Manufacturing industry lost one third of its work-force in seven years and now employs less than a quarter of the working population (Central Statistical Office, 1988). It was initially argued that many of these economic changes were cyclical in nature, that is that they were part of an economic downturn that would, through the process of the business cycle, turn up again. However, such was the decimation of British manufacturing industry during this short period that this analysis began to look increasingly unsound. Whilst it may be true that slimmed down firms may be more efficient and thus more competitive, the same can hardly be argued for firms which have gone out of business altogether. Now that the service sector employs two thirds of the domestic labour force and manufacturing facilities have grown up in many parts of the Third World (particularly the 'new Japans', e.g. Taiwan, South Korea and the Phillipines) there must be some doubt about Britain's ability to once again be an important manufacturing nation. The barriers to entry in manufacturing are much higher than in the service sector and it is widely accepted that domestic finance capital does not like the long-term horizons required by manufacturing industry for return on capital (Walker, 1985; Fifield, 1987). Furthermore, there is overwhelming evidence to suggest that Britain does not have the highly skilled labour force that would be capable of supporting a high tech/high value-added manufacturing industry (Keep and Mayhew, 1988).

During these years of economic turmoil the information technology revolution began to have an effect by radically changing the nature of jobs. In one or two cases the change was dramatic. The printing industry underwent a fundamental revolution. Hot metal technology and letterpress printing were replaced by computerised typesetting, changing both the skills required of the printer and the economics of the business. An equally dramatic change was witnessed in the trading of financial services and this was epitomised by the change to screen-based trading on the Stock Exchange. The changes arising from new technology have been greatly exaggerated (Jamieson and Tasker, 1988; Webster and Robins, 1986; Wellington, 1987) but the potential for a radical restructuring of jobs, work skills and organisation structures is certainly there.

It was these economic and technological changes that were the prime cause of the re-evaluation of the content of education, and it was a re-evaluation that had the broad support of all the political parties. However, it is possible to chart a growing loss of confidence in the education system from a broad spectrum of political life. For those on the political Right, educational standards were not high enough (and were even falling) although it was difficult to find much evidence to support the latter view. The political Right and Centre were also inclined to put at least part of the blame for the high levels of youth unemployment on the education system – it wasn't producing young people with the right blend of skills, attitudes, knowledge and competencies. Such a view was not supported on the political Left who saw the lack of jobs as a straightforward supply side problem. The political Left were more concerned that the comprehensive schools had apparently not provided the avenue for social mobility for the sons and daughters of the working class. A major reason for this, it was argued, was because the comprehensive schools had adopted a curriculum and ethos of the old grammar schools (Reynolds and Sullivan, 1987).

Certainly there was increasing concern that the curriculum of the maintained schools needed reform. Teachers working in the system recognised that there was an increasing 'revolt from below'. Students in the bottom 40 per cent of the ability range, who were formally neglected by the public examination system, began to show increasing unrest with the traditional academic curriculum. A variety of 'solutions' were proposed. From very different traditions, Bantock (1971) and Hargreaves (1982) both supported a curriculum which stressed the arts, including the practical arts, and links with the local community.

Hargreaves proposed this for all children whilst Bantock reserved his offering for the less able.

Because there was a widespread belief that there must be a close connection, if not a direct link, between economic performance and the education system, the education systems of Britain's successful economic competitors were closely scrutinised. As the UK was a member of the European Community, particular attention was paid to the educational procedures of member countries. New developments in Pre-vocational and Vocational Education, in transition pro-grammes, and in alternance programmes (where work and education are combined) were studied (CEDEFOP, 1984). The National Economic Develop-ment Office published *Competence and Competition* (NEDO, 1984), which presented a detailed examination of the education and training systems of Japan, West Germany and the USA. The common thread to all of these developments is the importance of the vocational dimension to education. The new vocationalism is not the product of a special set of circumstances in Britain in the late 1970s and 1980s – it is a phenomenon of nearly all the advanced industrial nations. Although its features may differ in detail, the countries of the European Community as well as Australia and Canada and the USA are all experiencing similiar developments.

The New Vocationalism

The term the 'new vocationalism' is used to describe the large number of developments that have occurred in Britain from the middle of the 1970s to the present time. There are so many initiatives and developments that it is almost impossible to chart them all, let alone place them in chronological order and see how they fit together. It is in fact difficult to see how many of them do fit into a coherent whole and this must be our first observation. The economic crisis caused a turmoil in society, and educational initiatives were launched and relaunched by a wide variety of bodies to remedy the ill – the result was often uncoordinated chaos (CBI, 1988).

The various arms of government have been the prime movers of most of the important developments and this in itself is something new. In the devolved system of education in England and Wales it has traditionally been the LEAs in partnership with schools and colleges which have initiated curriculum change, or the LEAs in partnership with the teacher unions and government working together in a body like the Schools Council.

The government was faced with a dilemma. It believed that radical change was needed in the education and training field if some of Britain's economic (and educational) problems were to be solved, and yet it saw itself as a relatively powerless actor. The traditional role of the DES was to act as paymaster to the

LEAs and to offer advice on how the money should be spent. It became increasingly clear that not only were very many LEAs not heeding that advice, but that few had any detailed knowledge of what went on in their own schools.

One of the first moves by the government was to launch the Lower Achieving Pupils Project (LAPP), a DES sponsored project, launched in 1982, which offered money directly to LEAs in return for the delivery of a programme of direct action in schools. The LAPP programme for 14- to 16-year-olds was designed to help lower-attaining pupils 'who are not benefiting fully from school' in basic skills acquisition and appreciation of industry, commerce and technology. The programmes were designed to be deliberately experimental, with LEAs exploring new ways of delivering education 'with a practical slant'.

The Technical and Vocational Education Initiative

LAPP was a DES initiative, but one of the most important policies in the field of Pre-vocational and Vocational Education did not come from the education ministry. In 1982 in a speech to the House of Commons the Prime Minister expressed '. . . a growing concern about existing arrangements for Technical and Vocational Education for young people', and asked the Manpower Services Commission (MSC), together with the DES, to develop a pilot scheme. This was the birth of the Technical and Vocational Education Initiative (TVEI) which started as a pilot scheme in 14 LEAs and by the mid 1990s should cover most maintained schools in England, Wales and Scotland. The objectives of the TVEI are to help young people to prepare for the world of work; to contribute to the life of the community; and to learn to adjust to the changing occupational environment. In curriculum terms young people are to experience a broad curriculum which integrates general and technical/vocational education (with work experience) through an integrated provision for the 14–18 age range.

Several features of the TVEI are worth highlighting because they have implications for the whole way in which the education system is to be run. The government's main technique for dramatic change in the system (and few deny that the TVEI is a dramatic change) is through the device of 'categorical funding' (Harland, 1987). The government has made enormous sums of money available for the TVEI and for related in-service training provision (TRIST/GRIST). In fact, by 1988 the sum stood at over £1 billion. The LEAs only have access to this if they spend the money in ways that meet the priorities and criteria set down by central government. In a period when LEAs have been under severe financial constraint few have resisted the 'golden hook'.

In curriculum terms TVEI has been seen by some as the 'technician's revenge' and an attempt to raise the status of a range of technical subjects which have hitherto operated on the fringe of schools. The two most important subject areas for many of these initiatives have been Technology and Business Studies. Both of these have been 'Cinderella' areas in the secondary school curriculum – from either side of the gender divide. Technology arose from male dominated craft subjects, whilst Business Studies has evolved from female dominated typing, office skills and commerce. Both subjects have always stressed the employment relevance of their work and they have thus fitted easily into the TVEI programmes. They have been assisted by the fact that new technology was transforming both areas of work and by TVEI's attack on the gender bias of these and other occupationally related areas of study.

Business Studies

Business Studies, or the business dimension, underpins a good deal of the study of occupational sectors which pervades the new vocationalism. Whether students are studying the travel and tourism industry, financial services or the service sector more generally, the business dimension is usually an important one. This area of work has also been helped by the growing interest in the business world and in the economic dimension of life that has accompanied the rise of the Conservative administration which was elected in 1979.

Business Studies is a leading curriculum area for the development of 'enterprise education', particularly the operation of mini-enterprises where students set up and run their own small companies (Jamieson, 1984). More generally Business Studies makes heavy use of practical and business-related assignments, e.g. market research or costing activities. Periods of work experience in a relevant business are also common, indeed one of the national criteria for Business Studies is that students are acquainted with 'current business practice'.

Economic Understanding

One of the factors which has transformed Business Studies in recent times is the gradual move away from a description of business and commercial institutional structures towards a greater emphasis on economics and economic factors. However, the importance of the economic dimension in the pre-vocational and vocational curriculum is not confined to Business Studies. Economic Literacy or Economic Awareness is rapidly becoming the most important of all the cross-curricular initiatives.

The importance of Economic Understanding in the curriculum has been recognised only since 1976 with the Ruskin speech of Mr Callaghan. The idea was taken up and developed most fully by Sir Keith Joseph during his period as Secretary of State for Education. His view 'that all young people should be taught the economic facts of life' became an enduring one throughout his period of office. The Economic Literacy movement argues that economics is central to our understanding of modern life, and this fact stems from the classic economic dictum that 'every nation's resources are insufficient to produce the quantities of goods and services that would be required to satisfy all of its citizens' wants' (Lipsey, 1983).

It is widely accepted that a study of Economics *per se* would be neither acceptable nor desirable for all pupils, so ways have to be found to integrate Economic Understanding into the existing subject curriculum. The problems which are encountered in this strategy are similar to those faced by all the cross-curricular initiatives. The first problem is that of definition – whilst the 'economic facts of life' might have been unproblematic for Sir Keith Joseph, he appears to be in a minority. The phrases Economic Literacy and Economic Capability appear to have few adherents (Scott and Sieber, 1985). The Economics 14–16 Project, sponsored by the Economics Association and launched in 1976 prefers the concept of Economic Understanding, whilst the SCDC Economic Awareness Project launched in 1987, covering the 5–16 age range, naturally prefers the phrase Economic Awareness. The 14–16 project has produced an extensive range of materials which can be fitted into a wide range of subjects, and both projects champion a blend of concepts, skills, knowledge and personal capabilities developed through active learning strategies.

The Certificate of Pre-vocational Education

As a 14–18 programme, TVEI goes beyond the sphere of compulsory schooling and enters the two very different worlds of the school sixth form (Years 12 and 13) and further education (FE). The sixth form (Years 12 and 13) has been the traditional pinnacle of *academic* work in schools – a place where knowledge was pursued for its own sake, or more immediately for the sake of the universities. Yet during the 1970s the character of the school sixth form began to change. As the job market for school leavers gradually collapsed, more and more disillusioned youngsters remained in school. The schools were faced with a problem: most of these students were neither able nor motivated enough to take traditional A-level courses; on the other hand, a growing number of teachers couldn't see a lot of sense in these students retaking CSE or GCE courses. What seemed to be required was a course that would improve the chances of these young people obtaining those jobs which were available. The courses had therefore to have close links with the world of work, and they had to be flexible in nature to account for the fact that students would leave them as soon as they found employment.

Individual schools up and down the country began to construct courses to cope with this 'New Sixth'. The courses had many things in common: they were often both constructed and delivered with the help of local industry; they nearly all contained extensive periods of work experience; they were student-centered with a major emphasis on active, experiential learning; most had very flexible structures, many had a modular structure.

Following pilot schemes in 1984 the Certificate of Pre-Vocational Education (CPVE) was introduced nationally in 1985. CPVE was designed to rationalise and codify the proliferation of one year post-16 courses which had grown up in the 1970s. The course framework was drawn up and the course certificated by two of the non-traditional examination bodies, the Business and Technician Education Council (BTEC) and the City and Guilds of London Institute (CGLI). These validating and examination bodies, along with organisations like the RSA, have become increasingly important in the accreditation of post-16 education. Significantly they are dominated by employers rather than academics or teachers, and this is reflected in their curricula. CPVE is a good example of the way in which the conceptual map of relevant knowledge bears little relationship to traditional academic subjects. The stress is on the development of practical skills and competencies applied to work situations. Work experience is a central element of the course.

Further Education and the Youth Training Scheme

CPVE is as much a feature of the further education and tertiary college curriculum as it is of schools. The FE world has always been strongly influenced by the needs of local employers, and this has been reflected in the character of its governing body, the background of its lecturing staff, and the provision of a wide variety of industrially related courses. Although FE colleges have always made provision for academic A-levels, they have become increasingly concerned with the provision of pre-vocational and vocational qualifications. BTEC courses now hold a dominant position in most colleges and their mode of operation – modular, cross-curricular, student-centred and employment-oriented – has influenced much other provision.

The world of further education has been the traditional site of Vocational Education. It has been affected in recent years by two bodies which have wielded enormous influence in Pre-vocational and Vocational Education. The first is the Further Education Unit (FEU), the second is the MSC (now known as the Training Agency) and more particularly the Youth Training Scheme (YTS). The FEU, which was set up in 1977, is formally independent of the DES and the MSC, although it has very close links with both bodies. Its remit as an advisory body runs throughout FE and it is centrally concerned with vocational preparation, mainstream Vocational Education and associated staff development programmes. Its influential report, *A Basis for Choice* (FEU, 1979), laid the groundwork for much of the recent thinking in Vocational Education.

The two year Youth Training Scheme, which now accepts around a half of all young people who leave school at 16, has become the central feature of post-16 vocational preparation. The scheme aims to help students (which it calls trainees) to acquire competence in a range of job and occupational skills, to transfer these core skills to new situations where necessary, and to develop personal effectiveness. These goals are to be achieved through work-based learning in selected occupational training families. FE colleges have provided the major share of off-the-job training (in increasing competition with private training companies who compete for this work). The growing impact of YTS has meant that MSC, now known as the Training Agency, increased its stake in post-16 education such that it now controls some 25 per cent of Non-Advanced Further Education (NAFE).

There are a number of other influences on Vocational Education that are important to chart and most of these relate to the increasing penetration of industry and commerce into the education system. From the 1970s onwards it was possible to refer to an education–industry movement in the UK. This movement has been described as 'a diverse collection of employer and trade union groupings; and especially constructed educational or quasi-educational "projects"' (Jamieson, 1985).

Many of these projects were set up as charitable trusts, usually with funding from industry and more recently from the Department of Trade and Industry. These organisations encouraged schools and colleges to develop the skills, knowledge and attitudes of young people. They did this not just by trying to influence the subjects on the formal curriculum, but by persuading schools and colleges to offer their students a variety of experiences as well. Leading examples of these projects include: Project Trident, which organises work experience for young people (amongst other things), and Young Enterprise, which helps young people set up and run a small company. These charitable trusts have been joined by large companies, professional associations, the CBI and TUC, and a host of others, all offering to enhance, enrich and extend the academic curriculum of schooling in a more vocational direction.

This heterogeneous collection of organisations constitute the 'supply side' of the education–industry movement. They operate on the 'Heineken' principle of curriculum change – they attempt to reach the place where the ordinary curriculum of schooling cannot penetrate. Alongside these organisations has grown up an LEA brokerage system which attempts to mediate between the 'supply side' and the 'demand side' – the schools and colleges. These brokers are known as SILOs or EILOs (Schools/Education Industry Liaison Officers) and practically every LEA in England and Wales has such an appointment – some large LEAs have several. The task of these SILOs is to put schools in touch with those organisations which can best help to develop their work.

Examination and assessment structures have traditionally reflected the academic–vocational divide. Employers and trade unions have been firmly in control of certificating the apprenticeship system, whilst employer-led bodies like the Royal Society of Arts (RSA) have certificated a range of commercial skills. By contrast, in schools and colleges academic courses have been certificated by the university-related examining boards. The rise of Pre-vocational and Vocational Education has seen the concomitant rise of industrially dominated examining boards. The RSA, the Business and Technician Education Council (BTEC) and the City and Guilds of London Institute (CGLI) have all made significant inroads into schools and colleges by offering a wide range of pre-vocational and vocational courses. CPVE is offered by the Joint Board for Pre-vocational Education (JBPVE), a hybrid constituted from BTEC and CGLI. The National Council for Vocational Qualifications (NCVQ) has now been set up to oversee and rationalise all vocational qualifications.

All these changes in curricula and certification make it very difficult for 'end-users' like employers to understand and use the system. In order to attend to this problem the government has instituted a review of vocational qualifications (NRVQ) with the intention of achieving a greater degree of unification between education and industry-based qualifications.

Table 2.1. (pp. 26, 27) outlines the major pre-vocational initiatives at present.

The New Vocationalism: A Curriculum Model

It has been argued that the term the 'new vocationalism' can be applied to the large number of educational schemes which have been launched by various agencies since around the middle of the 1970s (all of which have the intention of drawing the curriculum closer to the world of work). The main features of the 'new vocationalism' in curriculum terms are as follows:

● The age range covered by these schemes runs from 14 to 18 + .
● The courses tend to be taken by lower-achieving young people, typically those in the bottom 40 per cent of the achievement range.
● The schemes are not built around traditional academic subjects with their heavy emphasis on knowledge; rather the stress is placed on the acquisition of certain skills which are thought to underpin a wide range of adult behaviour, particularly but not exclusively, work-related behaviour. Basic numeracy and literacy, communication skills, problem-solving skills, and social skills figure strongly in most of the schemes.

- There is a strong orientation to the world of work in these schemes. Relevance and the application of knowledge to the 'real world' are stressed. In Pre-vocational Studies students will be encouraged to sample areas of work in order to assist with the process of vocational choice. In Vocational Studies students are likely to concentrate on the generic skills required in one vocational area.
- Most schemes place an emphasis on the use of Information Technology wherever this is possible.
- Work experience on employers' premises features strongly in nearly all the schemes. If this is not available then the students are expected to experience a series of simulated vocationally related experiences.
- All schemes are required to have career and vocational guidance built into the programme of work.
- The pedagogy of the new vocationalism is strongly cast in the active mould – this means a stress on experiential and experience-based learning, group work, and a desire to create autonomous learners out of the students/trainees. Teachers and lecturers refer to their own role in the process as that of facilitators.
- The curriculum is usually organised in a modular form, partly to aid motivation and partly to reflect the fact that in many schemes students may leave the course before the end to enter employment.
- Assessment tends to be criterion rather than norm referenced. Most students are continuously profiled with the stress being placed on skill acquisition and the ability to successfully perform certain vocationally relevant tasks. Certification is largely via the non-traditional examination boards and rarely takes the pass/fail form.

The New Vocationalism: The Major Issues

The new vocationalism has raised a large number of issues both for those working within the education system and for those who are more concerned with its performance in relation to the rest of the society. Two issues dominate recent debates. The first asks what is the relationship between the education system, and particularly the new vocationalism, and economic performance. The second asks whether the new vocationalism can claim to be about education rather than training.

There is a consensus in British society that our educational arrangements have not served the economy well. It is argued that this has been true for at least a century and probably longer (Sanderson, 1988). What is much less clear however is exactly what the nature of the linkage is between particular educational configurations (both of structure and curriculum) and economic

Table 2.1 Basic Features of the Pre-vocational Initiatives

	Age range	Target	Objectives	Main curriculum focus	Assessment/certification	Mode
		Ability range				
YTS	16–18+	Statutory-age school leavers of all abilities	To help trainees to achieve: competence in job and range of occupational skills; competence in transferable core skills; ability to transfer skills to new situations; personal effectiveness	Work-based on learning in selected occupational training families	Terminal certificate; Record of Achievement relating to the four outcomes (currently being piloted)	24 months full-time including minimum 26 weeks off-job
CPVE	16–17	Wide ability range	To form vocational interests; develop competences applicable to work and adult life; extend general education	Core and vocational studies – use of vocational focus to achieve personal development/work-related aims	Certificate carrying summative statement of experience and attainment under development; formative assessment/profiling	12 months full-time 24 months part-time

Table 2.1 (cont.)

	Target		Objectives	Main curriculum focus	Assessment/certification	Mode
	Age range	Ability range				
TVEI	14–18	'Across the ability range'	To help young people to prepare for the world of work; to contribute to the life of the community; to learn to adjust to the changing occupational environment	'Broad' curriculum integrating general and technical/vocational education with work experience	Uses existing and recognised qualifications; also use of profiling, leading to Record of Achievement covering full range of curriculum recommended	4 years full-time
LAPP	14–16	Lower 40% 'for whom GCSE not designed'	To help lower-attaining pupils 'who are not benefitting fully from school' in basic skills acquisition and appreciation of industry, commerce and technology	Education 'with a practical slant'	Formative reviewing processes, including profile recording	Built into full-time (compulsory) curriculum
JUPVE	14–16	Wide ability range	To help children continue general education through a range of occupational focuses	Practical skills focus in the area of people, technology, art and design, and money	Through case-studies throughout the course	2 year course full-time, usually offered as an option

(Adapted from Evans. K and Watts. A. G. [eds.], (1985) *Education and Training 14–18: Policy and Practice* (CRAC/Hobsons) performance. Simplistic national comparisons have not been helpful in this regard because it is easy to show that economically successful countries have widely different educational systems (Japan is a particuarly good example – a successful economy with a completely non-vocational system of compulsory schooling: the vocational training comes after compulsory schooling). There are three major worries about the economy that are relevant to the debate about the new vocationalism. Firstly, there are very rapid changes which are occurring in the industrial and commercial infrastructure of the economy. Secondly, and very much related to the first point, is the rapid advance of new technology. Finally, there is the fact that Britain is facing increasing competition in world markets. It is easy to see how many people are tempted to assume certain features of the new vocationalism from this economic scenario. For example, the stress on new technology and the emphasis on transferable vocational skills.

In fact such a 'reading back' exercise is fraught with difficulties. It makes certain assumptions about the sort of economy that Britain requires or wants. It assumes for example that Britain has decided that it is in the high value-added, high quality end of world markets – along with most of the rest of the 'first industrial nations'. It is probably the case that such an economy needs a very highly skilled labour force in order to cope with the demands placed on it by complex manufacturing and commercial systems. Yet the British economy does not exhibit all the signs that it is firmly in this market. Much of British industry is still competing in the mass production, low quality and low skill end of the world economy. But even if it was clear what sort of economy we as a society wanted, it is not clear that the new vocationalism can deliver. In the first place the evidence from other countries does not look encouraging. Norton Grubb has long argued that in the USA there is no evidence to suggest that the heavy emphasis on vocationalism in American education has paid economic dividends (Norton Grubb, 1987). British employers and academics have begun to ask some searching questions about the heavy emphasis on *skills* in the new vocationalism, particularly the idea that there are certain 'core skills' which can be transferred across a range of similiar occupations (Jonathan, 1987). Finally, there is general agreement that the enormous complexity and haphazard nature of the current range of initiatives that go to make up the new vocationalism do not as yet form a coherent system that is likely to much improve the present state of our economy. (For a full review of this debate see *Oxford Review of Economic Policy*, vol. 4. no. 3, 1988).

The second major debate about the new vocationalism is concerned with the *educational* value of the new curricula. It has been traditional to contrast education with training. In training, it is thought legitimate to concentrate on a narrow task, to specify aims and objectives in a rigorous way and to engage in repetition until the student has reached the required standard. But education, it is generally held, has a different agenda. Its central concern is with self-development rather than skill acquisition; it should be open-ended and liberating rather than narrow and constricting. Pring considers the differences between the two approaches in relation to the area of 'life skills', where the two contrasting philosophies can be easily compared. He rhetorically asks:

> What is it to prepare *persons* for life? Is it to spell out exactly how they should behave, what particular thoughts they should have, what specific skills they should own, what precise values they should hold dear? Or is it to recognise that, as persons, they should be encouraged to develop some *autonomy* of purpose, a *rational capacity* to think through issues of transition, *self-confidence* in their beliefs and relationships, a *sense of dignity* and personal worth even when the world seems against them, a worked out and defensible set of *moral principles*?   (Pring, 1987)

A further complication is that the traditional conception of industrial training is itself changing. Older forms of training focused unambiguously on the needs of employers to have existing jobs performed competently. This training model became difficult to sustain in an era of rapid change. The new problem was how to train and develop the capacity of individuals to adapt and respond to hypothetical jobs which did not yet exist. One version of the answer is embedded in the new vocationalism and is the basis of Lord Young's claim that the aim of Vocational Education must be to break down the 'artificial barrier between education and training' (cited in Pring, 1987).

Not everybody accepts the view that the distinction between education and training no longer holds. Although one line of argument is that training has drawn closer to education, another view sees the new vocationalism as much as an attack on the outmoded academic curriculum which, it is alleged, dominates compulsory schooling. Holt and Reid argue that to embrace the new 14–18 curriculum 'is to show your enthusiasm not so much for a particular initiative or programme, but indeed for a whole way of curriculum life. At a stroke, you show your readiness to cast aside schooling in terms of examination-validated knowledge and the irrelevance of academe, and to replace it with the skills to make British industry great again' (Holt and Reid, 1988). There is general agreement that the system of secondary education needs overhauling, but whether the alternative to the academic curriculum is some form or other of the new vocationalism is by no means accepted. Nor is the contention that the major vehicle for this overhaul should be state direction.

Perhaps an educational litmus test of the new vocationalism is whether the curriculum could be justified in its own right, that is, if it was not feeding into the occupational structure. It does seem difficult to justify very many of the low-level employment-related skills in educational terms. This form of education often seems based on a narrow, middle class and rather British view of the worker – that of an obedient drone. There is surely too much emphasis on technical aspects of job-related skills (the so-called 'can do' skills), and very little emphasis on wider questions about the values embedded in such jobs, the nature of the world of work, or the wider roles which students will also play as adults, those of consumers and citizens. Part of this impoverishment has come about because the traditional academic disciplines have shunned the world of work as an area of study. If this could be remedied, perhaps along the lines suggested by Spours and Young, then Vocational Education could be something which every student would value and want to study (Spours and Young, 1988).

Since the late 1960s Britain has pursued a policy of comprehensive schools for all. Although there had been some tracking of able and less able children within compulsory schooling some form of rudimentary common curriculum was beginning to emerge and the National Curriculum will strengthen this. What the new vocationalism appears to have done is to introduce strong divisions in post-16 education. This distinctive tracking has led some writers to argue that tripartite education is re-emerging in post-16 education. The academic A-level stream leads to higher education, management and the professions; a middle technician track is based on BTEC and TVEI influenced courses; YTS is the new tertiary modern sector, leading to a range of short-term or careless jobs. If the government wishes to avoid this, there must be greater integration and coherence within the 5–16 National Curriculum and post-16 education so that Pre-vocational Education, if it is to become a permanent valued part of the curriculum for *all* pupils and students, is properly linked with the liberal and academic traditions which are also part of our educational heritage.

References and Further Resources

G. Bantock, 'Towards a Theory of Popular Education' in R. Hooper (ed.), *The Curriculum: Context, Design and Development* (Oliver and Boyd, 1971)

CBI, *Building a Stronger Partnership Between Business and Secondary Education* (CBI, 1988)

CEDEFOP, *Alternance Training: Training Contracts for Young People in the European Community* (CEDEFOP, 1984)

Central Statistical Office, *Social Trends* 18 (HMSO, 1988)

P. Cohen, 'No Kidding – It's Really Useful Knowledge' in *Social Science Teacher*, vol. 15, no. 3, 1986

N. Crafts, 'British Economic Performance over the Long Run' in *Oxford Review of Economic Policy*, vol. 4, no.1 (1988)

K. Evans and A. G. Watts (eds.), *Education and Training 14–18: Policy and Practice* (CRAC/Hobsons, 1985)

C. Feinstein, 'Economic Growth since 1870: Britain's Performance in International Perspective' in *Oxford Review of Economic Policy*, vol. 4, no. 1 (1988)

D. M. Fifield, 'The Implications and Expectations of Ownership' in *Business Graduate Journal*, vol. 17 (1987)

FEU, Further Education Curriculum Review and Development Unit, *A Basis for Choice* (FEU, 1979)

D. Gleeson (ed.), *TVEI and Secondary Education: A Critical Appraisal* (Open University Press, 1987)

D. Hargreaves, *The Challenge for the Comprehensive School* (Routledge and Kegan Paul, 1982)

J. Harland, 'The TVEI Experience: Issues of Control, Response and the Professional Role of Teachers' in Gleeson (1987)

M. Holt and W. A. Reid, 'Instrumentalism and Education: 14–18 rhetoric and the 11–16 Curriculum' in A. Pollard, J. Purvis and G. Walford (eds.), *Education Training and the New Vocationalism* (Open University Press, 1988)

I. M. Jamieson, 'Schools and Enterprise' in A. G. Watts and P. Moran (eds.), *Education for Enterprise* (Hobsons, 1984)

I. M. Jamieson (ed.), *Industry in Education: Developments and Case Studies* (Longman, 1985)

I. M. Jamieson and M. Tasker, 'Schooling and New Technology: Rhetoric and Reality' in *World Yearbook of Education* (Kogan Page, 1988)

R. Johnson, 'Really Useful Knowledge' in J. Clarke *et al.* (eds.), *Working Class Culture: Studies in History and Theory* (Hutchinson, 1979)

R. Jonathan, 'The Youth Training Scheme and Core Skills: an Educational Analysis' in M. Holt (ed.), *Skills and Vocationalism: The Easy Answer* (Open University Press, 1987)

E. Keep and K. Mayhew, 'Education, Training and Economic Performance' in *Oxford Review of Economic Policy*, vol. 4, no. 1 (1988)

R. Lipsey, *An Introduction to Positive Economics* (Weidenfeld and Nicholson, 1983)

National Economic Development Office, *Competence and Competition* (MSC/NEDO, 1984)

W. Norton Grubb, 'Responding to the Constancy of Change: New Technologies and Future Demands on US Education' in G. Burke and R. W. Rumberger (eds.), *The Future Impact of Technology on Work and Education* (Falmer Press, 1987)

H. Perkin, *The Origins of Modern English Society 1780–1880* (Routledge and Kegan Paul, 1972)

R. Pring, 'The Curriculum and the New Vocationalism' in *British Journal of Education and Work*, vol. 1, p. 3 (1987)

D. Reeder, 'A Recurring Debate: Education and Industry' in G. Bernbaum (ed.), *Schooling in Decline* (Macmillan, 1981)

D. Reynolds and M. Sullivan, *The Comprehensive Experiment* (Falmer Press, 1987)

W. D. Rubinstein, 'Social Class, Social Attitude and British Business Life' in *Oxford Review of Economic Policy*, vol. 4, no. 1 (1988)

R. Ryba, 'Integrating Economic Learning into the Social Science Curriculum: The Contribution of the 14–16 Project' in *Social Science Teacher*, vol. 16, p. 1 (1986)

M. Sanderson, 'Education and Economic Decline, 1880–1980s' in *Oxford Review of Economic Policy*, vol. 4, no. 1 (1988)

W. H. Scott and A. Sieber, 'Teaching for Economic Understanding' in *Social Science Teacher*, vol. 16, p. 1 (1986)

K. Spours and M. Young, 'Beyond Vocationalism' in *British Journal of Education and Work*, vol. 2, p. 3 (1988)

D. A. Walker, 'Capital Markets and Industry' in *Bank of England Quarterly Review* (December, 1985)

F. Webster and K. Robins, *Information Technology: A Luddite Analysis* (Ablex, 1986)

J. J. Wellington, 'Employment Patterns and the Goals of Education' in *British Journal of Education and Work*, vol. 1, no. 3 (1987)

M. White, *Making Connections* (Policy Studies Institute, 1988)

Key Teacher Resources

K. Evans and A. G. Watts (eds.), *Education and Training 14–18: Policy and Practice* (CRAC/Hobsons, 1985)
A map of most of the relevant initiatives in the field with contributions from policy makers, HMI, MSC, academics and practitioners. There are some specific examples of most of the important education programmes 14–18.

D. Gleeson (ed.), *TVEI and Secondary Education: A Critical Appraisal* (Open University Press, 1987)
By far the best attempt to summarise and comment on TVEI. Many of the authors have been involved in aspects of the evaluation of this initiative and nearly all the facets of TVEI are covered. There are chapters on gender, teaching and learning styles, post-16 provision, management, work experience and the political genesis of TVEI.

M. Holt (ed.), *Skills and Vocationalism: The Easy Answer* (Open University Press, 1987)
Maurice Holt, the leading protagonist to attack Pre-vocational and Vocational Education in schools and colleges, leads a strong team of authors into a sustained assault on almost every aspect of vocationalism.

I. M. Jamieson, A. Miller and A. G. Watts, *Mirrors of Work: Work Simulations in Schools* (Falmer Press, 1988)
A description and analysis of the major ways in which the school curriculum attempts to reflect aspects of the working world. It concentrates on design simulations, mini-enterprises, work practice units, business games and the use of work tasks inside schools.

B. Law, *The Pre-Vocational Franchise* (Harper and Row, 1986)
An unusual and inventive book in which the author sets out a practical vision of the potential for Pre-vocational Education. Based on existing practice in schools and colleges, Law shows how teachers, students, parents, employers and others can accept the franchise and work to create a new and more invigorating education system.

Key Classroom Resources

S. Besley and J. McMinn, *CPVE: A Course Framework* (Longman, 1987)

BTEC, *The CPVE Education Handbook* (BTEC, 1985)
This is a large collection of handbooks on almost every aspect of CPVE.

CRAC, *Insight into Industry* (Hobsons, 1986)
An excellent book full of industrially related problem-solving activities.

Durham University Business School (1985–)
The school produces a number of useful publications in the field of Enterprise Education, for example *Enterprise: An Educational Resource for 14–19 year olds*. This consists of student and teacher workbooks; all the exercises are in the active learning framework.

Framework Press
This publisher specialises in pre-vocational and vocational books for students and teachers. The age range covered is 14–19 and all the materials involve active learning.

B. Law and J. Storey, *Is it Working?* (BP Educational Services, 1986)
An educational learning pack of text and a cassette encourages young people to learn more about themselves and work by active involvement in a variety of work situations.

Longmans Resources Unit
Longmans is probably the largest publisher of student material in the pre-vocational/vocational field.

R. Ryba, S. Hodkinson *et al.*, *Understanding Economics* (Longman, 1985)
30 resource packs, 6 computer assisted learning units and 3 teacher handbooks.

Key Addresses

Business and Technician Education Council,
Central House,
Upper Woburn Place,
London WC1H 0HH

Careers Research Advisory Council,
Sheraton House,
Gloucester Street,
Castle Park,
Cambridge CB3 0AX

Education for Economic Awareness,
SCDC,
Newcombe House,
45 Notting Hill Gate,
London W11 3JB

Joint Board for Pre-vocational Education,
46 Britannia Street,
London WC1Z 9RG

Longmans Resources Unit,
33–35 Tanner Row,
York YO1 15P

Royal Society of Arts,
8 John Adam Street,
London WC2N 6EZ

School Curriculum Industry Partnership,
Newcombe House,
45 Notting Hill Gate,
London W11 3JB

3

PERSONAL AND

SOCIAL EDUCATION:

TIMETABLE GHETTO OR
WHOLE-SCHOOL PRACTICE?

Chris Brown

Personal and Social Education (PSE) has only become a recognised element of the curriculum in most comprehensive schools within the last decade. This is true of England and Wales but less so of Scotland where a subject called Modern Studies prevails, although some aspects of Social Education are to be found in Scotland (MacBeath *et al.*, 1981).

PSE has a variety of titles including: Personal and Social Development (PSD) (Assessment of Performance Unit, 1981); Social Education (Brown *et al.*, 1986); Personal, Social and Moral Education (PSME) (Wakeman, 1984); Lifeskills (Hopson & Scally, 1981); Preparation for Life (Wilcox *et al.*, 1984). This diversity of titles is confusing and in 1988, HMI called for a single name for the subject (HMI, 1988). The variety of nomenclature is testimony to the way in which PSE has grown upwards within the school system. There is no agency handing down content and syllabuses; still less do universities define PSE through the exam system. Indeed 'official' encouragement for PSE has been so non-specific as to be almost vacuous. To some extent this has been rectified by the recent publication of an HMI Survey on PSE, which concludes: '... there are grounds for expecting PSE courses to make an increasingly valuable contribution within the pattern of a school's whole curriculum' (HMI, 1988).

The Development of PSE

There was a time when few schools put PSE on the timetable. They would have claimed that personal education arose out of relationships between the pupils and the teacher, especially in extra-curricular activities (Newsom, 1963), and that social education was achieved through the experience of schooling itself – learning to live with others, to share experience in sport, drama etc., to develop loyalty and a sense of pride and identity. That being so, it is worth considering how and why PSE has penetrated the formal curriculum.

When the tripartite system of education was introduced by the Education Act, 1944, a new concept of schooling came into existence in the shape of the secondary modern school. Here was a recognition that the old classical curriculum was not necessarily relevant to every pupil in the new free system of compulsory education. In the end, the secondary modern school never developed such an independent concept and its practice increasingly resembled the grammar schools. Nevertheless, it became possible to talk of 'relevant' schooling, meaning subjects which bore directly on contemporary experience, and for a while 'Social Studies' flourished (Gleeson and Whitty, 1976; Lawton and Dufour, 1973).

In some versions this was an amalgam of History and Geography, but in others, elements of a somewhat tepid Sociology appeared. A handbook for teachers published in 1950 and reprinted three times, recommended that Social Studies courses should start with the individual (note: not the actual individual pupil as might be the case with PSE) and then go on to widen the focus of study through the family, the neighbourhood, the nation, the Commonwealth to, finally, the world (Dray and Jordan, 1950).

Social Studies was always an 'academic' based subject. It rarely sought to make connections between its subject matter and pupils' experiences or opinions. It remained a subject that was 'taught' like any other. Eventually it supported an enormous range of GCE and CSE examinations and at its 'higher ability' end laid the basis for the introduction of Sociology into schools.

In 1971 the school-leaving age was raised to sixteen and this had a profound influence on the theory of curriculum 'relevance'. At a time when young people were maturing earlier both physically and socially (for example, following the reduction of the voting age) they were to be required to stay at school longer. At the time it seemed as if the 'child-oriented' ethos of schools would be seriously challenged by this new group of young men and women. To meet this expectation a major curriculum exercise took place under the acronym ROSLA and activities such as car maintenance and community service came to seem appropriate (Sames, 1986; Scrimshaw, 1981). However, in a period of high youth unemployment public examinations were still paramount and ROSLA eventually expended itself in a burgeoning of Mode III CSE courses, including Social Studies and Community Studies. Thus PSE in its present form did not emerge directly out of ROSLA but relationships between teachers and the new sixteen-year-olds created the environment in which PSE could be envisaged.

The spread of comprehensive schooling had a similar effect. Mixed-ability teaching further weakened the hold of academic values and the enlarged nature of comprehensive schools led to the introduction of systems intended to ameliorate the effects of size on pupils. Most important in this respect was the tutor period in which a teacher met with a class every day for perhaps thirty minutes and was supposed to create a sense of a home-base to allay anxiety and foster a feeling of security. Here, virtually for the first time on any scale, timetable resources were now allocated to activity which was definitely not to be 'teaching' of a subject and had aims related to the 'personal'.

As post-ROSLA secondary schools settled into a common structure of lower school and upper school, the Fourth and Fifth Year (Years 10 and 11) came to be seen as a unit for exam purposes and it was possible to create relatively coherent timetable slots running through both years. At the same time the comprehensive intake meant that the 'academic' subjects were not suitable for many pupils, so the concern for the personal needs of these pupils and for their social adjustment in society gave rise to attempts to find new 'subjects' suitable for them. In some cases this was still Social Studies but increasingly it was a 'circus' of topics such as Health Education (mainly Sex Education and then Drugs appeared), Careers Education, Leisure and so on.

What finally exploded this development to the point where most secondary schools now have some form of PSE was the dramatic collapse of the youth employment market. Many teachers felt real concern for the plight of the 14- to 16-year-olds, while others feared the consequences for their own authority and discipline. By now PSE had a track record and resources were becoming available in large quantities. In the early 1980s a planned, sequential scheme for tutor periods had attracted wide publicity and been taken up in a large number of schools (Baldwin and Wells, 1979–1983). The scheme emphasised inter-personal skills and engaged the teacher as a facilitator rather than the normal didactic, authority figure (Bolam and Medlock, 1985). Largely for this reason the scheme collapsed but some elements of its process could be transferred to the new PSE. More importantly it reinforced the validity of a Personal and Social Education as an entity distinct from the rest of the curriculum and yet capable of fitting into existing school learning structures.

Finally the explosion of PSE was coterminous with the impact of the MSC on schools through TVEI. Here was the apparatus of Skills Education on a massive scale so that many of the process aspects of TVEI could easily be accommodated within PSE.

The Place of PSE in Schools

The 1988 HMI Survey was based on visits to 21 secondary schools throughout England in 1986–7. The table on page 37 shows what HMI found in PSE courses. They found a variability in the time and resources given to PSE. Only six of the twenty-one schools visited offered PSE in all five years; most seemed to think PSE was only suitable for 14- to 16-year-olds. The number of time-

Main themes and topics included in PSE courses	Approximate percentage (%) in PSE courses
Health education	80
Careers education	60
Political education and world issues	55
Moral and religious education	50
Personal relationships and responsibilities	45
Community and social studies	40
Legal issues	35
Study skills	35
Economic issues	25
Education for parenthood	15

(HMI, 1988)

tabled periods ranged from four 35-minute periods per week in all five years to just one 35-minute period in the Fourth and Fifth Years (Years 10 and 11). In three-quarters of the schools the same teacher stayed with a class for all the PSE in one year; sometimes this was in a form period. In the remaining schools, teachers specialised in their own section of the course. Thus, PSE differed widely in schools in terms of the resources it used and the way it was organised. Surprisingly none of the schools allowed PSE to be optional, though this may be a consequence of the way the schools were selected for the survey. But despite being a core course in most schools, as the table shows, PSE remains a rag-bag of different topics that receive the most cursory treatment. Many PSE teachers complain of lack of resources, low priority in timetabling and staffing, and lack of INSET.

This low status of PSE is illustrated by HMIs who criticised the teaching and organisation of PSE on a number of grounds:

● planning is seldom more than elementary so that teachers are left to 'do their own thing' and there is no co-ordination with other areas of the curriculum
● senior management does not monitor PSE adequately
● controversial issues are avoided or treated superficially
● assessment of pupil performance is weak or non-existent
● evaluation of courses is weak and class teachers are rarely involved
● a number of teachers are reluctant conscripts to PSE while in other cases teachers who are anxious to teach PSE are not able to do so
● INSET is often not available or not used; thus quite often key areas such as Religious Education and Political and Health Education are taught by teachers with no specialist knowledge in these areas

This last point is a particularly good example of the simplistic nature of much PSE. From the subject matter it seems fairly clear that PSE is intended to help young people both understand and be more effective in society. Yet schools hardly ever draw upon the Social Sciences to provide such a study with informed argument and conceptual structure. If they tried to teach about the natural world without drawing on Physics, Chemistry and Biology they would be thought totally unprofessional. Some blame for this must lie with social scientists, especially sociologists. Social Science courses in schools are often too content-determined for PSE, where there is a much greater emphasis on skills and personal involvement. Of course, it is true that many schools do not have social scientists to use but this is rarely seen as a drawback. In the ideology of PSE there is no recognition that the Social Sciences could be a major source of material (Harber and Brown, 1983). It is not surprising therefore that HMI identify another weakness of PSE as a lack of rigour and challenge. The dominant view is that PSE can be taught by any teacher without much planning or any training.

One consequence of the absence of any input from the Social Sciences, especially Sociology, is that PSE courses are heavily dominated by an individualist philosophy. Hilary Burrage has put this point particularly well in relation to Health Education:

> One common strand in all the approaches to health ... is that they emphasise the role of the *individual*. It is as if health were an apolitical issue, somehow divorced from social, environmental or economic contexts. Such an individualised approach to health, couched in terms of personal responsibility, morality and normative judgements, presents something of a problem for teachers in schools and colleges who are sociologically inclined. On the one hand, we are (rightly) expected, if we teach A-level Sociology and the like, to present health, disease and medicine as greatly influenced by epidemiological and social factors; but on the other hand we may also, as 'teachers' (transmitters?) of Personal and Social Education, be expected to present our pupils and students with a notion of health which derives almost exclusively from ideas about personal responsibility. (Burrage, 1987)

This approach of individualism probably explains why the Social Sciences are absent from PSE – they constitute too great a threat to the sense of personal responsibility which runs through PSE. It may also partly explain why issues of equal opportunities are not usually found in PSE. They receive no mention as a category in the HMI survey but it is revealing that in mentioning some 'additional topics' HMI refer to 'prejudice'. Prejudice is, of course, a very individualised perspective on equal opportunities. To discuss anti-racism and anti-sexism effectively in PSE would require an analysis of social structures which has no place in a PSE programme designed to influence individual attitudes and behaviour.

The HMI survey reported that many courses shared the overriding concern of helping to prepare pupils for adult life. It is worth quoting HMI in full:

> Many of the courses shared similar aims and objectives. Their overriding concern was to help to prepare pupils for adult life. Thus the courses aimed to enable pupils to develop self-awareness, to extend their understanding of the nature of personal and social relationships, and of the social, economic and political world in which they lived and in which they would be adults. More specifically, courses were designed to enable pupils to develop effective skills in utilising their personal qualities, in managing their relationships, and in making choices when faced by dilemmas, were they moral, political or vocational. In short, they intended to give pupils a range of skills, and confidence, to help them cope with a rapidly changing social world. Some courses also made explicit a wish to encourage pupils to develop positive attitudes in caring for themselves – their health and their relationships – and in caring for and respecting others in their immediate relationships and in the wider community.   (HMI, 1988)

Although HMI appear satisfied that most schools were able to achieve these objectives (although they say this was more likely when PSE was linked with tutor periods) it is hard to see what level of achievement could be reached in relation to the overriding concern of PSE courses – preparing pupils for adult life. Perhaps this is the problem. Instead of having some ultimate goal in mind, PSE courses should always be oriented to the immediate needs of pupils, including success in school. Some schools evidently understand this, but developing self-awareness is a time-consuming and expert process requiring sensitivity and insight on the part of the trainer. It requires a supportive, non-threatening environment, not the authoritarian, coercive institution which some schools can be. Nor do schools often promote these skills in their own staff. PSE teachers need training in groupwork and other human relationship skills while management themselves need training in communication and participative decision-making skills. If staff feel valued, have high self-esteem and share in the ownership of courses they would run more effective PSE courses.

Preparation for adult life is a complex business. The influences on young people come from many sources; the school's influence may be fairly limited. This means that the claim for PSE that it, unlike other aspects of the curriculum, is relevant to pupils, is highly dubious. Ultimately it can only be relevant if it meets the expressed needs of the pupils, not the needs of white, middle-class society.

PSE and Social Control

PSE is a very recent phenomenon as an 'across-the-board' subject and most adults who now live or have ever lived have managed perfectly well without it. Why do we feel apparently that everyone should be exposed to PSE now and yet still not give it the resources which would be necessary to make it effective? We saw at the beginning of the chapter some possible explanations of how PSE has developed. But why, though widespread, is it still dogged by low status? What we are faced with here is the 'ambivalence of social control'. Ever since mass schooling came into existence, the hidden curriculum of education has been the socialisation of young people into the prevailing norms and ideologies (Hargreaves, 1982). It might be training for class roles or gender roles or work roles. It nearly always involved conscious attempts to initiate young people into their 'national heritage' and to foster patriotism and a national identity (Brown, 1984). This hidden curriculum has existed as an unacknowledged function of schooling which works both through the formal curriculum and the rules and customs which define school life. In the past, the hidden curriculum has been adequately effective, but for a variety of reasons related to economic recession, to the growth of the media, especially television, to the emergence of an awareness of the pluralistic nature of society, the hidden curriculum with its assumptions about moral and social consensus can no longer be guaranteed to deliver a tractable and well-integrated new generation. As an ILEA booklet puts it:

> We live in a pluralistic society in an age of rapid social and technological change. The traditions, customs and practices – and the assumptions, attitudes and institutions which stand behind them – of the various communities which make up our society are frequently called into question.   (ILEA, 1987)

In particular there are problems such as drugs and unemployment which pose particular threats to social order and are not covered within the hidden curriculum. PSE then is a sort of emergency social control dealing with particular problems as defined by the adult groups which dominate schooling. This explains the 'rag-bag'. In one sense, it is perfectly coherent – it is a list of prevailing moral panics – sex, drugs, AIDS, jobs, the credibility of the work ethic, the legitimacy of the party political system, the decline in moral standards (as evidenced by football hooliganism), the challenge to Christian values, the rise in crime, the failure of manufacturing industries to attract able recruits, broken homes, child abuse and so on. 'Lager louts' and 'acid parties' were troubling decent folk in the late 1980s. Some moral panics are longstanding; others come and go – and so does the money for training teachers to 'deal' with them.

So these things have to be brought out of the realms of the hidden curriculum and tackled head-on. The 'social control system' now comes to operate openly. The trouble is that, out in the open, the 'messages' are far less effective. Some pupils may feel that some topics are adults' problems, not theirs. Pupils may perceive teachers to be preaching alien values. In some cases teachers may engage in the very behaviour which they are supposed to deplore. On the face of it, PSE presents particular difficulties because many of the issues it deals with are likely to be highly controversial. Contraception, abortion, homosexuality, sex and marriage, and AIDS involve feelings and attitudes which are strongly held by most adults but where there are deep differences. In some cases, like abortion, there are major social institutions – the Roman Catholic church and the evangelical churches in particular – who are effective lobbyists and are able to ensure that issues are either not seen as appropriate for schools or, more likely, that their particular views are well and effectively represented. In other cases, like homosexuality, groups may have access to power in such a way that they may be able to push through legislation which supports their particular view of the subject. Thus it is now illegal, in schools, to advocate homosexual relations, according to education circulars based on the 1986 Education Act. While few teachers have ever advocated such a thing, many schools and teachers may avoid the issue altogether in case they get into awkward situations.

Political issues also have the potential to give rise to accusations of bias. Peace Education has been particularly attacked as indoctrination (Cox and Scruton 1984). However, a senior HMI, John Slater, reporting on a study of Peace Education, said that the evidence showed that the vast majority of teachers were desperately anxious to be professionally correct and academically respectable (*Guardian*, 15/11/83).

No published criticism of PSE has yet been able to provide any evidence that such bias exists beyond one or two isolated and sometimes bizarre anecdotes, often drawn second-hand from the popular press. The concern of the critics seems largely to be to suppress rational discussion of certain issues for fear that young people might become critical or cynical about established arrangements and orthodoxies, or, conversely, that their uncritical acceptance of 'official' values and practices becomes problematic (Harber and Brown, 1986). This would seem to be indoctrination in reverse. Even Sir Keith Joseph did not go that far:

> His (the teacher's) presentation needs to be as objective as he can make it, in the sense that he ensures that what is offered as a fact is indeed true; that the selection of facts gives a picture which is neither unbalanced nor superficial; the facts and opinions are clearly separated; and that pupils are encouraged to weigh evidence and argument so as to arrive at rational judgements.
> (Sir Keith Joseph, 1984)

This analysis goes a long way to explain why PSE emerged in the first place but also why it is given such low status and regarded with suspicion by many in authority. It also explains why teachers are so often blamed for things like football hooliganism, vandalism, bad manners etc. HMI criticised schools for avoiding controversial issues if they could. Perhaps they *should* avoid them. If teachers are given no opportunities to develop their own knowledge of the issues, to explore techniques for handling controversial issues or, most important of all, for examining their own attitudes, they are wise to leave well alone.

PSE as a Process

This has been perhaps a pessimistic discussion. HMI report that pupils enjoy PSE if it is well structured; this does not clash with another finding that pupils regard PSE often as 'not real work' even if they do enjoy it. It is also true that PSE is very new in schools – more experience may improve some aspects of its delivery.

However, the processes discussed below are fundamental to PSE. If the HMI analysis is correct, PSE as a curriculum subject is doomed to remain superficial, poorly resourced and ineffective. But there are other developments which see PSE in another light: PSE has more to do with whole-school relationships, teaching and learning styles and method or process, rather than subject or content.

Such developments are already present in PSE. In Health Education, for example, many materials are not directly about health matters but about personal confidence and interpersonal skills. An American course on Drug Education sponsored in this country by TACADE (see page 68), *Skills for Adolescence*, consists of six units designed to span the first three years of secondary school. Only Unit Six is directly about drug-related behaviour.

Many materials for Careers Education take a similar line. A recent publication from COIC is a good example. In the introduction it says:

> The basic thinking behind active and participative methods at this level is that pupils will benefit from working together in small groups, by learning from each other, by developing their own values and perceptions, by growing in confidence as they are learning to communicate more effectively in safe, non-threatening situations.   (COIC, 1987)

The World Studies project adopts an explicit stance based on experiential learning (Whittaker, 1984), and in practically all areas of PSE such methods are advocated. This does not mean that they are necessarily implemented. HMI found that active participation by pupils in lessons was a characteristic in only two schools. And it is clearly not easy to successfully run active learning in PSE and revert to the more formal, didactic approach in other subjects. This must confuse many pupils – in some lessons they are expected to question whereas in the next lesson they could be reproved for asking why they are doing a particular topic. To many teachers there seems to be no reason why active learning should not be adopted in all subjects.

If PSE was defined as a process of active learning as much as a study of certain essential themes, then the thrust of development could move away from the curriculum of moral panics to the development of a teaching–learning relationship where learners have real responsibility for their own learning, and the teacher's role is one of facilitator or manager of learning.

These approaches to PSE can be seen as having four characteristics (Brown *et al.*, 1986). They are:

● person-centred because the emphasis is on personal growth and on a form of partnership between learner and teacher
● group-based because groups provide a necessary framework for developing interpersonal skills, for encouraging learning through dialogue and for making learning fun
● experiential because experience, real or simulated, confers ownership on learning and provides a basis for reflection on learning
● problem-solving because PSE is skill-based, its approach to knowledge is tentative, and solving problems builds self-confidence

Developing educational processes along these lines could go further to 'prepare pupils for adult life' than a drab list of adult horrors 'taught' in a conventional lesson. Moreover, what would be the point of training teachers to be facilitators in PSE lessons and ignoring the rest of the timetable?

There are trends in this direction. What some PSE teachers have learned to do can now be transferred to academic subjects. The rhetoric of GCSE stresses active learning. TVEI has imported a whole range of participative techniques from education contexts outside schools. Strategies such as student-centred learning (Brandes and Ginnis, 1986) and problem-solving (Blagg *et al.*, 1988) are gaining a foothold in schools. Many employers are now looking for individuals who can work in groups, cope with stress and use initiative.

Examples of Good Practice in PSE

Some indication of how 'PSE as method' can work in practice are given in the HMI survey. Although these examples all relate to PSE topics it is possible to see how the elements of group-work, participation, experience and problem-solving are manifested in good practice. From this it is possible to see the possibilities of continuing this process into the rest of the curriculum.

One Fifth-year class (Year 11) had spent some weeks on a module of work entitled 'Personal effectiveness', which was related to employment opportunities. By the time of the HMI inspection, a situation had been reached where pupils, in groups of four, had established themselves as employers in imaginary firms. The nature and employment requirements of the firms had been clarified, and it had been decided what jobs would be offered to school leavers. Teachers had provided documentation to help pupils to decide what sort of questions they would ask, and what qualities they would look for in interviewees. A group prepared furniture in the school for interviews – each 'firm' had its table, together with its name clearly displayed. The course co-ordinator introduced the session, and to give an example of what was required, took the role of an employer interviewing a young woman (performed by the Deputy Head) for a barperson's job. That this could be done at all, and taken seriously, was indicative of the good, relaxed relationship between staff and pupils. Following this role-play which was realistic, carefully prepared and which created an appropriate atmosphere, the pupils set about their own interviewing, arranged in such a way that everyone had a chance to interview and be interviewed. Discussion of the interviewee's performance took place after each interview and assessment sheets were completed. Eventually, each group decided on an applicant and had to justify the choice in a plenary session, where such reasons were given as 'she was enthusiastic', 'he had experience of this sort of thing', and 'she explained things carefully'. The session concluded with the co-ordinator drawing out the main points. The school then arranged for local business people to come to the school to give mock interviews for pupils who were interested. This whole session was highly participative, and it had both pace and challenge. It enabled pupils to develop some understanding of the appointment of people to firms, and to develop skills of decision-making, of interviewing and of being interviewed.

Some lessons described in the HMI survey dealt more with industrial issues, such as different production methods. In one Fourth-year class (Year 10), pupils spent short periods of time making coloured paper discs, first on their own and then in pairs. The teacher acted as quality controller and rewarded the best work. Subsequent pertinent discussion examined why co-operative working appeared in most cases to have been more effective, and the relative merits of different ways of organising work in industry. The virtues of specialisation, the use of robots, and current practice in the furniture and car-making industries were all considered.

In the field of Political Education, a number of topics were concerned with political participation and decision-making. One group of lower-attaining Fourth-year pupils (Year 10) was seen studying how political decisions are taken. The teacher usefully summarised previous work on decision-making in relation to self, the family and the local community. For further work on local government the teacher introduced a case-study, complete with relevant documentation, on an application for planning permission (the conversion of a stable to a disco in a quiet, village community). Each document was read aloud to the class, emphasising its implications; then the class divided into sub-groups for a form of role-play exercise, in which pupils spoke to the different documents rather than acting as personalities involved in the controversy. The room was then reorganised to resemble a council chamber with the teacher acting as chair. Pupils were invited to contribute their own viewpoints, and over half did so. At the end of the lesson a vote was taken (overwhelmingly approving the disco). This realistic, well-structured and well-paced lesson successfully motivated pupils. Sufficient guidance was provided by the teacher to enable pupils to participate, and to explore appropriately various aspects of political behaviour.

Other political and social issues were also explored. A Fourth-year (Year 10) mixed-ability group was seen considering the subject of violence. The teacher skilfully encouraged pupils to think for themselves in a purposeful way, without imposing her own ideas. Discussion focused on the violence precipitated by the industrial dispute at Wapping in 1986–7, and, following excellent contributions from pupils a general consensus emerged that it was wrong for union members and others to use violence. The teacher then outlined the story of the *Lord of the Flies*, by William Golding, and read the extract dealing with the murder of Simon, one of the children. In the discussion which followed one boy admitted he had been involved in the killing of a pheasant: 'it was exciting at first but afterwards we all felt ashamed.' The pupils went on to talk about how fire, war-paint and dancing contributed to the children in the story becoming 'psyched up', and to forgetting civilised modes of behaviour; the teacher pointed out parallel situations in contemporary society. The class considered reasons for violence and whether it could be prevented. This was a rigorous and challenging lesson which raised some fundamental questions about the origins, nature and prevention of violence. Pupils responded very well, arguing that violence is inherent in human nature, that social conditions may exacerbate it, but that home and school influences might help to control it.

HMI summarise their view of good practice in a way which echoes the four approaches to PSE as method which were described earlier:

In general the *best lessons* seen were characterised by a number of particular features. Pupils were encouraged to participate in learning through a range of appropriate activities clearly related to the objectives of the lesson, and supported by relevant materials. Lessons were well paced and rigorous, requiring pupils to grapple in some depth with issues related to ideas, principles and values. The approach and content of lessons built on pupils' current interests and related these to preparation for adult life.

Speakers and visitors, together with planned experience outside the school, enhanced the relevance of what they were learning. Lessons arose from careful individual and collective planning by teachers, and there was a concern to identify systematically both what pupils needed to learn and what they had learned. Care was devoted to establishing good relationships. In this way not only was learning in general promoted but opportunities were created for encouraging pupils to take personal responsibility for their work, for assessing their own progress and for contributing to course elevation.   (HMI, 1988)

PSE and the National Curriculum

Ultimately PSE is about treating each other with respect. HMI found that relationships were good:

Overall, the relationships between teachers and pupils, and amongst pupils themselves, were good, and reflected the quality of relationships within the school as a whole. In one school, the positive nature of the relationships between tutors and pupils helped to maintain order within a very poor course. The type of relationship did vary from school to school – in one case quite open and sensitive, in another more paternalistic – but in all schools there was generally a respect for the integrity of others.
                                                                                              (HMI, 1988)

This may be surprising since some secondary schools still seem to be dominated by an authoritarian, coercive management style in which pupils experience scant respect and even less consultation. Even PSE courses are rarely devised after consultation with pupils. Within this framework many teachers and students do manage to create relationships which encourage growth and development, but if active learning is to characterise the secondary school as a whole, radical changes will be required of senior management. The increased role for parents and others in governing schools will reduce the power of existing school oligarchies centred around the Head. PSE teachers would be wise to enlist these governors as their allies. But this extension of democracy outward to the community will need to be extended inwards as well to teachers and pupils alike. Prescriptions about subject matter and regular public assessments will certainly not reflect the openness and permissiveness that characterises a plural society. Nor, as its proponents desire, will it eradicate this permissiveness and reassert moral authority; reformers of the last thirty years know only too well that education cannot compensate for society, whether we are talking about actual material deprivation or supposed moral anarchy.

So in the era of the National Curriculum what is the future of PSE? There is, of course, no place for it in the core or foundation curriculum as a separate subject. It is possible, however, that schools will devise a way of retaining much or all of their existing PSE programmes within the area of the National Curriculum which remains unspecified and within the cross-curricular themes. Given the strength of the forces that propelled PSE into the curriculum in the first place, it seems quite possible that this will happen. The government's preference is for a cross-curriculum delivery of PSE – Health Education in Science, RE etc.; Political Education in History and so on. However, experience in this sort of permeation approach does not necessarily lead one to be optimistic about it. Normally whatever is being permeated actually just trickles away.

However, if PSE is defined principally as a method and a relationship between learner and teacher, it might be possible to preserve this aspect of PSE through the way in which the subjects of the National Curriculum are delivered. As we have seen there is no inherent requirement that academic knowledge can only be learned through didactic teaching. Academic knowledge can be rendered interesting and relevant if learning is understood as a collaborative process rather than a transmission process and in so doing most of the objectives of PSE could be achieved.

Students would learn about politics, power and decision-making from the democratic processes in the school, though some could take Politics courses if they wished. Students would cease to be the passive recipients of largely irrelevant and nearly always half-understood facts and would learn to take responsibility for their own learning. Finally students would have greater opportunity to explore the knowledge and skills which interested them and would thus be more self-motivated and probably more successful.

This scenario for PSE could seem unrealistic, even at a time when official ideologies encourage personal initiatives and private enterprise. The truth is that these ideologies do not extend as far as the classroom. But if educational reform has reduced curriculum choice and strengthened central control, it has not prescribed specific teaching–learning strategies directly (although statutory testing may make it more difficult for teachers to embark on radical change to their teaching methods). Whatever obstacles the National Curriculum creates there could still be room for a personal and social education which mobilises the whole school and not just the PSE teacher. In the end, each school will have to choose.

Acknowledgements

I would like to thank Angela Mukhopadhyay, Adviser, Sandwell LEA, and Susan Poole, Advisory Teacher, Walsall LEA, for their helpful advice and Barry Dufour for his advice and forbearance.

References and Further Resources

Assessment of Performance Unit (APU), *Personal and Social Development* (DES, 1981)

J. Baldwin and H. Wells (eds.), *Active Tutorial Work, Books One–Five and Sixteen–Nineteen* (Basil Blackwell, 1979–1983)

N. Blagg *et al.*, *The Somerset Thinking Skills Course* (Blackwell, 1988)

R. Bolam and P. Medlock, *Active Tutorial Work: An Evaluation* (Basil Blackwell, 1985)

D. Brandes and P. Ginnis, *A Guide to Student-Centred Learning* (Blackwell, 1986)

C. Brown, 'National Identity and World Studies' in *Eductional Review*, vol. 36, no. 2 (1984)

C. Brown *et al.*, (eds.), *Social Education: Principles and Practice* (Falmer Press, 1986)

H. Burrage, 'Sociology and Health Education in the Curriculum' in *Social Science Teacher*, vol. 17, no. 1 (1987)

COIC, *Group Exercises for Career Education* (MSC, 1987)

C. Cox and R. Scruton, *Peace Studies: A Critical Survey* (Institute for European Defence and Strategic Studies, London 1984)

J. Dray and D. Jordan, *A Handbook of Social Studies* (Methuen, 1950)

D. Gleeson and G. Whitty, *Developments in Social Studies Teaching* (Open Books, 1976)

C. Harber and C. Brown, 'Social Education and the Social Sciences' in *Curriculum*, vol. 4, no. 1 (1983)

C. Harber and C. Brown, 'Sociology, Politics and the Wayward Curriculum' in *Social Science Teacher*, vol. 16, no. 1 (1986)

D. Hargreaves, *The Challenge for the Comprehensive School* (Routledge and Kegan Paul, 1982)

HMI, *A Survey of Personal and Social Education Courses in Some Secondary Schools* (DES, 1988)

B. Hopson and M. Scally, *Lifeskills Teaching* (McGraw–Hill, 1981)

ILEA, *The Teaching of Controversial Issues in Schools* (ILEA, 1987)

Sir Keith Joseph, *Educating People for Peace* (National Council of Women of Great Britain, 1984)

D. Lawton and B. Dufour, *The New Social Studies* (Heinemann, 1973)

J. MacBeath *et al.*, *Social Education: The Scottish Social Education Project* (Scottish Social Education Project, 1981)

J. Newsom, *Half Our Future* (DES, 1963)

J. Sames, 'Social Education Method' in C. Brown *et al.* (1986)

P. Scrimshaw, *Community Service, Social Education and the Curriculum* (Hodder and Stoughton, 1981)

B. Wakeman, *Personal, Social and Moral Education* (Lion Publishing, 1984)

P. Whittaker, 'The Learning Process' in *World Studies Journal*, vol. 5, no. 2 (1984)

B. Wilcox *et al.*, *The Preparation for Life Curriculum* (Croom Helm, 1984)

Key Teacher Resources

D. Brandes and P.Ginnis, *A Guide to Student-Centred Learning* (Blackwell, 1986)
Reputedly one of the best ever selling books for teachers. Practical explanations of everything a teacher needs to start on student centred approaches.

C. Brown *et al.*, *Social Education: Principles and Practice* (Falmer Press, 1986)
Chapters on assessment organisation etc. and then a survey of the main elements of a PSE programme – Health Education, Political Education, Media Studies etc. – with a special emphasis on active methods and suitable resources.

B. Hopson and M. Scally, *Lifeskills Teaching* (McGraw–Hill, 1981)
A most valuable book containing clearly written background analysis and extensive practical advice on specific strategies, e.g. groupwork.

I. Instone, *The Teaching of Problem-Solving* (Longman, 1988)
A very useful account of the use of problem-solving teaching methods in a secondary school.

P. Lang (ed.), *Thinking About Personal and Social Education in the Primary School* (Blackwell, 1988)
One of the first attempts to develop a more formal approach to PSE in primary schools which will particularly interest secondary teachers responsible for transition and others teaching PSE in the lower school.

J. Ryder and L. Campbell, *Balancing Acts in Personal, Social and Health Education: A Practical Guide for Teachers* (Routledge, 1988)
A practical text designed to be the basis of INSET activities run by teachers themselves.

J. J. Wellington (ed.), *Controversial Issues in the Curriculum* (Blackwell, 1986)
An excellent discussion of these difficult issues partially linked to specific areas of the PSE programme, e.g. Peace Education.

Key Classroom Resources

B. Maxfield and M. Oddy, *Assignments in Social and Life Skills* (Edward Arnold, 1986)
Suitable for all 14+ age groups but inspired by CPVE.
T. Bond, *Games for Social and Life Skills* (Hutchinson, 1986)
A good example of ways of making PSE both fun and effective.
Lifeskills Associates, *Lifeskills Teaching Programmes* (currently numbers 1–4) (Ashling, Back Church Lane, Leeds LS16 8DN)
A series of exercises on a variety of PSE themes which come in loose-leaf format and can be photocopied.
Development Education Centre, *Values, Cultures and Kids* (2nd edition, 1985) (Gillett Centre, Selly Oak Colleges, Bristol Road, Birmingham B29 6LE)
A handbook for teaching about child development and the family with a valuable multicultural perspective.

N. Leech and A. Wooster, *Personal and Social Skills: A Practical Approach for the Classroom* (Religious and Moral Education Press, 1986)
Spiral bound materials for younger pupils.

P. Smith, *Simulations for Careers and Life-Skills* (Hutchinson, 1986)
A comprehensive course based on simulations.

J. Thacker, *Steps to Success: An Interpersonal Problem-Solving Approach for Children* (NFER–Nelson, 1982)
A carefully designed sequence for lower secondary schools.

Key Addresses

Association for the Teaching of the Social Sciences,
P.O. Box 461
Sheffield S1 3BF
Publishes: *Social Science Teacher*

National Association for Pastoral Care in Education,
Education Department,
University of Warwick,
Coventry CV4 7AL
Telephone: (0203) 523809
Publishes: *Pastoral Care in Education*

National Organisation for Initiatives in Social Education,
Birmingham Polytechnic,
Westbourne Road,
Birmingham B15 3TN
Publishes: *Noise*

The Economics Association,
Maxwelton House,
41–3 Boltro Road,
Haywards Heath,
West Sussex RH16 1BJ
Telephone: (0444) 455084
Publishes: *Economics*

• 4 •

HEALTH EDUCATION:

EDUCATION FOR HEALTH?

Hilary Burrage

Introduction and History

Health Education as an identified entity is, along with many of its companion subjects in the personal and social curriculum, a fairly recent innovation, although its roots stretch back over at least the last century, and arguably, indeed, to ancient times (McBride, 1983).

Modern times have, however, seen something of a shift away from traditional legal–prescriptive instruction backed by religious sanction (in health as much as other areas of experience). Substantial work on preventive and public health, underwritten particularly by findings during the First World War, demonstrated more publically than ever before the poor health of many ordinary working people. Likewise, the mid 1930s saw the establishment of the Central Council for Health Education and, by the 1950s, the involvement of the (then) Ministry of Education. More recently, research on health care and inequalities in health, reported by Black (1980) and Smith and Jacobsen (1988), has reinforced the perception that much preventive work remains to be done.

In the past decade the Health Education Council (HEC), reconstituted since 1987 as the Health Education Authority (HEA), has taken on a substantial role in the development of Health Education in schools, and (to a lesser extent) colleges – as well as with the general public. Area and Regional Health Authorities now have a duty to support health promotion by the appointment of appropriate personnel and the provision of resources (usually via their Health Education Units). At the same time, Health Education has become the subject of university research, central government development and focused professional training.

Despite its importance, Health Education remains a 'Cinderella' subject within the school and college curriculum. The Health Education activities of the Health Education Authority and Local Health Authorities are directed at the general populace and, although school- and college-based Health Education is

51

an identified part of their work, much of this is also done through health promotion programmes which have little to do with formally constituted education. The perspectives and career paths of most Health Education professionals are rooted within Health rather than Education Authorities.

Similarly, few Local Education Authorities have Advisers or Inspectors with a brief in Health Education alone (it is often combined with subjects such as Science or Home Economics). Few school or college staff members have a significant qualification in this 'subject'. Indeed, the Health Education Council and Authority have themselves been marked by an absence in their highest echelons of significant numbers of professionals with first-hand experience of work in schools and colleges. This isolation from wider educational issues has been exacerbated by the Council/Authority's increasing (government-led and -funded) concern with a number of apparently singular issues such as AIDS and drug abuse (HEA, 1988b) – sometimes (though not always) at the expense of broader 'social' issues which, as much in schools and colleges as elsewhere, are the basis of any meaningful and integrated programme of Health Education.

In its development outside the normal contexts of curriculum, Health Education stands apart from almost the whole of the remainder of that curriculum. It is delivered, for the most part, by staff with other subject specialisms who have to transmit the received wisdom of medical, political and other personnel who sometimes have little direct connection with mainstream curriculum development. There is little opportunity (despite the best efforts of some LEA Advisers and, indeed, of a number of HMI (DES, 1986)) under the funding and political–structural arrangements of the immediate past, for teachers collectively to influence or own the 'health' curriculum.

The debates in Health Education continue to flourish though: is it about medical 'facts' (where babies come from, why you need vitamins), is it about social and behavioural prescription (don't smoke, do take exercise), or is it about feelings and contexts (making your own choices, developing skills of communication and negotiation)? The crucial factor in decisions about Health Education is that these must involve not only those who teach but also those who represent, directly or indirectly, the interests of learners. An understanding of what Health Education is and could be, and of the ways that it might be delivered, must become currency far beyond the inner circle of 'health professionals' if this is to occur.

General Issues and Contexts in Contemporary Health Education

The Education Reform Act, 1988, has given the debate about control of the curriculum new impetus and meaning. Nonetheless, the Health Education Authority (Council, as was) – effectively the only organised curriculum leader in this field, and certainly the major source of funding for Health Education curriculum development – continues to perceive its role as addressing the Health Education needs of those both outside and inside the formal education system.

Whilst large numbers of professional educators (and others) believe strongly that education should indeed be on-going throughout life, quixotically the most significant upshot of this belief for Health Education is that it remains effectively outside the mainstream curriculum. The delivery of the 'health' curriculum is best achieved by the active involvement of teaching staff (with other professionals such as health educators or school medical personnel) in the empowerment of their students (Anderson, 1986). Yet much material continues to be packages (leaflets, films, etc.) presented at best by interested non-specialists who are also staff in the institution in question, and sometimes, with varying success (McCafferty *et al.*, 1987), by people who are both total strangers to the institution and not, themselves, teachers.

The first thesis of this chapter, then, is that health is far too weighty a matter to be left to the vagaries of visiting speakers, odd sessions, leaflets, films, etc., (which may or may not be easily accessible) and the whim of individual teaching staff, Heads or even governing bodies. Education for Health must be a central theme within the curriculum of any institution which takes the needs of its pupils or students seriously. It follows from this:

1   that Education for Health (as we shall henceforth call it) needs clear acknowledgement of its place within the curriculum
2   that the mode(s) of delivery of the health curriculum require careful consideration

Further, adequate curriculum delivery requires a critical appreciation of the intended aims and outcomes of this curriculum and of the contexts (classroom and institutional) in which it may effectively be negotiated and delivered (Balding, 1986).

Our second thesis is therefore that meaningful (or even plausible) Education for Health can only be achieved in institutions where the teaching staff as a whole have a competent grasp of curricular issues and where the *mores* of those institutions themselves support an alert and sensitive response to the social and personal needs of learners. Isolated 'lessons' on the 'nightmares of adults' (to use Chris Brown's apt term) are unlikely to meet effectively the aims of an informed and humane programme of Education for Health.

Ultimately, health can be viewed as a positive feeling of well-being (World Health Organisation, 1978), a philosophy which, whilst equipping the individual to survive and learn from the knocks which life inevitably imposes, also facilitates a strength and confidence to make the best, for oneself and for others, of whatever the situation has to offer. Such a definition has the advantage that it does not emphasise physical fitness at the expense of all else. It offers space for pupils and students with disability and for those who experience discrimination or disadvantage; it offers space for professionals with responsibility for curriculum development and educational administration to move beyond the straightforward physical and medical aspects of Education for Health. Equally important are those psychological, social and, indeed, politico-economic aspects of health which are fundamental to the enhancement of well-being.

A corollary of this is that any institution which means what it says about Education for Health will recognise the necessity for:

1   a curriculum which acknowledges the overlap between different aspects of social and personal experience
2   an adequate allocation of resources – financial and personnel – to develop and deliver such a curriculum
3   careful attention to the dignity and welfare of all who are involved in work or study within it

Such an institution will of course provide pastoral care and guidance to its students (and, where appropriate, to its employees), but it will also recognise its own wider role in offering respect and unobtrusive support to those within it. In such an intimate area as health and well-being, above all, integrity and continuity between the overt and the hidden curriculum become imperative (Tones, 1987).

In a wider context, despite the fairly conventional 'medical' (individualised and apparently apolitical) models of health in the higher echelons of Health Education, there exists a middle tier of workers (researchers, ex-teachers, community physicians, etc.) with some sympathy for health 'messages' which reflect notions of active learner empowerment and well-being. But the majority of developments in Health Education continue to occur outside the context of the mainstream curriculum, and certainly outside the professional remit of those who manage formal educational organisations. Our last point, then, is that the present isolation or marginalisation of health matters in the curriculum and in educational organisations as a whole may account for the lack of impact which many health messages appear to have on their intended recipients.

Curricular Aspects of Education for Health

Although there is some danger that any list of health 'topics' may deflect attention away from the central importance of the facilitation of well-being, it is only by an examination of the actual content of possible curricula that decisions about what to include can be made, and modes of delivery for given parts of that curriculum chosen. It has been argued elsewhere (DES, 1986; David and Williams, 1987) that there is ample scope, within a cross-curricular framework, for the delivery of health messages and skills, specifically via the more general personal and social curriculum (Tones, 1986; Wise, 1986) and through subjects such as Home Economics (DES, 1985), Physical Education (Dowling, 1986), Science (Payne, 1987), Social Studies/Sociology (Burrage, 1987a) or even perhaps Religious and Moral Education. But the extent to which this can be achieved through the present National Curriculum is, most commentators agree, doubtful (Burrage, 1987a; Finn, 1988). What will most concern us here, however, are issues of a broader nature concerning, for instance, the general aims of Education for Health and the sorts of curriculum and delivery appropriate to learners of both sexes and different ages, abilities and cultural backgrounds.

Topic Areas Comprising the Health Curriculum

There are a number of areas which any content list for Education for Health should include and ideally this list is irreducible; but personal or intimate topics 'taught' by teachers who are not comfortably familiar with the material they offer are probably nonetheless best omitted. (For this reason, yet again, it is crucial that teaching staff be active, well-versed participants, not passive vessels of conveyance – even mere film projectionists and arrangers of sessions by outside speakers – when they are involved in the transmission of the health curriculum.)

The following areas, then, comprise the core of the health curriculum:

● drug use and abuse (where drugs include nicotine, alcohol, tranquillisers, pain killers, etc.)
● Sex Education (the biological 'facts of life'), contraception (sometimes) and sexually transmitted disease (including AIDS more recently)
● nutrition ('balanced diet', if not obesity and eating disorders)
● hygiene and care/maintenance of self, including physical fitness, dental hygiene, cancer, etc. (plus care of others, first aid and childcare)

To this list could be added, in more liberal or ambitious programmes, for example:

● coping with stress (examinations, personal problems, assertiveness)
● 'the right to say No' (in respect of child abuse, touching, etc. – also obviously includes assertiveness skills)
● sexuality (but this is a matter of legal and political contention where it refers to homosexuality, because of clause 28 of the Local Government Act, 1988; but this does not, in fact, apply to schools according to the DOE, circular 12/88)
● mental health and illness (particularly in respect of the demystifying of certain psychiatric conditions)

- constructive and creative use of leisure and recreation time
- health and safety in the home and workplace (including, perhaps, knowledge of the functions of trade unions and of the Health and Safety Inspectorate (HSI), as well as strategies to reduce workplace hazards); plus wider health risks such as pollution
- health-related rights and responsibilities of the individual and the state (ranging from, say, a responsibility to ensure adequate immunisation of one's children – to issues concerning welfare benefits)

Not all these latter health curriculum areas are commonly addressed, but they all inform choices in Education for Health, whether consciously or not. At one extreme lies the decision to provide the minimum of information to permit the learner to understand the basic, mostly physiological, functions of his or her body; at the other extreme, the decision may be taken to introduce the concept of health as a personal experience and as being affected by social, political and economic factors.

We shall now look at some of these areas briefly before examining how Education for Health can work with wider trends in curriculum development and educational practice.

DRUG USE AND ABUSE

'Drugs' in this sense means both legal and illegal substances, ranging from so-called hard drugs through soft illegal drugs and solvent abuse, to legally available drugs like tobacco, alcohol, aspirin and prescribed medicines. Amongst the areas of particular current concern in Drugs Education are solvent abuse (glue sniffing), alcohol-enhanced riotous behaviour (plus, in older adolescents, driving over the alcohol limit) and transmission of AIDS through intravenous drug injection.

Agencies such as The Teachers' Advisory Council on Alcohol and Drug Education (TACADE) and the Institute for the Study of Drug Dependence (ISDD) have demonstrated a particular sensitivity to drug-related socio-cultural issues and to the necessity of differentiating between groups of users of legal and illegal drugs. But whatever material is used, there is evidence that the general curricular context within which children receive information on drugs is important. Thus, for instance, Evans and Lee (1986) suggest that children are more likely to be deterred from (as opposed to simply frightened by) illegal drug use or smoking if they discuss it in their Personal and Social Education lessons, rather than just receiving tuition about it in Science classes.

An issue which cannot be avoided in Drugs Education is the behaviour of adults. This ranges across matters such as smoking policy in schools (including staffrooms?) (Reid, 1985) through questions of the media and the advertising of legal drugs, to the discovery of children in possession of illegal drugs, or to really fraught issues concerning, e.g., suspected alcoholism in staff or child abuse resulting from parents' drinking or alcoholism. For these, as well as for more general curricular reasons, it is crucial that each school develop, within the parameters of legal requirements and LEA policies, an agreed, mature and considered overall policy on drugs which will serve to guide and protect both pupils and staff in a variety of unpredictable but always possible contingencies.

SEX EDUCATION

Sex Education is almost the only area of the curriculum which has in recent years been the subject of substantial (if not coherent) specific legislation apart from the Education Reform Act, 1988. It is arguably both the most contentious and the least well integrated 'topic' within the health curriculum. Traditionally, many schools (and colleges of further education, insofar as they attend to the issue at all) have dealt with Sex Education through a combination of Biology lessons and visiting speakers. This approach, whilst relatively 'safe' from the perspective of the Head/Principal and the established teaching staff, has several disadvantages from the alternative perspective of those (often less well informed than we imagine (Goldman and Goldman, 1988)) who are subjected to it. Further, the appearance of a relatively anonymous visitor to explain the essentials of where babies come from and (usually) how to avoid having them, is likely to confirm in young people's minds the impression that most of the 'ordinary' staff in the institution are not willing to discuss such matters.

Recently, however, there has been considerable political debate about some aspects of Sex Education such as sexuality (heterosexual or homosexual), contraception, sexually transmitted disease (including AIDS), and parental rights (if not children's): the Education Act (Number 2), 1986, requires governors to decide, and, if necessary, produce for parents a statement on their school's Sex Education curriculum. (This Act does not, however, permit parents to withdraw pupils from Sex Education classes without the consent of individual governing bodies.)

Whilst this debate has sometimes reinforced teachers' fears about their professional position if they provide children with the opportunity to learn about these important areas, it is also recognised that sex, sex roles, sexual relationships and sexuality are all parts of a reality which individuals experience as a whole. In moving away from straightforwardly medical–biological definitions of sex, we are more able to describe a life experience which means something to students; and it is now also essential that children and young people understand about AIDS and other sexually transmitted disease (STD). This simply cannot be done without some kind of understanding of sexual activity and its contexts. The Health Education Authority has, after some political difficulty, produced a government-approved pack on *Teaching about HIV and AIDS* (HEA, 1988b).

It is with AIDS, of course, that the confusion in the 1986 Conservative Government's attitude to sex and sexuality is so apparent. On the one hand there is clear acknowledgement by the government that students should become aware of AIDS as an issue. Yet many of their circulars and initiatives have had the effect of reducing school discussion. The DES Circular 11:87 (DES, 1987a) was widely interpreted as limiting teachers' remit in Sex Education, especially in regard to sexuality. Likewise, the Education Act (Number 2), 1986, has, uniquely, made provision for Sex Education solely at the discretion of individual school governing bodies. Further, Section 28 of the Local Government Act, 1988, attempts to prevent any positive acknowledgement of homosexual life styles through sanctions against those who may be judged to 'promote' homosexuality. After considerable confusion this Act is now adjudged not to apply to schools, which are still under the jurisdiction of the 1986 Act (DOE, Circular 12/88: 1988).

But despite all this it is generally agreed that AIDS must be understood by young people *before* they begin sexual activity, especially in terms of what constitutes 'high risk' sexual contact (this being not only homosexual), and which sorts of physical intimacy – including sexual contacts, needles shared by drug users, etc. – are likely to increase that risk. Recent legislation has, however, created an atmosphere of uncertainty and professional risk which hardly invites concerned teaching staff (the only informed adults some young people meet on a regular basis) to discuss these matters openly and supportively with their students.

Nonetheless, and contrary to some expectations, young people who have the opportunity to discuss sex and sexual relationships openly with their parents and teachers may cope better with their developing sexuality (Allen, 1987) and may even initiate sexual activity later, or have fewer early conceptions (Went, 1985).

Further, for the minority of young people who are, or may be, homosexual, the opportunity to discuss sexuality and sexual orientation with a responsible adult in a non-threatening, supportive and esteem-enhancing way may reduce considerably the (occasionally literally life-threatening) distress which a number of them experience (Trenchard and Warren, 1987). If, as has been suggested (Bayliss, 1988), teachers are being intimidated by recent legislation and guidelines not to discuss sexuality, the consequences for a number of young people may be grave.

Likewise, much of the health curriculum adopts the perspectives of white, middle class, middle aged men, and so is paternalistic or androcentric (Rocheron and Whylde, 1983; Burrage, 1986; Szirom, 1988). It is often assumed that teenagers who become pregnant are either unprepared or silly: whereas the opposite may be the case. In socio-economic circumstances that offer little prospect of a future, having children may have been a conscious and positive decision. A further assumption is the unspoken one that parenthood for mature women is an end in itself in a way which it is not for men.

Similarly with our assumptions about marriage. The Education Act, 1986, requires that Sex Education emphasise moral considerations and the 'value of family life', but many children are conceived (and a significant number born) out of wedlock and/or stable unions, and others are the subject of sexual or other abuse (National Children's Homes, 1988). The imposition on children of rigidly moral views about adult sexual behaviour is therefore both dishonest and potentially cruel.

Certainly, sex within a stable, supportive and equal relationship may be the ideal, but, as the HMI publication on *Health Education in Schools* (DES, 1977) infers, it is not for teaching staff to be overly judgemental of people who do not live up to this ideal, when some of them are likely to be the parents of the children whom we teach. Similarly, a more recent HMI commentary, *Health Education from 5 to 16* (DES, 1986), noted that '. . . many children come from backgrounds which do not correspond to this ideal (of loving relationships and respect for others), and great sensitivity is needed to avoid causing personal hurt and giving unwitting offence.'

Nor may we make socio-cultural assumptions which may not be appropriate for people from other cultures (Christopher, 1980), or neglect the special problems with sexual relationships of some young people with physical disability (Anderson, Clark and Spain, 1982) or with mental handicap (Fraser, 1987; Dixon, 1988).

Sex is sometimes an embarrassing or painful topic for adults but we must remember that it can be one of the most positive aspects of any person's experience. Carefully considered, Sex Education in the context of a professional and caring attitude (David and Wise, 1987) will assist young people in their development of a responsible and balanced view of this perplexing but deeply important part of life.

NUTRITION

'. . . so many people . . . with the most influence understand so little about food in practical terms. Most are middle-aged men who rarely go shopping or cook.' Thus remarked Caroline Walker (1988), former Secretary of the National Advisory Committee of Nutrition Education, whose report in 1983 pressed the government to take steps to reduce fat and sugar in the national diet. Caroline Walker took the view that financial, organisational and political pressures combine to restrict ordinary people's access to good quality food.

This view must be set against government ministers' tendency to blame the public, despite the frequent lack of real choice and the continued inadequate or indecipherable labelling of food, for their poor eating habits. School Catering Services can, however, have a very positive influence (London Food Commission, 1986), and should provide nutritionally balanced meals for meat-eaters, vegetarians and those with religious or cultural requirements.

In the classroom, nutrition and food hygiene are amongst only a small number of Health Education topics which are offered as examination courses for older children (eg. GCSE and Royal Society of Health). It is also quite possible to integrate 'healthy eating messages' into many other parts of the curriculum. 'Food topics' for this purpose might include additives, sugar or fibre, but we must acknowledge in tackling any food issue that cultural (or regional) influences on students' eating habits must be approached supportively (HEA/Coronary Prevention Group, 1988).

Finally, it appears that young people are particularly prone to eating-related disorders such as obesity and anorexia. Parents and staff alike must be aware of these potentially serious conditions and of the sensitivities they may arouse.

HYGIENE, SAFETY AND CARE / MAINTENANCE OF SELF AND OTHERS

Even very young children need to be taught the basics of physical and personal growth, hygiene and self-care. Physical Education staff have a clear role here and the Schools' Council Health Education Project (5–13) provides worksheets and information on such matters as personal hygiene and dental health and leisure and recreation – now supplemented also by a programme for the 16–19 age range (Schools Council / HEC, 1987). (For slow learners aged 5–16, a parallel project produced by the Schools Council with the Health Education Council is available, entitled *Fit for life*.)

Apart from personal hygiene and care, children of 13 upwards may be taught the basics of life-saving and first aid (whether in Health or PSE lessons, or in time allocated to Sport and Physical Education). They should also begin to learn about health and safety in the workplace (Watterson, 1986) – just as they will already have begun to learn about road safety: the local Police Force Schools Liaison Officer or the Royal Society for the Prevention of Accidents will advise on the latter and, for the former, the Health Education Authority and trade union organisations such as the TUC or NALGO may be able to provide materials and advice.

Schools may also choose to teach adolescents (male and female, able and less-able) something of childcare and possibly of care of other dependent people (GCSE courses are available). The Learning Materials Service resource packs on *Childhood and Family Lifestyles* (1985) may prove useful here.

STRESS

There are different types of stress. Whilst many people may see it only as a personal problem to be overcome by self-discipline (for example, by time management) there is the danger that one may fail to recognise a number of other factors which cause stress, many of them outside personal control, which everyone experiences from time to time.

Examinations are one common reason for stress, and strategies to assist students in 'coping' should be integrated into the teaching of every appropriate subject (Mechanic, 1979; Nash, 1984).

Other causes of stress are, however, by their nature almost invisible at school, although they may be very much part of a pupil's home life. Examples might include family violence, drug addiction or alcoholism, unemployment, redundancy, poverty and/or illness (Smith, 1987), mental or physical handicap, etc.

All educational establishments therefore need staff trained as counsellors. Policy and implementation in respect to stress management must be matters of importance to all staff, students, governors and parents; as should policy and training on referral of individuals with problems. The British Association for Counselling provides advice for schools and colleges in these areas.

Finally, assertiveness training may facilitate both staff and students in presenting their views or positions clearly without aggression or apology. Whilst this sort of training is not part of the traditional health agenda, it is increasingly becoming acknowledged as important.

Making Education For Health part of the New Curriculum

It will by now be apparent that the integration of Education for Health with other aspects of the curriculum can only be achieved when the issues have become clear to those staff, governors, parents, and perhaps students, who will be involved, and when a fair amount of time and energy has been invested in considering 'who will do what'. A cross-disciplinary area such as Health covers areas as varied as Physical Education, Home Economics, Science, Social Studies and Pastoral Care, with the resultant danger (unless a senior member of staff has a specific remit here) that it can fall between all of them. In this the Education Reform Act, 1988, is not helpful.

There has, however, been some progress, albeit unco-ordinated. The National Curriculum proposals on *Science for Ages 5 to 16* notes that responses to the previous Interim Report saw:

> . . . (the) educational approaches outlined . . . as compatible with good Health Education. It was hoped that the final report would stress the importance of developing in children the ability to understand the consequences of action for self and others. [. . .] Our Science theme relating to living things and their interaction with the environment was seen as having a central role in promoting an understanding of health-related areas of the curriculum. There was (also) a need for Science to link

with Personal and Social Education, which often played a vital role in the
delivery of Health Education in schools.   (DES, 1988)

This approach, balancing to some extent knowledge for personal responsibility
against social aspects of health, offers some hope that the issues explored above
will not be lost. Further, other programmes such as the Certificate in Pre-
Vocational Education, whilst their relationship to the National Curriculum
remains unclear, do include core elements which may be taken to relate to health
(as, of course, do some GCSE and other examined subjects).

Essentially, however, the new curriculum appears to be led by aspects of
educational experience which can be tested. Indeed, the first stages in the debate
about the National Curriculum were conducted in these terms.

If the 'serious' curriculum is effectively defined by what can be tested, it could
lead to the disappearance of whole areas of Health Education. It is certainly
possible, given proper co-ordination, to test (and therefore legitimately to
deliver) knowledge about physiology or the physiological effects of given
substances and behaviour, but it is less easy – and, many would feel, professionally very questionable – to test publicly individuals' attitudes to, say,
drugs, mental illness or contraception. There may even be a role for Records of
Achievement as students gain in understanding of health issues, but the
experience of the past decade in Health Education is that the most important
feature of effective work in this area concerns attitudes and peer group cultures.
Though a heavy responsibility, staff, governors and parents must work
together, within whatever national guidelines, to decide what attitudes they
wish to see inculcated in pupils and students of different ages and abilities, etc.
This is very different from examining formally the 'attainment' of these
individual learners in such personal matters.

But one important feature of effective Education for Health is that it changes
behaviour as well as attitudes. Evaluation of *programmes* of Health Education *is*
therefore a legitimate target for appraisal (Perkins, 1987) even though evaluation of only certain aspects of individual learning may be ethically defensible.
Health educators and teachers must work with community physicians to
develop understanding of underlying issues in health and illness (Kolbe, 1984;
Burrage, 1987b) and to become more conscious of how our pupils and students
themselves perceive the issues. (Useful enquiry instruments here may be the
Health Related Behaviour Questionnaire and *Health Topics Questionnaire* of the
HEA Schools Health Education Unit, University of Exeter.) Then we must
evaluate our programmes for Health Education for their immediate efficacy and
later, again with the epidemiologists, examine what longer-term effects on
behaviour and health our teaching may be having. Training to effect such
evaluation must therefore be a priority in all Education for Health initiatives.

Ultimately we must knit an understanding of the support young people need in maintaining their well-being with the tools to evaluate and improve our work. The real questions in Education for Health evolve around the will to provide space and resources to define aims, integrate curriculum and evaluate outcomes. In some schools and colleges, and especially in those which pursue clearly stated organisational health promotion policies and ensure effective co-ordination of health elements in the curriculum, excellent practice will continue to develop. But there is as yet little to encourage the hope that national educational structures, combining the experience of health promotion personnel, health educators and classroom teachers firmly within the context of the National Curriculum, will soon emerge to encompass and consolidate this good practice. In such circumstances the vigilance and support of concerned staff, governors and parents remains crucial.

Acknowledgements

I am grateful to a number of friends and colleagues, amongst them Jan Cornish, Nick Dorn, Wendy Farrant, Linda Finn, Hilary McBride, Alex Scott-Samuel and Ann Thorpe, for information and advice concerning this chapter. Its content and any errors or omissions are, however, entirely my own responsibility.

References and Further Resources

I. Allen, *Education in Sex and Personal Relationships*, Policy Studies Research Report no. 665 (Policy Studies Institute, 100 Park Village East, London NW1 3SR, 1987)

E. Anderson, L. Clark and B. Spain, *Disability in Adolescence* (Methuen, 1982)

J. Anderson, 'Health Skills: the power to choose' in *Health Education Journal*, vol. 45, no. 1 (1986)[*]

J. Balding, 'Planning the Curriculum: Health-related behaviour studies in schools' in *Health Education Journal*, vol. 45, no. 1 (1986)[*]

S. Bayliss, 'New laws "frighten off" queries on Sex Education' in *Times Educational Supplement* (23 September 1988)

D. Black, *Inequalities in Health* (DHSS, 1980), also published as P. Townsend and D. Davidson, *Inequalities in Health: The Black Report* (Penguin, 1982)

H. Burrage, 'Health Education: The Androcentric Agenda' in *Journal of the Institute of Health Education*, vol. 24, no. 3 (Institute of Health Education, 14 High Elms Road, Hale Barnes, Cheshire, 1986)

H. Burrage, 'Sociology and Health Education in the Curriculum' in *Social Science Teacher*, vol. 17, no. 1 (1987a)
   The bibliography for this paper is located in *Social Science Teacher*, vol. 18, no. 1[**]

H. Burrage, 'Epidemiology and Community Health: A Strained Connection?' in *Social Science and Medicine*, vol. 25, no. 8 (Pergamon Journals, 1987b)

H. Burrage, 'Social Science in the National Curriculum' in *Social Science Teacher*, vol. 17, no. 3 (1988)*

J. Chambers, *Men, Sex and Contraception* (Birth Control Trust, 27–35 Mortimer Street, London WC1N 7RJ, 1984)

E. Christopher, *Sexuality and Birth Control in Social and Community Work* (Temple Smith, 1980)

K. David and T. Williams (eds.), *Health Education in Schools*, 2nd edition (Harper and Row, 1987)

K. David and C. Wise, 'Challenges for Sex Education in Schools' in K. David and T. Williams (eds.), *Health Education in Schools*, 2nd edition (Harper and Row, 1987)

DES, *Health Education in Schools* (DES, 1977)

DES, *Curriculum Matters 5: Home Economics from 5 to 16* (HMSO, 1985)

DES, *Curriculum Matters 6: Health Education from 5 to 16* (HMSO, 1986)

DES, *Sex Education at School*, circular 11/1987 (DES, 1987a)

DES, *National Curriculum: Task Group on Assessment and Testing: A Report* (DES, 1987b)

DES, *Science for Ages 5 to 16: Proposals of the Secretary of State for Education and the Secretary of State for Wales* (DES, 1988)

H. Dixon, *Sexuality and Mental Handicap: An Educator's Resource Book* (Learning Development Aids, obtainable from Healthwise (FPA bookshop), 27–35 Mortimer Street, London W1N 7RJ, 1988)

DES, on non-application of Section 28 to schools, circular 12/1988 (DES, 1988)

F. Dowling, 'The Changing Face of Physical Education' in *Health Education Journal*, vol. 45, no. 1 (1986)*

V. Evans and J. Lee, 'An Integrated Approach to Drug Education' in *Health Education Journal*, vol. 45, no. 1 (1986)*

L. Finn, 'Responsible Learning: Omitting PSE from the National Curriculum could damage our health' in *Times Educational Supplement* (27 May 1988)

J. Fraser, *Not A Child Anymore* (Brook Advisory Centres, obtainable from Brook Education and Publishing Unit, 24 Albert Street, Birmingham B4 7UD, 1987)

R. Goldman and J. Goldman, *Show Me Yours* (Penguin, 1988)

C. Griffin, *Typical Girls? Young Women from School to the Job Market* (Routledge and Kegan Paul, 1985)

HEA, *Working for Health: A Consultation Document* (Health Education Authority, 1988a)

HEA, *Teaching about HIV and AIDS* (obtainable from Health Education Units of Local Health Authorities, 1988b)

HEA/Coronary Prevention Group, *Heart, Health and Asians* (Health Education Authority, 1988)

L. J. Kolbe, 'Improving the Health Status of Children: An Epidemiological Approach to Establishing Priorities for Behavioural Research' in G. Campbell (ed.), *Health Education and Youth: A Review of Research and Developments* (Falmer Press, 1984)

London Food Commission, *School Meals: What can you do?* (Publications Department, London Food Commission, 88 Old Street, London EC1V 9AR, 1986)

H. McBride, *Tracing the Origins of Health Education* (unpublished dissertation submitted for the diploma in Health Education, Polytechnic of the South Bank, London, 1983)

I. McCafferty *et al.*, 'Health Education Units and the Use of Visitors in the Classroom' in K. David and T. Williams (eds.), *Health Education in Schools*, 2nd edition (Harper and Row, 1987)

D. Mechanic, *Students Under Stress* (Wisconsin Press, 1979)

W. Nash, 'The Perceptions of 14–15 Year Old Pupils Concerning Stress: A Pilot Study' in G. Campbell (ed.), *Health Education and Youth: A Review of Research and Developments* (Falmer Press, 1984)

National Advisory Committee on Nutrition Education, *A Discussion Paper on Proposals for Nutritional Guidelines for Health Education in Britain* (Health Education Council, 1983)

National Children's Homes, *Children in Danger* (National Children's Homes, 85 Highbury Park, London N5 1UD, 1988)

V. Payne, 'Challenges and Implications of Introducing Social and Ethical Issues into the Science Curriculum' in P. J. Kelley and L. J. Lewis, *Education and Health* (Pergamon, 1987)

E. R. Perkins (ed.), 'Research and Evaluation in Health Education' (Section 8) in G. Campbell (ed.), *Health Education, Youth and Community: A Review of Research and Developments* (Falmer Press, 1987)

D. Reid, 'Prevention of Smoking Among Schoolchildren: Recommendations for Policy Development' in *Health Education Journal*, vol. 45, no. 1 (1985)[*]

Religious and Moral Education Press, *Values: Sex Education Issue*, vol. 2, no. 1 (Religious and Moral Education Press, Hennock Road, Exeter EX2 8RP, 1987)

Y. Rocheron and J. Whylde 'Sex Education' in J. Whylde (ed.), *Sexism in the Secondary Curriculum* (Harper and Row, 1983)

S. V. Rosser, *Teaching Science and Health from a Feminist Perspective: A Practical Guide* (Pergamon, 1986)

Schools Council/HEC, *Health Education Pack: Health Education for 16–19* (National Extension College, 18 Brooklands Avenue, Cambridge CB2 2HN, 1987)

R. Smith, *Unemployment and Health: a disaster and a challenge* (Oxford Medical Publications, 1987)

A. Smith and B. Jacobsen (eds.), *The Nation's Health* (Oxford University Press for the King's Fund, 1988)

T. Szirom, *Teaching Gender? Sex Education and Sexual Stereotypes* (Allen and Unwin, 1988)

K. Tones, 'Promoting the Health of Young People – the role of Personal and Social Education' in *Health Education Journal*, vol. 45, no. 1 (1986)[*]

K. Tones, 'Health Promotion, Affective Education and the Personal – Social Development of Young People' in K. David and T. Williams (eds.), *Health Education in Schools*, 2nd Edition (Harper and Row, 1987)

L. Trenchard and H. Warren, 'Talking about School: the experiences of young lesbians and gay men' in G. Weiner and M. Arnot (eds.), *Gender Under Scrutiny: New inquiries in education* (Hutchinson/Open University, 1987)

C. Walker, as reported in her Obituary, *The Guardian* (24 September 1988)

A. Watterson, 'Occupational Health and Illness: The Politics of Hazard Education' in A. Watts and S. Rodmell (eds.), *The Politics of Health Education: Raising the Issues* (Routledge and Kegan Paul, 1986)

D. Went, *Sex Education: Some guidelines for teachers* (Bell and Hyman, 1985)

C. Wise, 'Tensions and Trends in School Health Education' in C. Brown, C. Harber and J. Scrivens (eds.), *Social Education: Principles and Practice* (Falmer Press, 1986)

World Health Organisation, *Declaration of Alma Ata* (1978), the European goals of which are discussed in Faculty of Community Medicine of the Royal College of Physicians of the UK, *Health for All by the Year 2000: Charter for Action* (FCMRCP, 1986)

Health Education Journal is available from the Health Education Authority, Hamilton House, Mabledon Place, London WC1H 9TX

**Social Science Teacher* is the Journal of the Association for the Teaching of the Social Sciences and is available from the Executive Secretary, ATSS, PO Box 461, Sheffield S1 3BF

Key Teacher Resources

Health Education Authority, *Health Education for Young People: a guide to projects and resources*; Resources Catalogues (on a wide variety of topics); *Schools Health Education Project 5–16*, a Training Manual.

HEA Schools Health Education Unit, *Education and Health* (journal); *Services to Schools, Health Authorities, Local Education Authorities*, a catalogue of research instruments and findings

Institute for the Study of Drug Dependence, Publications List; Curriculum Guide (part of *Drugwise*)

North Western Counties Physical Education Association, *Health Related Fitness: Its Place in the Curriculum* (2 Vanderbyl Avenue, Spital, Wirral L62 2AP)

School Curriculum Development Committee/Equal Opportunities Committee, *Genderwatch!* (stage 3: Health Education section) (SCDC Publications, Newcombe House, 45 Notting Hill Gate, London W11 3JB)

Secondary Science Curriculum Review, *Health and Science Education: Proposals for Action and Consultation* (SSCR, Newcombe House, 45 Notting Hill Gate, London W11 3JB)

Training in Health and Race, Resources List (National Extension College, 18 Brooklands Avenue, Cambridge CB2 2HN)

Key Classroom Resources

BBC and IBA – radio and television health programmes for children and young people

Concord Films Council Ltd. – large variety of resources (201 Felixstowe Road, Ipswich IP3 9BJ)

Institute for the Study of Drug Dependence / Lifeskills Associates / Teachers' Advisory Council on Alcohol and Drug Education, *Drugwise: Drug Education for Students 14–18* (1986) (includes materials for classroom use, a Curriculum Guide and a Training Manual for teacher/parent workshops)

Learning Materials Service, *Childhood and Family Lifestyles* (ring-bound packs for older teenagers) (Centre for Continuing Education, PO Box 188, Milton Keynes, MK7 6DH, 1985)

Schools Council Health Education Project 5–13, *All about me* (for 5–8s) and *Think well* (for 9–13s) (packs include Teachers' Guides, Resource Sheets and Spirit Masters) (Thomas Nelson and Son, 1977/1983)

Schools Council / Health Education Council, *Fit for Life* – for slow learners (Macmillan Education, Houndmills, Basingstoke, Hampshire RG21 2XS, 1983)

N.B. The materials listed here are largely already established; resources in Health Education are frequently revised, and up-to-date catalogues from the HEA, and local Health Education Units should be consulted to check current availability and whether the material has been superseded.

Key Addresses

British Association for Counselling,
37a Sheep Street,
Rugby,
Warwickshire CV221 3BX
Tel: (0788) 78328/9

Brook Advisory Centres,
Central Office,
153a East Street,
London SE17 2SD
Tel: (01) 708 1234/1390

Family Planning Association,
27–35 Mortimer Street,
London W1
Tel: (01) 631 0555

Health Education Authority,
Hamilton House,
Mabledon Place,
London WC1H 9TX
Tel: (01) 631 0930

HEA Schools Health Education Unit,
Department of Education,
University of Exeter,
Heavitree Road,
Exeter EX1 2LU
Tel: (0392) 264722

Institute for the Study of Drug Dependence,
1–4 Hatton Place,
Hatton Garden,
London EC1N 8ND
Tel: (01) 430 1991

Local Health Authority Health Education Units
(see local telephone directories)

Teachers' Advisory Council on Alcohol and Drug Education (TACADE),
Furness House,
Trafford Road,
Salford M5 2XJ
Tel: (061) 848 0351

• 5 •

MEDIA EDUCATION:

CRITICAL TIMES?

Mike Clarke

Origins

A key factor in the early development of Media Education was a widespread public concern about the supposed harmful influence of the media on impressionable individuals. In the 1930s (before television) this was articulated by figures as diverse as the critical theorists of the German 'Frankfurt School' and, in Britain, F. R. Leavis and others associated with the literary review *Scrutiny*.

The Frankfurt School included Herbert Marcuse, Theodor Adorno and Max Horkheimer. They sought to explain Germany's descent into fascism by the effects of the media: differences between people were suppressed by the media's tendency to present society as a homogeneous mass; traditional identifications with class or political party disappeared, leaving isolated individuals with no defences against the Nazi propaganda. These writers' cultural pessimism, understandable given their circumstances, is reflected in the title of one of their papers, *The Culture Industry: Enlightenment as Mass Deception* (Adorno and Horkheimer, 1977).

In Britain, Leavis and Denys Thompson criticised the media's 'exploitation of the cheapest emotional responses' which they saw as an aspect of the destruction of rural community life by industrialisation. The antipathy they felt towards many aspects of modern society is evident in their early pamphlet, *Mass Civilisation and Minority Culture* (Leavis, 1930). Nevertheless, in *Culture and Environment*, they could be said to have founded Media Education by calling on teachers to bring media texts into the classroom, albeit so that their pupils could be 'trained to discriminate and resist' (Leavis and Thompson, 1933).[1]

Leavis and his followers saw their mission as the preservation of fundamental human values which were beyond (above) politics; Marcuse and his followers in Germany were concerned to make a political analysis of historical events. However, both groups' blanket hostility to mass art and mass culture reveals a shared cultural conservatism, a commitment both to 'high art' and to the values of an earlier, supposedly better, era.

The succession of 'moral panics' which have surrounded various popular forms, including music hall, films, horror comics, television crime programmes and video 'nasties', have also given some impetus to Media Education. Despite the inconclusiveness of their results, the innumerable research reports on the damaging effects of sex and violence on television have fostered a desire to protect vulnerable members of society, particularly children.[2] Often the outcomes of these campaigns have been increased censorship (e.g. the Video Recordings Act, 1984) but they have also been turned towards a more constructive engagment with how children watch television programmes and what it is that they understand from them.

From the left of the political spectrum, concerns in recent years have been more to do with the increasing centralisation of control over the media, especially through conglomerates such as those owned by Rupert Murdoch and Robert Maxwell, and with the nature of media products themselves – specifically, their representation of such key areas as gender and race. The issue of representation has emerged most forcibly in campaigns about the relative absence of black people on British screens (other than as stereotyped characters in situation comedies) or about the degradation of women through 'national institutions' like page 3 of *The Sun*.

It is notable that virtually all these currents within 'public opinion' begin from a negative attitude to some aspect of the media. In education the picture is not quite so bleak, although many teachers share some or all of these worries. The formation of Media Education in schools and colleges was undoubtedly influenced by earlier developments in Higher Education, particularly in the fields of Sociology and Film Studies, and later from Communication Studies. From Sociology came an interest in the workings of the media organisations themselves.[3] Questions of ownership and control were explored in a series of papers by Graham Murdock and Peter Golding, in which they argued that an understanding of the *political economy* of the media (i.e. issues of ownership and control) was essential to an analysis of modern society.[4]

The legacy of Film Studies is complex. Film Studies became concerned with the study of *cinema* as a system for the production, circulation and consumption of *meanings* (i.e. the ideas and ideologies contained in films). This approach developed in Britain particularly through the work of *Screen* in the 1970s.

What distinguishes the Film Studies influence on Media Education from the sociological one is its emphasis on textual analysis – detailed examination of the workings of specific media products, as opposed to the macro-economic study of media organisations. The contribution of Communication Studies in secondary and further education is less easy to pinpoint. Broadly speaking it approaches both practical 'production' work and questions of audience consumption of media products.[5]

The history of Media Education in schools and colleges is a relatively short one but the principal line of development can be traced fairly clearly from Film Studies (taught at CSE and O/A-level in the 1970s) through Film and Television Studies to Media Studies (now available at GCSE and A-level). Agencies such as the Education Department of the British Film Institute (BFI) and the Society for Education in Film and Television (SEFT) have played a vital role, through the teaching materials they have made available. With the shift from Film Studies to Media Studies has come an increasing recognition of the role and importance of practical activity, which not only bridges the traditional, damaging mental/manual divide in school work but also enables a more concrete, active understanding of theoretical concepts.

Media Studies as such has always been a minority activity, typically an optional subject at 4th and 5th year level (Years 10 and 11). A key moment in the movement towards a more broadly based notion of Media Education was the publication by the DES in 1983 of *Popular TV and Schoolchildren*. This was the report of a working party set up by the then Secretary of State for Education, Sir Keith Joseph, with a brief to examine the images of adult life being presented to children by the broadcasters. Out of an initial concern for children's moral welfare (the familiar anxious and negative standpoint that children are corrupted by television) came several highly positive recommendations. In particular, it recommended that teachers, parents and broadcasters should get together to examine their roles in relation to children's developing understanding of the world, and that '... specialist courses in Media Studies are not enough: all teachers should be involved in examining and discussing television programmes with young people' (DES, 1983). The latter recommendation has been frequently quoted in support of the drive to establish Media Education across the curriculum and throughout children's schooling.

Key Debates

In 1980, Macmillan published Len Masterman's *Teaching About Television*, which might reasonably be described as the first book of the modern era of Media Education (despite the fact that it bases much of its argument on the teaching of a CSE course in Television Studies in the 1970s and, indeed, explicitly rejects Media Studies as such). Several commentators on *Teaching About Television* took up the question of 'discrimination'. Prominent amongst these was Roger Knight, editor of *The Use of English* – the magazine founded by Denys Thompson, co-author of *Culture and Environment* and also of *Discrimination and Popular Culture* (1964). Many people, including teachers, were outraged that questions of value were apparently being banished from the classroom. How could Masterman contend that discrimination and appreciation had no place in Television Education, and that its real business was solely to analyse the images and ideological content and to ignore the issues of quality, value and merit?

In fact, from the perspective of the early 1990s, this seems like a non-debate. Masterman's hidden agenda was not in fact the dissolution of values, but the displacement of one literary set of values with another ideological one. An important teaching point was nevertheless made: that careful and detailed *investigation* of any media text must precede any judgement of it. The criteria on which such judgements might eventually be made (and the teacher's role in relation to these) remain, necessarily, controversial. Different teachers will have their own views about what constitutes a good television programme, for example, as will their students. Each framework has its own moral and political implications and the course is a difficult one between on the one hand, indoctrination, and on the other, the abdication of any responsibility.[6]

The debate which followed Masterman's later publication, *Teaching the Media*, took a different turn. Both this and the more or less contemporary *Making Sense of the Media* (Hartley *et al.*, 1985) were charged, in effect, with being overly sociological, and with laying too much emphasis on 'external' factors (like ownership and control) and too little on questions of subjectivity. It is only fair to add that the authors of both responded vigorously to these reviews, principally by denying the interpretations of their work on which the criticisms were based. Whether or not they were 'guilty as charged', the nature of the supposed 'crimes' is worth exploring in more detail.

In his review of *Teaching the Media*, David Buckingham (1986) attacked the notion of 'demystification' as an appropriate target for Media Education. The objections to this are twofold. Firstly, it assumes that the student is, in fact, mystified; secondly, it implies that there is a clear and correct view. So, if one demystifies, say, the television soap *Coronation Street*, one reveals the underlying truths of what the programme is saying. In a sense, this is completely unobjectionable: one aim of any worthwhile education is a deepening of understanding. Where it falls down (as a description of what Media Education should be doing) is in its suggestion that there is, somewhere, a *simple* way of summing up the complex operations of a soap opera.

However, the problem with demystification is not only this reductionism but also the accompanying concept of the viewer as someone who is duped (mystified) by the media. What this calls to mind is the notion of 'false consciousness', or ideology, used in Marx's earlier writings and later rejected both by him and by other writers within the same tradition. Adherents to the wider forms of this theory argue that the deliberate and regular distortion of ideas and reality by the controllers of the media leads to a lack of sympathy or understanding of socialism among the general public – without the distortion and manipulation, there would be widespread support for socialism. Unfortunately, there is little empirical evidence of such a conspiracy – indeed, where a deliberate campaign to misinform is discovered (e.g. during the Falklands/ Malvinas conflict in 1982), what this precisely establishes is the rare and exceptional nature of calculated media manipulation. 'False consciousness' is not only misleading in this sense, it is also counter-productive pedagogically speaking – students do not grasp the idea and many do not support the notion. When approaching a media text, students must feel that their view of it is valued by the teacher. Indeed, the teacher needs to regard their pleasure in particular programmes or publications not as the products of media mystification, to be expunged as soon as possible, but as the vital raw material for debate in which a variety of 'readings', or interpretations, can be brought forward and examined, with a view not to correcting them but to making the meaning clearer.

More recent volumes attempt to take account of the importance of the concept of pleasure – and the theoretical shift from a notion of media audiences as mere dupes to an understanding of viewers as active participants in consumption (that is, members of social formations who bring their own cultural predispositions to bear on media products).[7] David Morley's useful publication, *Family Television* (1986), documents this active engagement on the basis of a small-scale research study.

To over-simplify considerably, it might be said that the debate around *Teaching the Media* and *Making Sense of the Media* was about the importance of 'process' in Media Education as opposed to 'content'. Whether or not Masterman and Hartley *et al.* actually espoused the views attributed to them, it is not surprising to find a range of opinions on this issue. If part of the aim of Media Education is to help students to become more critically aware and more critically autonomous, one of the corollaries of this is that they must be able to challenge not only media texts but also those presented by the teacher. An approach which puts a great deal of emphasis on factual knowledge, whether of multinational holdings or of the technical specifications of the latest whizz-bang technology, is unlikely to foster such critical autonomy. On the other hand, if students are disabled from considering the choices that have been made in the presentation of a news item because they simply do not *know* enough about how editing works, then, again, no useful purpose is served.

Making Sense of the Media was one concrete outcome of a series of important initiatives in Wales. What eventually became known as the Clwyd Media Studies Unit was established in the 1970s to support the work of teachers in schools, particularly that which led to a joint O-level/CSE examination in Mass Media (succeeded by the WJEC GCSE Media Studies syllabus). As more schools and teachers were involved, the need for certificated in-service training became apparent and the Polytechnic of Wales came up with the Diploma in

Teaching Media, the course materials for which contributed substantially to *Making Sense of the Media*. Another course, the Diploma in Media Studies in Education, ran for a short period at Leicester University School of Education. However, the most substantial and sustained work at this level has taken place at the London University Institute of Education, where many hundreds of teachers have developed their understanding of Media Education through Diploma courses, PGCE courses and the MA in Film and Television Studies for Education.

The development of GCSE courses both demonstrated and contributed to a growing consensus about the nature of Media Studies. All the early syllabi laid stress on the importance of conceptual knowledge and all involved practical work as well as written coursework. More or less contemporaneously, TVEI came upon the scene. This was regarded with grave suspicion in many quarters (with ILEA refusing to be involved at all for several years) but it has undoubtedly contributed substantially to the recent growth of interest in Media Education. To put it at its most crude, teachers of the Arts and Humanities saw large amounts of money being spent on hardware in Science, Technology and Business Studies and wanted a slice of the cake for their areas. The emphasis placed in the early stages by some authorities (even more than the MSC) on technological skills and vocational relevance created problems, however, as this version of Media Education seemed to conflict with the earlier critical emphasis. In some cases this led TVEI-inspired media courses to be called Media Technology, presumably in order to escape the requirement to examine cultural and political questions. What needs to be asked of such courses is what their real value is. Teaching students to use what is invariably domestic or amateur equipment has little vocational relevance in itself (despite the fascination which practical activity clearly holds for many youngsters). Equipment-led developments posed the question of the value and purpose of practical work in an acute form but the relationship between *reading* and *writing* (criticism and practice) in Media Education continues to be the subject of debate.

Current Practice

The principal concerns of Media Studies might be broadly described as the *forms* of the media; *representation*; and *institutions* and *audience:*

- *Forms* include the various codes and conventions employed to create meanings in the different media, as well as the characteristics of particular genres. The complex issues surrounding the various types of realism ('Hollywood', documentary, etc.) may be raised here.
- *Representation* covers both the relationship between media images and the

social groups they portray, and the process whereby such media images are produced (who is depicted, how, by whom, for whom?). Questions of social justice are prominent.

● *Institutions* and *audience* tackle not the individual media image ('product' or 'text') but the context of media production, circulation and consumption.

It is possible to think of there being three elements in the practice of Media Education: *reading* (critical response to media products), *writing* (making media products) and *learning* about institutions. However, many teachers have been loath to see the last as a separate activity, preferring that students should see the relevance of other issues (such as ownership and control, selection and editing) to actual newspapers, programmes, etc. So, for example, the question of how a film is sold would be tied into the viewing of a particular feature; television production practices might be linked with the study of an actual programme, say *Boys from the Blackstuff*. In other words *reading* is not something which can be learnt out of context, and *writing* needs to be related to professional production.

Some more concrete examples may be helpful at this point. A simple, basic activity of *reading* would be one like the 'Teddy Bear' exercise in the BFI teaching pack, *Reading Pictures*. A series of four slides are shown to the group, the first of which shows a small part of a photograph. Students are asked to describe what they can see as fully as possible. If necessary, they may be prompted to consider the position of the camera, the nature of the lighting, and so on. Although their answers at this point may be tentative, it is nevertheless worth asking 'institutional' questions such as: 'Have you any idea what sort of photograph this is? Where might you come across one like this? Who do you think might have taken it?' At an appropriate point, the next slide is shown, which reveals a little more of the image. Some possibilities will now seem less likely, while new ones may emerge. The third slide shows the whole photograph, which is still somewhat enigmatic, even though it is clearly 'set up' with studio lights, etc. Most viewers see that it is most likely to be an advertising image, although what the product is it is difficult to say. Once everyone who wishes to has contributed, the full page can be shown, revealing it to be an advertisement for make-up. It is then possible, and often useful, to look again at the first slide, in order to raise more precisely the question of the teddy bear's role in this mini-narrative. This is the moment when the teacher may feed in the information that the advertisement appeared in a range of teenage and women's magazines with a predominantly female readership between the ages of ten and fifty. Who then is it supposed to appeal to? Is it saying the same thing to a 13-year old as it is to her mother? What are their concerns likely to be?

The point of the exercise, which can last up to half-an-hour, or even longer, is to make students aware of the ways in which pictures make sense to us – or, if you prefer, we make sense of them. Depending on the group of students, it may be possible to explore the differences between their interpretations of the advertisement and to see whether any patterns emerge. For example, do the girls find it easier than the boys to understand the advertisement? The normal process of looking at a picture of this kind (i.e. more or less instantaneously as one flips the pages of a magazine) is disrupted; in this exercise we puzzle over what the image means. It is possible to extract far more in discussion than would usually be the case: the process is one of investigation and description, where everyone in the group has a right to justify a particular perception.

This is described here as a basic activity of 'reading' a media product, which might conceivably lead on to studying short segments of television (such as title sequences, for example).[8] It might also be a way into learning about techniques as part of a topic on advertising. Whatever its purpose, if it is to work successfully, questions of value have to be postponed. Nothing will destroy the activity more certainly than premature questions about the advertisement's 'quality' – how can this be judged until an understanding of how it works has been reached? – or about the morality of advertising in general. To this extent, Len Masterman is correct in his contention in both *Teaching about Television* and *Teaching the Media* that appreciation and discrimination and value judgements have no place. Where one might challenge this view is in follow-up work – perhaps not exactly Media Education in itself – where precisely such issues might need to be raised.

This sort of *deconstruction*, or process of analysis, can be a very useful prelude to students' own production work. If they have had a chance to think concretely about the sorts of appeal that different advertisements make to their audience, and the ways in which they make them, they are far better placed to produce their own advertising images. There is no reason why these should have to ape the professionals' (some interesting work has been done on 'anti-advertisements', e.g. for cigarettes). But there is every reason why students should at least be aware of the conventions they may choose to flout. Lest it be misunderstood, this is not an argument for didactic teaching or conventions, abstracted from any purpose or context, nor is it an argument for the teaching of narrow, technical skills. To use an analogy from English teaching, perhaps appropriate in the light of the Kingman Report (1988), teachers need an understanding of the 'grammar' of different audio-visual languages. When, or indeed whether, this 'grammar' should be made explicit to students is a matter of judgement: students need space to explore modes of expression for themselves, and too much emphasis on particular 'rules' is at best irrelevant (therefore ignored) and at worst stifling, leading to a slavish copying of professional practices.

Practical production is an area which many teachers have felt wary about. Certainly it requires careful management – not everyone can use the camera or the word processor at once. However, the benefits in terms of levels of motivation and of active, concrete understanding of basic principles make some considerable effort well worthwhile. Perhaps the most important first principle is to start small. For example, if the first assignment is a promotional video about the school, to be shown to the Chair of Governors and the Chief Education Officer, it is hardly surprising if it causes a great deal of anxiety. There has in the past been a popular misconception that practical work is a soft option, or that it is particularly suitable for 'less-able' children. Neither is true. Practical work is certainly different from writing, although it is often difficult to avoid writing in the planning stages, but it is no less of an intellectual challenge, whatever the ability of the students involved.

For this reason, it is often valuable to introduce practical activities in stages. Photoplay activities, where students select and order a sequence of images from a set provided, can assist with the later work of producing a storyboard for students' own productions. Simulations, such as *Radio Covingham* (producing a local radio magazine programme) or *Choosing the News* (compiling a newspaper front page), allow students to consider some of the issues involved without at the same time having to confront all the delays and difficulties of actual production.[9]

Another temptation in schools where such facilities exist, is to think that every production has to involve using the video camera. Properly used, this is certainly one of the most valuable and versatile items of equipment a school can have, but it is all too easy to spend a great deal of time without very much real learning taking place. A more tightly structured, more manageable introduction to using visual images can be achieved if students are enabled to use a stills camera to tell a story or explain a process. Ironically, if the school does have access to video, the relatively 'low tech' stills camera is much more expensive to run. However, whether the sequence of photographs takes the form of a display, a book, or even a tape/slide programme, many of the basic principles of audio-visual production can be learnt without the added complication of movement and editing.

Whenever students are involved in planning and producing their own media artefacts – either to a brief (e.g. designing an advertisement) or as an experiment with a popular generic form (e.g. opening of a horror film) – reflection on the process and their own product is an important part of the activity. If what they are doing is presenting a scientific experiment, they may be encouraged to think about how films and television programmes represent science for example, *Frankenstein, Tomorrow's World*, Schools Programmes. For, of course, what they produce is video, not television. There may be a passing similarity in the technology employed but there is all the difference in the world in the institutional status of the two products – in their economics, their audiences and the ways in which they are regulated, for example.

Examples of good practice focusing entirely on institutional questions are harder to come by, since many media teachers do their utmost to incorporate such issues into activities involving textual analysis or production work. However, Len Masterman's *Television Programme Planning* simulation may be cited as a useful exercise designed to bring out some of the factors influencing broadcast schedules. *The Film Industry*, described as a 'simulation game', explores the process of film production.[10] It is only fair to point out that the latter, particularly, requires a good deal of work and knowledge from the teacher if it is to succeed, unlike a simulation such as *Radio Covingham*, which virtually runs itself.

One consequence of Media Education perhaps needs to be spelt out more explicitly. If the aim is to encourage students to be critical of what they see and hear, teachers certainly need to be prepared to justify their own procedures, but what they also need to recognise is that the 'innocent' use of photographs or television programmes as 'windows on the world' is no longer possible or desirable (if, indeed, it ever was). Whatever students are presented with, it should be possible for them to question what it is saying and whose interests it serves. Some may regret this: there are sure to be others like the teacher who brought *The War Game* into school and followed it by announcing to the class, 'Well, I think that says it all.' Whether he was aware of how prescriptive this was is uncertain, but it was a wonderful way of stifling discussion![11] Even if we all recognise that such an approach is unacceptable, there are bound to be many people who will question whether there is time to analyse classroom materials (including books) in this fashion. To which the response must be, if there is not sufficient time to use materials properly, why use them at all? And, on the other hand, it also needs to be said that analysing the way in which an image or a programme communicates (its form) is the best possible method of trying to ensure that its 'message' (content) is understood and remembered.

Media Education in the 1990s

The 1990s is a crucial time for Media Education. A great deal of uncertainty surrounds the future (with not only the National Curriculum but also Local Management of Schools). Indeed, *Initiatives 9* (Lusted, 1988) featured a long article by David Lusted entitled 'Media Education in an Age of Uncertainty', which pictured media educationists as split between a vision of hope for the future and a blind despair about the very survival of their area of work.

The reasons for this uncertainty, not to say confusion, are diverse. Not least, surely, is the conflict between the evident importance attached to education and 'standards' by the government (as measured by the political effort that has been expended on the ERA) and the accusation that teachers, the very people whose co-operation is essential to any significant innovation, have been demoralised. Aside from this general point, however, the future of Media Education is difficult to see because what was once viewed in some circles as dangerously radical has now achieved a degree of respectability, even official acceptance, partly as a result of some most unexpected alliances. TVEI and the MSC (now the Training Agency) were not the most likely bedfellows for media teachers. The recognition in 1988 that City Technology Colleges might be as relevant if they emphasised Arts Technologies as if they specialised in Science was a surprising acknowledgement – no doubt conditioned by a variety of factors – of the value of media work as a motivating force, even with disaffected youngsters, and of the increasing importance, both economic and cultural, of the leisure and communications industries.

If the above seems to imply an inability to predict the future of Media Education on the part of the writer, so be it. What it does not entail, however, is indecision about how teachers, and media educationists in particular, should act. Even if the constraints appear to pinch tightly within the National Curriculum there is still scope for astute and determined teachers to justify what they do, even if it represents an unfashionable view.

There are several key issues to be addressed:

1 Teacher training in Media Education, both pre-service and in-service. How available is it? What does it emphasise? Who delivers it (cf. the recognition in the Kingman Report, 1988, that trainers would themselves need educating)?
2 Continuity and progression (5–16 and beyond). As Media Education becomes more widespread, how do we avoid unproductive duplication and at the same time ensure a rational sequence of learning experiences for children?
3 Links with established and new subject areas. Media educators have to learn from colleagues, as well as attempting to influence their practice.
4 The status of examinable Media Studies courses if cross-curricular Media Education becomes more established. Despite their growing significance in both status and entry numbers at the present time, what is the future for specialist options? A parallel may be drawn here with the situation of Computer Studies, which, because it was in competition for relatively scarce hardware and teacher resources, came to be seen as a threat to the development of Information Technology (IT) across the curriculum.
5 The organisation and management of Media Education within the school. Without the massive support of specific Education Support Grants which have fuelled the development of IT, can we envisage the appointment of Media Education co-ordinators? If not, how will approaches and resources be developed?

With so many pressing questions the need for unifying organisations is obvious: in Media Education as elsewhere there is still too much re-invention of the wheel. Some of the current difficulties and uncertainties are probably inevitable as Media Studies adjusts to the new educational climate. We have to try to ensure that a distinctive contribution to other areas is made as Media Education spreads across the curriculum. Although dilution is a danger, a retreat into radical élitism is an option that is neither available nor desirable.

Notes

1   This very sketchy account of 'Leavisism' owes a good deal to the useful and much fuller summary in Masterman (1985).
2   A useful critical account of the research literature is given in G. Murdock and R. McCron, 'The Television and Delinquency Debate', in *Screen Education*, no. 30 (Spring 1979).
3   See, for example, P. Schlesinger, *Putting 'Reality' Together* (Constable, 1978).
4   Two of the principal texts here are:
    G. Murdock and P. Golding, 'Capitalism, Communication and Class Relations' in J. Curran *et al.* (eds.), *Mass Communication and Society* (Edward Arnold, 1977)
    G. Murdock and P. Golding, 'Ideology and the Mass Media: The Question of Determination' in M. Barrett *et al.* (eds.), *Ideology and Cultural Production* (Croom Helm, 1979).
5   The Project section of the AEB A-level in Communication Studies is one example of this.
6   This issue is considered further in Lusted and Drummond (1985) – see References section – and in Clarke (1987).
7   See, for example, Alvarado *et al.* (1987) – see References section – and Clarke (1987).
8   As suggested in the teaching pack *Starters* (BFI).
9   *Radio Covingham* may be found in Volume 1 of *Graded Simulations* by Ken Jones (Oxford, Blackwell, 1985). *Choosing the News* is available from SEFT.
10 *Television Programme Planning* is in Masterman (1980). *The Film Industry* is available from SEFT.
11 To be fair to the person involved, it should perhaps be mentioned that there are very real problems in dealing critically with a text as emotionally charged as *The War Game*. Perhaps the only way is to allow some time to elapse, so that all concerned have an opportunity to become more objective about the experience.

References and Further Resources

T. Adorno and M. Horkheimer, *The Culture Industry: Enlightenment as Mass Deception* in J. Curran, M. Gurevitch and J. Woollacott (eds.), *Mass Communication and Society* (Arnold, 1977)
M. Alvarado *et al.*, *Learning the Media* (Macmillan, 1987)

D. Buckingham, 'Against Demystification' in *Screen*, vol. 27, no. 5 (1986)

M. Clarke, *Teaching Popular Television* (Heinemann, 1987)

P. Cook (ed.), *The Cinema Book* (BFI, 1985)

DES, *Popular Television and Schoolchildren* (HMSO, 1983)

DES, Black Report (HMSO, 1988)

A. Hart, *Teaching Television: The Real World (a television study resource pack)* (Cambridge University Press, 1988)

J. Hartley *et al.*, *Making Sense of the Media* (Comedia, 1985)

Kingman Report, *Report of the Committee of Inquiry into the Teaching of English Language* (HMSO, 1988)

F. R. Leavis, *Mass Civilisation and Minority Culture* (Cambridge University Press, 1930)

F. R. Leavis and D. Thompson, *Culture and Environment* (Chatto and Windus, 1933)

D. Lusted and P. Drummond (eds.), *TV and Schooling* (BFI, 1985)

D. Lusted, 'Media Education in an Age of Uncertainty' in *Initiatives*, Issue 9 (Summer, 1988)

L. Masterman, *Teaching About Television* (Macmillan, 1980)

L. Masterman, *Teaching the Media* (Comedia, 1985)

D. Morley, *Family Television: Cultural Power and Domestic Leisure* (Comedia, 1986)

D. Thompson, *Discrimination and Popular Culture* (Pelican, 1964)

Key Teacher Resources

M. Alvarado, R. Gutch and T. Wollen, *Learning the Media* (Macmillan, 1987)
Combines principles with examples of classroom activities though with the accent on the former.

BBC, *Get It Taped* (BBC Enterprises)
Videotape with notes on the use of the videocamera in many different areas of the secondary curriculum. Expensive, not by any means perfect, but well worth borrowing (e.g. from a local Teachers' Centre).

M. Clarke, *Teaching Popular Television* (Heinemann, 1987)
Contains chapters on different programme types (with ideas for classroom work at the end of each) and also on institutional questions.

P. Cook (ed.), *The Cinema Book* (BFI, 1985)
Excellent summaries of debates and approaches in Film Studies. Contains details of all film extracts available for hire from the BFI.

Leicestershire Centre for Educational Technology, *Media Kids OK?*, videotape with notes by Paul Merrison on primary Media Education (available from Leicestershire Centre for Educational Technology, Herrick Road, Leicester LE2 6DJ)
Shows a great variety of activities and is very useful in demonstrating possibilities of practical work even with quite young children.

D. Lusted and P. Drummond (eds.), *TV and Schooling* (BFI, 1985)
Essays which take up the issues surrounding the DES Report, *Popular Television and Schoolchildren* (reprinted at the end of their book).

Key Classroom Resources

Baxters: The Magic of Advertising (SFC)

Pack including videotape. Contains lots of useful information about a Baxters soup campaign, with material provided by the advertising agency (including their 'pitch' selling the concept to the company). Aimed at 6th form level (Years 12 and 13) but can be adapted to younger students.

Selling Pictures (BFI)

Pack containing slides, pupils' book and teachers' notes. Follows on from the excellent introductory *Reading Pictures* and goes into questions of representation and stereotyping (particularly in relation to gender).

Talking Pictures (Mary Glasgow Publications)

Tape/filmstrip (which needs cutting up into slides) with notes. Also follows on usefully from *Reading Pictures*. Though now slightly dated (published 1981), it offers a range of interesting images for analysis.

Teachers' Protest (SEFT)

Basic pack contains class sets of photographs; filmstrip for cutting up and using as slides also available. This photoplay, which looks at the construction of bias in television news, is a companion to *The Visit* (about narrative suspense in a feature film).

The Media Pack (Macmillan)

Similar format to *The Television Programme*. Aims to be a complete GCSE teaching pack. Many helpful ideas but should be used selectively.

The Television Programme (Sheffield Media Unit, Central Library, Surrey Street, Sheffield S1 1XZ)

Loose leaf folder, photocopiable, with lots of practical ideas for organising production work, not only in video.

Key Addresses

BFI (British Film Institute Education Department),
21 Stephen Street,
London W1P 1PL
  For advice and teaching materials.

Clwyd Media Studies Unit,
Centre for Educational Technology,
Shire Hall Campus,
Mold,
Clwyd CH7 1YA
  For Welsh news and catalogue of teaching materials.

Department of English and Media Studies,
London University Institute of Education,
20 Bedford Way,
London WC1
  For information on courses and for TEAME (The National Association of Teacher
  Educators and Advisers in Media Education

Education Department,
Museum of the Moving Image,
South Bank,
London SE1 8XT
  For visits and teaching materials.

SFC (Scottish Film Council),
Dowanhill,
74 Victoria Crescent Road,
Glasgow G12 9JN
  For AMES (the Association for Media Education in Scotland) and teaching materials
  including *Baxters.*

SEFT (Society for Education in Film and Television),
29 Old Compton Street,
London W1V 5PL
  For *Initiatives*, the termly magazine for media teachers, and teaching materials.

• 6 •

PEACE EDUCATION:

ATTEMPTING TO TEACH
FOR A
BETTER WORLD

David Hicks

The Quest for Peace

The pursuit of peace as a goal in human relationships is as old as humanity itself. The institution of war, however, may be much more recent, having occurred for only 'two per cent at most of our history' (Barnaby, 1988). The pursuit of peace is a response not just to the destructiveness of war but, more broadly, to any manifestation of violence. Both the problems of violence and the quest for peace can thus be studied on scales ranging from the intrapersonal and interpersonal to the national and global. Whilst the problem of war may accordingly be a main focus for peace movements and peace educators it is far from their only concern.

> A peaceful world is not necessarily a world without conflict. It is a world which solves these conflicts without recourse to violence . . . Inevitably there are many ideas about the kind of social structures needed and the best routes to try. There are many issues . . . and they include nuclear disarmament, stopping the sale of arms, conflict resolution, security, general disarmament, development here and abroad, independence and liberation, and moving towards a more just, more equitable and more sustainable society. The organisations which make up the peace move-ment are as diverse as the issues they cover.   (Houseman, 1984)

Hutchinson (1986), in his consideration of the philosophical origins of Peace Education, points out that cosmopolitan and peace-related ideas can be traced back to early Christian and Asian religion and philosophy. Since then, such concerns have always had a part to play in spiritual and ethical thinking and have also often been seen as a proper concern of education. Hutchinson cites Erasmus, Comenius and Condorcet, amongst others, as educators with a particular interest in such ideas.

Although the early years of this century saw a proliferation of organisations dedicated to the idea of peace, and many people believed the abolition of war to be a real possibility, two world wars followed. Osborne (1987) has suggested that this failure by peace educators and by the peace movement generally was a result of innate conservatism and cautious aims. Little wonder then that peace movements from the 1950s onwards have generally been more militant in their stance and more radical in their analysis of the issues.

By the beginning of the 1980s, with the escalation of the arms race and the Soviet invasion of Afghanistan, peace movements were growing rapidly in Europe, North America, Australia and elsewhere. At the same time teachers in the UK became interested because many were increasingly feeling that issues of peace and conflict were a proper concern of education. The growth of Peace Education, whilst undoubtedly encouraged by this climate, had more to do however with the earlier developments in the fields of education for international understanding and World Studies.

Converging Strands: The Development of Peace Education

The major formative influence on Peace Education has been World Studies, and the origins of this field have been interestingly mapped by Richardson (1986). He identifies two main forces behind World Studies:

1 various experiments in *child-centred education* around the turn of the century
2 a growing interest amongst educators in the 1920s and 1930s in 'international understanding' and 'world citizenship'. One of the leading organisations in this field, the Council for Education in World Citizenship (CEWC), was set up in the late thirties (Heater, 1984). The term World Studies was coined by James Henderson in the sixties and the One World Trust ran the first World Studies Project during the 1970s which was ably directed by Robin Richardson.

At the same time, during the 1950s and 1960s, the discipline of peace research was beginning to emerge at various European and American universities. Initially focusing on problems of overt violence and war, concern gradually shifted to embrace problems of structural violence, for example, the damage caused to people by unjust social, political or economic structures. Similarly attention moved from peace defined negatively as the absence of war, to peace defined positively as the presence of a wide range of welfare indicators. The International Peace Research Association was set up and, in Britain, the School of Peace Studies at Bradford University was established.

By 1980 a lot of work had been done in the field of Global Education, both by

85

the World Studies Project and by those involved in the field of Development Education. There was awareness amongst a critical number of educators of the need to promote within schools both issue-based and student-centred learning which emphasised a global perspective. Support for such concerns also came from various DES consultative documents which noted the need for pupils to understand the multicultural nature of society in an interdependent world. These concerns, and the need for active as opposed to passive learning, were later to be stressed in *The Curriculum from 5 to 16* (DES, 1985).

The first school in Britain to develop a programme of Peace Education was the United World College of the Atlantic in South Wales. As an international sixth-form college it offered a programme in Peace Studies for the International Baccalaureate exam in 1977. A major international conference was held at the college in 1981, attended by more than two hundred people. Key-note lectures were given by Adam Curle, Emeritus Professor of Peace Studies, Bradford University; James O'Connell, the current Professor of Peace Studies at Bradford; Robin Richardson, then Multicultural Educational Adviser for Berkshire, and Colin Reid who had been responsible for initiating The Atlantic College Peace Studies Project.

The conference was a major inspiration to all those present and it put Peace Education firmly on the map in the UK (Reid, 1984). At about the same time the Centre for Peace Studies had been set up at St Martin's College of Higher Education in Lancaster and the Centre for Global Education at York University. Both were to play a major part in legitimising and clarifying the role of Peace Education and World Studies in the curriculum of the 1980s. In particular, the highly successful Schools Council project *World Studies 8–13* came to be seen as one embodiment of good practice in Peace Education (Fisher and Hicks, 1985).

The first reference to Peace Education in the educational press had come in 1980: '"Sir, would you tell us if the bomb was going to drop?" When the first-former raised his hand at the beginning of the drama period, I had not expected his question to render me speechless' (Reidy, 1980). In 1981 the NUT and NATFHE issued a joint statement on Peace Education, and many Teachers for Peace Groups sprang up around the country. As a result of the Atlantic College conference, a Peace Education Network was set up, a group of teachers in Bristol began the Avon Peace Education Project, and several LEAs set up their own working parties on Peace Education.

Whilst the initial concern of teachers was whether, and how, they might teach about the nuclear debate, the question was soon broadened to become: 'Whatever subject I teach, whatever age children I teach, how can I help them to understand more clearly issues of peace and conflict on scales from the personal to the global?' The focus for Peace Education thus quickly widened to encompass both a range of issues and questions of what peaceful pedagogy actually looked like in the classroom. Most of the educational support for teachers came initally from outside the formal sector: from organisations such as CEWC, Pax Christi, the Peace Education Project of the Peace Pledge Union and the Campaign for Nuclear Disarmament (CND). Their resources were often used to balance the unsolicited materials on nuclear deterrence sent to schools by government sources. Of this period Young wrote:

> Since 1981, at least in parts of Europe, a Peace Education movement has emerged which is parallel to, but distinct from the disarmament action movements. By Peace Education movement I mean a movement of peace educators from the bottom up in local struggles of students and teachers and local authorities to introduce teaching for peace into the curricula of schools and in wider public education on peace issues. Only a few years ago those who became identified as peace educators were a prophetic minority – in Britain for example the term was not widely known. Now, a national network of peace educators has emerged . . .
>
> (Young, 1987)

Principles and Practice

It is important to recall at this point that the growing interest in Peace Education during the 1980s was an international, not just a national, phenomenon. Interested readers should consult sources such as Sharp (1984); Brock-Utne (1985); Toh & Floresca-Cawagas (1987) and Reardon (1988). Here we will consider the educational rationale for Peace Education, its assumptions and definitions, its content and form, as worked out in the UK. More detailed elaborations of this can be found in Hicks (1988).

Galtung (1976) succinctly described the problems of peace as those to do with: violence and war, inequality, injustice, environmental damage and alienation. He accordingly described some of the main values underlying peace as: non-violence, economic welfare, social justice, ecological balance and participation. Such a framework, whilst broad, provides a useful conceptualisation of both the field of peace research and of Peace Education.

Burns (1983) has suggested that three specific assumptions underlie Peace Education. These are:

1 that war and violent behaviour are not conducive to human well-being
2 neither are they the result of inevitable aspects of human nature
3 peace, i.e. alternative forms of being, organising and behaving, can be learnt

The aims of Peace Education can therefore be formulated as follows:

1   to explore *concepts of peace* both as a state of being and as an active process
2   to enquire into the *obstacles to peace* and the causes of peacelessness, in individuals, institutions, groups and societies
3   to *resolve conflicts* in ways that will lead towards a less violent and a more just world
4   to study ways of constructing different *alternative futures*, in particular those which embody a more just and sustainable world society

The overall aim of Peace Education is thus to develop the knowledge, attitudes and skills necessary to resolve conflict peacefully in order to work towards a more just, sustainable and less violent world.

It needs to be specifically stressed at this point that whilst occasionally (as in the case of Atlantic College) schools may have a timetabled slot called Peace Studies, this is extremely rare. Most practitioners see Peace Education as a cross-curricular concern which has implications for both curriculum content and the learning process. It can contribute to all core and foundation subjects, and many of them can, in turn, realise many of the learning objectives of Peace Education (see Table 6.1 below).

The rationale for Peace Education in the curriculum is a fivefold one. Firstly, the state of our planet demands it. Global inequality, violence and injustice are on the increase in a world which is also ecologically under threat. We are faced by a series of interrelated global crises that are ably described and mapped by Kidron & Segal (1988), Sivard (1987), Myers (1985) and Barnaby (1988). If we do not educate students about the state of their planet we do them a grave disservice. The conflict and violence that are so characteristic of the global stage also affect our own society both directly and indirectly. Acts of terrorism, high unemployment, racist attacks, sexual harrassment, issues of law and order, alienation amongst the young, increasing violence in schools, are all inescapable features of life in Britain today. Studying the causes of violence, the nature of effective conflict resolution, meanings of peace and the nature of justice are prerequisites for any creative and secure future, both within schools and in wider society.

Secondly, during the 1980s, there has been considerable consensus about the broad aims of education (DES, 1985). For example, education should aim:

● to help pupils develop lively, enquiring minds, the ability to question and argue rationally, and to apply themselves to tasks and physical skills
● to instil respect for religious and moral values, and tolerance of other races, religions and ways of life
● to help pupils to understand the world in which they live, and the inter-dependence of individuals, groups and nations

Central to good education in a democratic society is not only a focus on the personal and social but also a need to set these in their broader political and economic contexts. If we fail to do this we risk turning out a generation of young adults ill-equipped to make sense of a fast changing world or indeed to make appropriate decisions within it.

Thirdly, and following on from the above, there is the need for young people to have some understanding about the main controversial issues of the day. Students need to acquire the skills and insights needed to identify bias and indoctrination, whether from governments or pressure groups; they need to have been taught *how* to think, rather than *what* to think (Stradling *et al.*, 1984).

John Slater has commented that:

> The testing of fundamental values as well as their preservation lies at the heart of the educational process. Controversial issues cannot be avoided in schools ... the question is not whether (they) should be part of a school curriculum but when, how and with what resources they should be tackled ... Controversial issues can appear on the curriculum of children from the age of five. They are neither subject nor phase specific.
>
> (Slater, 1986)

Fourthly, we need to note and be aware of the critical role of childhood socialisation in the children's perceptions of the world. At, or even before, the infant level, children are forming their perceptions about countries and cultures other than their own, about gender, aggression and violence. Peer group and family pressure, comics, books, videos and television provide images which can be both racist and sexist (as well as condoning of violence). Images of war and peace also develop at an early age, with the latter often much less clearly understood than the former (Heater, 1980). By the end of primary school some children will also be worrying about the threat of nuclear war. More than half of secondary school children think nuclear war could happen at any time (Dyer, 1988). Such matters are not only specifically pertinent to Peace Education but to all teachers – whatever age children or subject they may teach.

Lastly, it must be noted that all statements about education embody particular and often very different views of education. Educational theorising, policy-making and classroom practice do not take place in an ideological vacuum. Broadly one can note at least four different traditions:

1 the 'liberal humanitarian' which is primarily concerned with passing on the basic cultural heritage from one generation to another
2 the 'utilitarian' which sees the main task of education as equipping students to fit into previously defined situations
3 the 'student-centred' which values the autonomy, self-development and personal growth of each student

4   the 'reconstructionist' which sees education as one potential tool for changing society.

This still begs the question as to whether education has any influence at all on wider society or whether it merely reflects and reproduces the structural inequalities of which it is a part. Peace educators, whilst noting the force of this argument, would see themselves as working very much within the student-centred and reconstructionist traditions. They would be concerned about education for liberation as opposed to education for domination. The National Curriculum and all that goes with it is, of course, based on the 'liberal' and 'utilitarian' traditions and such a view of education is one that many peace educators and others would wish to oppose (Richardson, 1988).

Peace Education thus has a strong rationale and Figure 6.1 (a checklist of learning objectives) begins to flesh out both the possible content and process as it occurs in practice, both at primary and secondary levels.

Figure 6.1 Peace Education: A Checklist of Learning Objectives

SKILLS

1 Critical thinking

Students should be able to approach issues with an open and critical mind and be willing to change their opinions in the face of new evidence and rational argument. They should be able to recognise and challenge bias, indoctrination and propaganda.

2 Co-operation

Students should be able to appreciate the value of co-operating on shared tasks and be able to work co-operatively with other individuals and groups in order to achieve a common goal.

3 Empathy

Students should be able to imagine sensitively the viewpoints and feelings of other people, particularly those belonging to groups, cultures and nations other than their own.

4 Assertiveness

Students should be able to communicate clearly and assertively with others, i.e. not in an aggressive way which denies the rights of others, or in a non-assertive manner which denies their own rights.

5 Conflict Resolution

Students should be able to analyse different conflicts in an objective and systematic way and be able to suggest a range of solutions to them. Where appropriate, they should be able to implement solutions themselves.

6 Political Literacy

Pupils should be developing the ability to influence decision-making within their own lives, in their local community, and also at national or international levels.

ATTITUDES

1 Self-respect

Students should have a sense of their own worth, and pride in their own particular social, cultural and family background.

2 Respect for Others

Students should have a sense of the worth of others, particularly of those with social, cultural and family backgrounds different to their own.

3 Ecological Concern

Students should have a sense of respect for the natural environment and our overall place in the web of life. They should also have a sense of responsibility for both the local and global environment.

4 Open-mindedness

Students should be willing to approach different sources of information, people and events, with a critical but open mind.

5 Vision

Students should be open to, and value, various dreams and visions of what a better world might look like both in their own community, in other communities and in the world as a whole.

6 Commitment to Justice

Students should value genuinely democratic principles and processes and be ready to work for a more just and peaceful world at local, national and international levels.

KNOWLEDGE

1 Conflict

Students should study a variety of contemporary conflict situations from the personal to the global and attempts being made to resolve them. They should also know about ways of resolving everyday conflicts in a non-violent way.

2 Peace

Students should study different concepts of peace, both as a state of being and as an active process, on scales from the personal to the global. They should look at examples of the work of individuals and groups who are actively working for peace.

3 War

Students should explore some of the key issues and ethical dilemmas to do with conventional war. They should look at the effects of militarism on individuals or groups, on scales ranging from the local to the global.

4 Nuclear Issues

Students should learn about a wide range of nuclear issues and be aware of the key viewpoints on defence and disarmament. They should understand the effects of nuclear war and appreciate the efforts of individuals, groups and governments to work towards a nuclear-free world.

5 Justice

Students should study a range of situations that illustrate injustice on scales from the personal to the global. They should look at the work of individuals and groups involved in the struggle for justice today.

6 Power

Students should study issues to do with power in the world today and ways in which its unequal distribution affects people's life chances. They should explore ways in which people and groups have regained power over their own lives.

7 Gender

Students should study issues to do with discrimination based on gender. They should understand the historical background to this and the ways in which sexism operates to the advantage of men and the disadvantage of women.

8 Race

Students should study issues to do with discrimination based on race. They should understand the historical background to this and the ways in which racism operates to the advantage of white people and to the disadvantage of black people.

9 Environment
Students should have a concern for the environmental welfare of people worldwide and the natural systems on which they depend. They should be able to make rational judgements concerning environmental issues and participate effectively in environmental politics.

10 Futures
Students should study a range of alternative futures, both probable and preferable. They should understand which scenarios are most likely to lead to a more just and less-violent world and what changes are necessary to bring this about.

The content of Peace Education is well summarised by the knowledge objectives set out above. Each of these issues has been described in some detail in Hicks (1988), together with examples of appropriate classroom activities. Excellent examples of how one subject, Geography, has responded to the needs of Peace Education can be found in *The Geography of Peace and War* (Pepper & Jenkins, 1985) and in *Teaching Geography for a Better World* (Fein & Gerber, 1988). Other subject areas are similarly able to match their own concerns with these learning objectives.

Many practitioners prefer to talk of Education *for* Peace as a reminder that the way in which we teach is equally as important as what we teach. Peace Education is thus also about an approach to teaching and learning, for if peace is the goal, then due attention must be given to ends and means. The relationship between content and form is seen as a dialectical one in which the form determines the content and the content the form. The medium is quite specifically the message. The form of Peace Education has to exclude both direct and structural violence in schools and classroom settings.

Structural violence occurs in school when the learner's needs, hopes and fears are not truly respected and listened to. It occurs when communication is one-way, often 'top-down' (from the teacher to the pupil) and learners are unable to develop interaction between themselves or indeed to reverse the communication flow. It occurs when learning is passive, when students are not consulted, when knowledge is treated as neutral and value-free, when teachers impose authority rather than acting as facilitators of young people's learning.

The process which is constantly stressed in Peace Education is, in essence, good active learning. Here the teacher will see her/his role as that of a facilitator, learning will take place in both experiential and participatory modes, there will be a lot of talking and arguing in pairs and in small groups. Students will take a lot of responsibility for their own learning, which will be designed to develop both hemispheres of the brain; it will be challenging and also fun. Such

93

approaches to education have been admirably described by Rogers (1983), Wren (1986) and Brandes and Ginnis (1986).

Peace Education is thus both issue-based and student-centred, with a particular focus on problems of peace and conflict. It attempts to look at positive alternatives to current dilemmas, whether personal or global, and to look at solutions as much as problems. Peace Education is future orientated and attempts to liberate and empower both student and teacher. It is seldom found as a subject on the curriculum but more often seen as a concern to be expressed through the whole life of a school. It has proved effective at infant, junior and secondary levels of education. Indeed some LEAs have appointed advisory staff; several have produced detailed guidelines for teachers, e.g. Ealing (Freeman, 1987) and Manchester City Council Education Committee (1987).

Deliberate Disinformation

As soon as Peace Education began to establish its bearings and credentials and the contribution that it could make to good primary and secondary practice it found itself under attack. In part this was because it simply looked and felt different and because the initial focus, in the early 1980s, was on teaching about nuclear issues. The arguments of the critics, generally of the political Right, hinged around the actual and alleged dangers of indoctrination and bias. Their contention was that controversial subjects are bound to be taught in a biased way and therefore they should not be taught at all. Underlying this, of course, are their own assumptions about education:

> The truly educational subject forces the pupil to understand something which has no immediate bearing on his (sic) experience. It teaches him intellectual discipline, by presenting him with problems too remote or too abstract to be comprehended within his own limited world. In other words, it asks him to stand back from his immediate concerns, and make a considered judgement of matters which are interesting in themselves, whether or not he can see their 'relevance'. (Cox and Scruton, 1984)

Indeed education must be about making considered judgements, but to suggest that the immediate lives of students should have no bearing on their learning experiences is to disregard the whole basis of good primary practice. The critics, it should be noted, bring their own ideological and value assumptions with them whilst claiming to be neutral and objective. The main critics, i.e. Cox and Scruton (1984) and Marks (1984), can be accused of tendentious argument creating a smoke-screen of public anxiety about Peace Studies.

Detailed refutation of these critics have been provided by Aspin (1986) and White (1988). Suffice here to comment briefly on the five main criticisms made by Cox and Scruton (1984). Firstly, they argue that Peace Studies is not a proper educational discipline and should thus not be taught as one. But very few teachers, as we have seen, are arguing for such a discipline.

Secondly, it is said that Peace Education favours foregone conclusions in relation to issues such as the arms race or global inequality. Clearly peace educators favour values such as non-violence, social justice and ecological balance, but they also favour participatory and experiential learning. What they do *not* promote, however, is one-sided treatment of debates. Rather than reducing the task to looking at 'the two sides of the argument' most teachers, as good professionals, encourage young people to see that there are a range of viewpoints about, say, defence and deterrence or about US food aid.

Thirdly, it is said that 'the subject' is taught in a way that discourages critical reflection and promotes prejudice. Yet the vast majority of teachers would agree that one of their tasks in a democratic society is to protect divergent viewpoints. This should mean that students will be exposed to a wide range of views. One cannot but suspect that what the critics fear is that students will thereby get the opportunity to explore views with which *they* disagree. If students are not encouraged to debate and discuss controversial issues at school then they are much less likely to challenge received wisdom, whether from the media or the government, on any issue.

Fourthly, it is said that Peace Education is but one part of a move to politicise the curriculum, to lower intellectual standards and to promote the interests of the Soviet Union. This presumes that questions of politics (i.e. how power and resources are used, shared and distributed in society) are totally divorced from education, that education takes place in a political vacuum and that children should not be given the opportunity to learn about the political nature of society. Active learning, the research suggests, enhances all aspects of education including intellectual development. HMI have yet to find any evidence that Peace Education promotes Soviet as opposed to British interests.

Lastly, it is said that the reality of Peace Education should not be confused with its apparent innocuous purpose, that its focus on good manners is but a cloak for its revolutionary ends. Certainly Peace Education is about much more than 'good manners'. It is about helping to create self-reliant, responsive and responsible young citizens. It is both about valuing what is good in the old order and cherishing it, but it is also about the struggle to change what is inequitable and unjust. Peace Education lies quite clearly in the reconstructionist tradition.

Changing Times

The campaign of disinformation waged by the political Right against Peace Education did have some measure of success. What it succeeded in doing, as it intended, was to obscure the issues. Some teachers and parents became cautious because they felt Peace Education itself was a controversial issue. The irony is that a survey by Galfo (1986) reported no signs of the indoctrination in schools feared by Conservatives. Indeed, he reported that students generally had a *better* grasp of arguments when they had been involved in Peace Education.

Peace Education in Britain, particularly during the early and mid 1980s, generated an enormous amount of enthusiasm amongst teachers. Whilst perhaps never more than the concern of a minority of teachers and educators, it was nevertheless a very significant minority, who acted as catalysts both at school and LEA level. In so doing they also drew on innovative work in World Studies and Development Education, crystallising the importance of matching curriculum content and form with both personal and planetary needs. Perhaps Lister (1987) is right when he argues that Peace Education and World Studies are part of a vanguard movement in the late twentieth century. Such a movement is certainly vital to education in the 1990s if we are going to make a peaceful transition to a new society.

If Capra (1983) and others are right, we may be witnessing some sort of global transformation. In essence, this is about moving away from the mechanistic world view of Newtonian science to one which is more holistic, organic and ecological. It is a 'systems' view in which the universe is no longer seen as a multitude of separate objects but as one indivisable dynamic whole whose parts are all inextricably related. Peace Education may be one of the elements at the heart of such changes.

References and Further Resources

D. Aspin, 'Peace Studies in the Curriculum of Educational Institutions: an argument against indoctrination' in J. J. Wellington (ed.), *Controversial Issues in the Curriculum* (Blackwell, 1986)

F. Barnaby (ed.), *The Gaia Peace Atlas* (Pan Books, 1988)

D. Brandes and P. Ginnis, *A Guide to Student-centred Learning* (Blackwell, 1986)

B. Brock-Utne, *Educating for Peace: A Feminist Perspective* (Pergamon, 1985)

R. Burns, *Education and the Arms Race* (Centre for Comparative and International Studies, La Trobe University, Melbourne, 1983)

F. Capra, *The Turning Point: Science, Society and the Rising Culture* (Flamingo/Fontana, 1983)

C. Cox and R. Scruton, *Peace Studies: A Critical Survey* (Institute for Defence and Strategic Studies, London, 1984)

DES, *The Curriculum from 5 to 16* (HMSO, 1985)

J. Dyer, 'What children know and feel about nuclear war: evidence from research' (Scottish Working Party on Psychosocial Issues and War, Edinburgh, 1988)

J. Fein and R. Gerber, *Teaching Geography for a Better World* (Oliver and Boyd, 1988)

S. Fisher and D. Hicks, *World Studies 8–13: A Teacher's Handbook* (Oliver and Boyd, 1985)

J. Freeman, *Peace Education in the London Borough of Ealing* (Ealing Education Committee, 1987)

A. J. Galfo, 'Influences of education in the formation of public views of the NATO–Warsaw Pact confrontation: a pilot study conducted in selected secondary schools of the United Kingdom' in *Journal of Educational Administration and History*, vol. 18, no. 2 (1986)

J. Galtung, 'Peace Education: problems and conflicts' in M. Haavelsrud (ed.), *Education for Peace: Reflection and Action* (IPC Science and Technology Press, 1976)

D. Heater, *World Studies: Education for International Understanding in Britain* (Harrap, 1980)

D. Heater, *Peace Through Education: The Contribution of CEWC* (Falmer Press, 1984)

D. Hicks (ed.), *Education for Peace: Issues, Principles and Practice in the Classroom* (Routledge, 1988)

Houseman, *Houseman's Peace Diary* (1984)

F. Hutchinson, 'Education for Peace: what are its philosophical origins?' in *Educating for Peace: Explorations and Proposals* (Canberra Curriculum Development Council, 1986)

M. Kidron and R. Segal, *The New State of the World Atlas* (revised) (Pan Books, 1988)

I. Lister, 'Global and International Approaches in Political Education' in C. Harber (ed.), *Political Education in Britain* (Falmer Press, 1987)

Manchester City Council Education Committee, *Education for Peace in Manchester: Guidelines and Case Studies* (1987)

J. Marks, *'Peace Studies' in Our Schools: Propaganda for Defencelessness* (Women and Families for Defence, 1984)

N. Myers (ed.), *The Gaia Atlas of Planet Management* (Pan Books, 1985)

K. Osborne, 'Peace Education and the Schools: What can we learn from History?' in T. Carson and H. Gideonse (eds.), *Peace Education and the Task for Peace Educators* (World Council for Curriculum and Instruction, 1987)

D. Pepper and A. Jenkins, *The Geography of Peace and War* (Blackwell, 1985)

R. Reardon, *Comprehensive Peace Education: Educating for Global Responsibility* (Teachers College Press, New York, 1988)

C. Reid (ed.), *Issues in Peace Education* (United World College of the Atlantic / D. Brown and Sons, S. Glamorgan, 1984)

M. Reidy, 'What should we tell our pupils?' in *Times Educational Supplement* (31 October 1980)

R. Richardson, 'The World Studies Story: projects, people and places, a conference paper' (1986)

R. Richardson, 'Opposition to Reform and the Need for Transformation: some polemical notes' in *Multicultural Teaching* vol. 6, no. 2 (1988)

C. Rogers, *Freedom to Learn in the 80s* (Charles Merrill Publishing Co, Ohio, 1983)

R. Sharp, 'Varieties for Peace Education' in R. Sharp (ed.), *Apocalypse No: An Australian Guide to the Arms Race and the Peace Movement* (Pluto Press, Sydney, 1984)

R. L. Sivard, *World Social and Military Expenditures* (World Priorities, Washington DC, 1987)

J. Slater, 'The Teaching of Controversial Issues in Schools: an HMI view (1986), paper published by School Curriculum Development Committee

R. Stadling, M. Noctor and B. Baines, *Teaching Controversial Issues* (Arnold, 1984)

S. Toh and V.Floresca–Cawagas, *Peace Education: A Framework for the Philippines* (Phoenix Publishing, Quezon City, 1987)

P. White, 'Countering the Critics' in *Education for Peace* (1988) (see Hicks above)

B. Wren, *Education for Justice* (SCM Press Ltd, 1986)

N. Young, 'Some Current Controversies in the New Peace Education Movement: debates and perspectives' in *Peace Education and the Task for Peace Educators* (World Council for Curriculum Instruction, 1987)

Key Teacher Resources

F. Barnaby (ed.), *The Gaia Peace Atlas* (Pan Books, 1988)
A comprehensive examination of all aspects of global peace and security with particular attention being given to sustainable future directions. Well illustrated with many tables and figures. An excellent resource book.

D. Brandis and P. Ginnis, *A Guide to Student-centred Learning* (Blackwell, 1986)
An excellent and detailed account of the theory and practice of active person-centred learning. Contains many practical exemplars, checklists and guidelines.

Green Teacher, a magazine for teachers on ecological and environmental related issues. Recent issues have been on Peace Education and future studies. Available from: Lys Awel, 22 Heol Pentrerhedyn, Machynlleth, Powys SY20 8DN.

D. Hicks (ed.), *Education for Peace: Issues, Principles and Practice in the Classroom* (Routledge, 1988)
The first full-length teacher's handbook on Peace Education in the UK. A clear introduction to the field with ten case-studies of particular issues, each with their own classroom activities, written by leading practitioners in England and Australia.

D. Hicks and M.Steiner (eds.), *Making Global Connections: A World Studies Workbook* (Oliver and Boyd, 1989)
A second resource book from the World Studies 8–13 Project with extended case-studies and many classroom activites. Also has good chapters on lessons from Political Education and on thinking about evaluation.

N. Myers (ed.), *The Gaia Atlas of Planet Management* (Pan Books, 1986)
A definitive guide to the current state of the planet in all its aspects. Beautifully and graphically illustrated with a wealth of data on global resources, their use and abuse. An excellent resource book.

G. Pike and D. Selby, *Global Teacher, Global Learner* (Hodder and Stoughton, 1988)
An exciting teacher's handbook and resource book with numerous classroom activities on different aspects of Global Education. Authoritative, practical and eminently usable.

Key Classroom Resources

D. Cooke, *Teaching Development Issues* (Manchester Development Education Project, 1987)
A set of seven pupil books on: *Perceptions, Colonialism, Food, Health, Aid, Population* and *Work*. Highly recommended for their informative text and wealth of practical activities. Available from Manchester DEP, c/o Manchester Polytechnic, 801 Wilmslow Road, Manchester M20 8RG.

M. Kidron and R. Segal, *The New State of the World Atlas* (Pluto Press, 1988)
An informative and beautifully illustrated atlas with a wide range of maps and accompanying notes. Together they illustrate all the main dilemmas associated with the state of the planet today.

M. Kidron and D. Smith, *The War Atlas* (Pluto Press, 1983)
Like its counterpart described above this atlas contains numerous informative and detailed maps. It focuses particularly on issues to do with war, conventional and nuclear, and militarism.

C. Leeds, *Peace and War: A First Sourcebook* (Stanley Thornes, 1987)
This useful textbook covers a range of issues from conflict at the personal level to the causes of the arms race and strategies for global peacekeeping.

Mark Goldstein Memorial Trust, *Teaching Resources for Education in International Understanding, Justice and Peace* (second edition) (Marc Goldstein Memorial Trust, University of London Institute of Education, 1988)
This detailed, cross-referenced resource list is available from: Anne Brewer, 6 Phoenice Cottages, Dorking Road, Bookham, Surrey KT23 4QG.

D. Selby, *Human Rights* (Cambridge University Press, 1987)
A clear and informative introductory textbook on questions to do with human rights. Well illustrated with cartoons, posters and photographs.

J. J. Wellington, *The Nuclear Issue*, (Blackwell, 1986)
This photocopiable book contains activity sheets designed for class use. It covers all the main aspects of the nuclear issue in a clear and informative fashion.

Key Addresses

Centre for Global Education,
York University,
York YO1 5DD

Provides resources for teachers and runs various curriculum projects on aspects of Global Education. A part-time Diploma in Global and Multicultural Education is available for teachers.

Concord Films Council,
201 Felixstowe Road,
Ipswich,
Suffolk IP3 9BJ

Extremely useful film and video library on a wide range of contemporary issues. Publishes an informative and detailed film catalogue, with updates.

National Association of Development Education Centres (NADEC),
6 Endsleigh Street,
London WC1H 0DX

Co-ordinating address for some fifty or so Development Education Centres around the country. Many sell resources useful to teachers on world development issues.

Peace Education Project,
Peace Pledge Union,
6 Endsleigh Street,
London WC1H 0DX

Publishes teaching resources and a newsletter on issues to do with peace, war, non-violence and conflict resolution.

GENDER EDUCATION:

CHALLENGING SEXISM IN EDUCATION

Janie Whyld

Working against Sexism: Then and Now

Ten years ago, I often used to wear a badge, *Fight Sexism in Schools*, to college, in order to provoke the question, 'What's sexism?' Nowadays, that is no longer an appropriate consciousness-raising strategy. Most people know what sexism means. They may not be able to define it clearly, or distinguish between 'anti-sexist behaviour' and 'feminist practice' – how many people use words with accuracy and precision, anyway? But it is one measure of change over the last few years that 'sexism' is now part of our vocabulary.

Challenging stereotyping of whatever sort, be it race or gender roles, for example, is a common media practice these days. The television programme *Right to Reply*, on Channel 4, is full of people challenging the racist or sexist bias of this or that report, comedy programme or advert. Many late night movie spots are dedicated to films by non-European, gay or female directors. But far from being confined to the fringes, challenging gender expectations is part of peak viewing time culture. The television soap, *Brookside*, for example, regularly deals sensitively with women-centred issues such as rape and abortion. Comédiennes such as Victoria Wood, Dawn French and Jennifer Saunders, (and many of their male counterparts) have succeeded in changing the butt of our humour from the mother-in-law to the macho-maniac.

So, sexism is definitely a concept of which we are aware. How far has it affected our behaviour, though? 'Not a lot', according to recent research from the University of Ulster on the behaviour of pre-school children. This shows that boys are still getting a better chance to develop manipulative skills, which may be important in many aspects of Science and Engineering. In the nursery playground, girls were frightened of crossing a plank but the 'boys used this equipment in a way bordering on recklessness and it was clearly a means to establishing lack of fear and general bravado. On one occasion the observer

101

helped one girl to cross by holding her hand, and this resulted in other girls demanding the same help, including those who had successfully and independently tackled the task before.' (*New Statesman*, 6 Nov. 1987). However, the same article also reports on a nursery school where staff are trained to avoid encouraging sex-differentiated behaviour. One college in Humberside which does community outreach work with an adult literacy group of parents of pre-school children has been encouraged by the group leader to look at sex roles. Changing attitudes is a slow job. Firstly, it requires that those who form the attitudes of the next generation should be prepared to change their own attitudes, for it is the reaction of others to our behaviour which causes us to maintain or change that behaviour. Also that behaviour is largely learned when we are very young, although not irremediably fixed, as some would maintain. 'But by the time we get them, it's too late; the damage is done' is a common complaint from teachers who consider sex-stereotyping to be a problem, whether they are working in higher education or with pre-school children. There are others who do not see sex-stereotyping as a problem, and maintain that they treat all children equally. One major stumbling block which could prevent the future progression of Equal Opportunities is that institutions would not want to admit that they do not provide equality of opportunity *already*, because this could cast doubt on the integrity of the teachers. It is now widely recognised that awareness training with staff will be essential. Sexism-awareness training has produced excellent initiatives from staff who have been involved in major projects. Judging by recent bids made by schools for INSET money, Equal Opportunities still has low priority, but it is definitely 'on the agenda' in a way which seemed unimaginable a decade ago.

In February 1988, the Equal Opportunities Commission (EOC) launched a formal investigation 'to find out what education colleges and other teacher training institutions are doing to ensure that student teachers are fully aware of their responsibilities as teachers, *to promote equal opportunities* and to comply with the Sex Discrimination Act' (EOC, *News Bulletin*, 1988, my italics). Governmental bodies do not usually take such action to challenge the establishment unless they are sure that a majority of institutions are already complying, and that their enforcement will have widespread support.

By comparison, in the late 1970s, several years after the Sex Discrimination Act, 1975, a few teacher training institutions were grudgingly allowing study of sexism in education and women's issues to count as an optional 'module' in the final year of Bachelor of Education degrees. In NATFHE, the college lecturers' union, a motion requiring lecturers involved in teacher education to ensure that their institutions offered some training in anti-sexist practice to all students was deferred several times because other issues were considered more important. Nowadays, Equal Opportunities has a much higher profile.

In the 1970s, the Women's Liberation movement drew attention to the vast inequalities of treatment and opportunities between the sexes, and prompted people to research the practices which maintained the *status quo* in a so-called egalitarian education system. By the early 1980s, consistent pressure from feminists active in politics and the unions, small pockets of teachers (mostly young) developing new ways of teaching, and political involvement from the top down in some LEAs meant that when there was a general demand for curricular change and new movements to make education more relevant for non-academic children and adults, Equal Opportunities was one aspect which was included, and there was already a lot of well-developed practice and expertise to draw on. Today, some teacher education colleges actually promote their courses as challenging sexism, as do many colleges offering training in Youth and Community work. All courses for secondary education need to include Equal Opportunities as a way to prepare students for TVEI and CPVE. Equal Opportunities must not, of course, be confused with promoting anti-sexist practice. But certainly TVEI and YTS, with their associated funds for staff development, and their formal requirements for Equal Opportunities, have brought Equal Opportunities training to not only the Humanities teachers who tend to be concerned, but also to the most traditional group in terms of teaching style and attitudes, the Craft teachers – both technical and domestic (Kelly *et al.*, 1987).

How Sexism occurs in Schools

Factors contributing to different performance between boys and girls at school may be broadly classified into three areas:

1 Syllabus content and the materials used to give information and provide examples
2 The organisation of the school, including the ratio of male to female staff at varying levels in the hierarchy and in curriculum areas; the organisation of registers; the distribution of resources; and the choice of subjects offered to boys and girls
3 Interpersonal relationships throughout the school (including between staff and students, and between boys and girls). The attitude of teachers has been the subject of many studies (Clarricoates, 1978; Spender, 1982; Stanworth, 1983), and is the most difficult to change. Individual teachers and some progressive LEAs have started to deal with this issue, and it is central to initiatives in anti-sexist work with boys.

The first area, that of the taught curriculum and its hidden messages, was the first area to be studied in depth (in the early 1980s). This was perhaps because, like the provision of statistics on student take-up, success in varying subjects and on staffing, it was an area which lent itself to statistical analysis, or could be undertaken without the permission or co-operation of school authorities. Various interest groups of feminist teachers, publishers, trade unionists and curriculum managers have examined the bias throughout the school curriculum (Educational Publishers Council (EPC), 1981; Whyld, 1983) and, in particular, curriculum areas such as Science, Technology (Kelly, 1981) and CDT (Grant, 1983; EOC, 1983).

The second area, that of school organisation, is theoretically the easiest area to change, because it is basically an issue of the distribution of material resources. However, many consider that while those who are in the position of distributing resources, predominantly white males, do not consider that they will benefit from such changes, there is little likelihood of change. Some institutions have changed, mostly those with a woman in a senior management position (see Beauchamp Community School, 1987; Bradford Gender Project Base, 1987) but they are very few, despite the existence of Equal Opportunities policies in many LEAs.

Lastly, with the area of interpersonal relationships, it has been the question, 'What about the boys?' which has prompted the most imaginative initiatives on 'attitude change' with students. Since sexism disadvantages boys, particularly in terms of their emotional development (Whyld, 1986), people wanting to work with boys have had to look at how to encourage young people to look at their own behaviour and attitudes in a non-threatening way. Some of this work has been done in schools (Askew and Ross, 1988a) although, perhaps because there has been so much else to do within education, and also because there is considerable antagonism from conservative-minded teachers about the propriety of influencing young people, much of the most progressive moves in this area have been made within the Youth Service (Lloyd, 1986). Working with young people in this way can be very threatening to the workers concerned, so initiatives usually start with staff sharing their own concerns and developing trust with colleagues. Many of the exercises developed for working with young people are equally applicable or easily adaptable for use with staff.

Working with Staff

Because the analysis of sex bias in reading materials (Writers and Readers, 1976) and examinations (Fawcett Society, 1987) has been so well established, I have had a tendency to pass over this issue when training teachers in sexism awareness, assuming, wrongly, that most teachers would be aware of the research. However, various influences over the last few years have meant that a large number of teachers are now being drawn into Equal Opportunities training. Even Maths, which many assume is a neutral, and bias-free subject, has been subjected to scrutiny in the ILEA publication, *Everbody Counts*, which has opened people's eyes to sex and race bias in frequently used Maths materials. The analysis of bias in teaching materials has progressed in recent years from the necessary but simplistic exercise of counting images of males and females, to a detailed analysis of the activities and characteristics attributed to males and females in current materials within particular curriculum areas, such as *Girls and Boys in Primary Maths Books* (Northam, 1987). Many staff-development programmes find that analysis of sex bias in materials is a useful starting point for awareness-raising with staff. It can also be a fascinating and legitimate exercise for students in any course which requires the identification of prejudice and bias. (For details of a lesson, see Whyld, 1986).

Staff development is an important tool for change, but it needs to be used carefully. With issues that involve attitude change, a generous amount of time is important! A rushed course (where people are simply told about the importance of Equal Opportunities, and what they should do) is worse than useless, because the uncommitted can simply go away believing that they had 'done Equal Opportunities' and that it has nothing to do with them. An awareness of where people 'are at', and what particular ideas they are refusing to accept is an essential skill in raising awareness. A useful model to help diagnose this, is the *discount matrix* developed by Elizabeth Hendry with the help of workshop participants from a conference on 'transactional analysis'! This is a form of therapy aimed at analysing human relationships and communication in every-day situations with the object of encouraging a more constructive way of interacting (Hendry, 1988).

At the Counselling and Career Development Unit (CCDU) of Leeds University, the sex-differentiation training team developed a two-day sexism awareness course, which devoted most of the first day to helping participants explore their own prejudices and experience of oppression, and to developing a consensus of what they were aiming for in creating a non-sexist society. In the final session, where participants were invited to devise plans for future action, a 'card-sort' exercise was used to help participants identify issues which they personally considered important. Those teachers who are just beginning to recognise that careers guidance may passively discourage girls and boys from trying out non-traditional occupations, cannot be expected to tackle more difficult and sensitive issues of sexual harassment by Third Year (Year 9) boys. *Gender Issues Training* (Bradford, 1987) also describes many general exercises for use with staff. A benefit of this type of training is that it 'models' exercises which can be taken back into school and used in PSE work. ('Experimental exercises' – involving games, activity simulation and role-play – are far less restricted by the age and ability of the participants than 'information input', since this requires a level of verbal skill and previous knowledge.) The most complete resource pack both for raising awareness, and for implementing change is *Genderwatch* (see Resources).

Special Projects and Current Practice

Initiatives on Equal Opportunities and money to fund them, arise in a variety of ways. In a medium-sized FE college in an industrial town, for example, a lecturer was given some remission each week for a term, and expenses, from staff development money set aside to develop 'open-learning' packages (distance learning or home study systems). The money had been allocated to colleges from the LEA, who had acquired it from the MSC. This lecturer knew of the money, saw how it could be used to implement Equal Opportunities, and approached his Head of Department, who welcomed the idea of taking on the project. Not all colleges would have greeted the idea with such enthusiasm. Initiating Equal Opportunities work depends upon a lot of factors, and a very important consideration can be the attitude of colleagues and immediate superiors. In this case, the LEA had a rather bland Equal Opportunities policy, which they needed to develop to get further MSC funding. The college's PSE curriculum development team had already expressed concern about Equal Opportunities, partly prompted by the publication of *Curriculum Development for a Multicultural Society* (FEU, 1985), and had used some of the ideas to look at race, disability and gender within the department's curriculum. They produced a report, which was approved by the department, and passed to the Academic Board for acceptance as college policy. The Academic Board approved it, and passed it on via the governing body to the LEA, who after keeping it for a year with their legal department, welcomed it, and suggested that other colleges adopt it.

The result of the policy in this lecturer's college was to add responsibility for Equal Opportunities to the duties of an existing senior manager, and to set up a new subcommittee of the Academic Board, which spawned three working parties (race, gender, disability). These working parties comprised of any interested people including students, and outside specialists were also invited to join. So this project was not set up as an isolated instance of concern about Equal Opportunities.

The aim of the project was to enable staff to review the old curriculum and create a new curriculum which reflected the Equal Opportunities policy of the college. Humanities staff, and new staff throughout the college were fairly aware of Equal Opportunities, but many staff in traditional areas of Engineering and Construction considered that they already implemented Equal Opportunities, and need do nothing else. The paperwork side of the project is now completed, but the Head of Department has acquired further money to monitor the progress of Equal Opportunities in student recruitment, curriculum issues and staff recruitment and promotion, and the PSE group secured GRIST (Grant Related Inservice Training) money for five days' Equal Opportunities training for themselves and other staff. Under YTS, the college has also set up a workshop for Asian girls in Industrial Sewing, with the aim of getting them in to the college, and hopefully persuading them to take up other college provision.

There are details of more extended projects looking at the effect of gender in schooling in Smail (1984), Agnew (1985), Millman (1987), Millman and Weiner (1985), Whyte (1986) and Chisholm and Holland (1987). Often known as 'intervention research', projects such as Girls into Science and Technology (GIST, 1984), the EOC/Sheffield LEA-Careers Intervention Project, and Girls and Occupational Choice (GAOC), have operated like extended staff development programmes, monitoring the attitudes of staff, and offering staff extensive opportunities for awareness-raising and support to develop and try out their own strategies for change. According to the aptitudes, subject specialism and areas of concern of the staff involved, these strategies range from an examination of materials used in the classroom for sexist bias, to investigating ways of classroom interaction, and devising structured ways of challenging boys' domination.

The Schools Council Sex Differentiation Project supported a variety of different intervention methods, ranging from attempting to influence the structure of schools with the help of the LEA, developing a whole-school Equal Opportunities policy, supporting a girls-only taster course in CDT, and looking at the role of the adviser.

The project identified four main areas for attention in secondary schools. These were:

1 changes in the option system (consideration of a common core of subjects)
2 consideration of the value of mixed and single-sex grouping in particular curricular areas (PE, Mathematics and Science, etc.)
3 new curricular developments for girls (assertiveness training, self-defence and extra support for girls taking Science); for boys (child development, the development of emotional sensitivity and self-sufficiency) and for both (new technology)
4 a review of Careers Education

Beauchamp Community School, Oadby, Leicestershire, one of the schools which took part in the Schools Council project, made gender a key issue, and has become something of a 'model school' in terms of what can be done to implement Equal Opportunities. The school has a woman principal, Maureen Cruikshank, a large proportion of the staff fairly committed to Equal Opportunities, and an LEA with a progressive Equal Opportunities policy. The Equal Opportunities initiative started when Beauchamp was invited to become one of the schools involved in the Schools Council Sex Differentiation Project. As a result of that, Beauchamp experimented with the following departmental initiatives:

● Drama – production of 'equal opportunity' plays for assemblies

- Youth Club – informal discussions and ideas and displays of Equal Opportunities information
- Science and English – an analysis and monitoring of exam results
- Careers – a gender analysis of job destinations
- Geography – an analysis of gender and ability factors operating at option choice
- Maths – a departmental analysis and curriculum review
- Typewriting – an examination of student attitudes
- PE – experiments with mixed groupings
- Computer Studies – lunchtime clubs
- Home Economics – a gender analysis with recommendations for change
- Languages – a gender analysis with recommendations for change
- Library – a one month survey of library use by gender

The school has produced a report monitoring the progress of Equal Opportunities, and showing how gender can be integrated across the curriculum (Beauchamp Comminity School, 1987). Marsha Jones, the school's Equal Opportunities co-ordinator, feels that there is a high level of awareness among the staff, and some change in attitudes in the school. In the fourth year, there are almost equal numbers of girls and boys taking Physics. All the school resources, both books and exam material from outside, and material produced by staff, are examined for bias. All tutors do PSE in tutorial time and use centrally-produced material which covers gender issues. However, Marsha feels that 'whenever we do something on gender stereotypes, we feel resistance. Fourteen is not a good time to start. Attitudes are already formed.' So she is now involved in a collaborative project with primary schools, organising initiatives like bringing people in non-traditional occupations into school to talk about their work. The most successful ways of introducing gender into the curriculum have been through the legitimate study of gender in Sociology, and in using it as a theme in assemblies.

Gender Issues

In order to find out how gender is being dealt with in the curriculum at present, I conducted a small scale survey in a number of schools.

In a medium-sized mixed comprehenisve school in Lincolnshire, serving a small town and a sparsely populated rural area, Equal Opportunities is not considered formally. There is no LEA policy, and in school, a couple of committed teachers raised the issue at the Curriculum Planning Board, but it got dropped and lost. Gender is dealt with in some specific subjects, such as English, Drama, Sociology and Geography depending on the concern of the individual teacher. A contact described how she would challenge sexism by personal example, use of language, confronting students' sexist assumptions and language, by choice of teaching material and displays, and through the physical arrangement of the classroom and questioning and discussion techniques. (She is the only teacher I have ever observed who has managed to divide her time equally between boys and girls.) In Years 8 and 9, sex-stereotyping is discussed in Social Studies modules, and in Years 10 and 11, gender is dealt with in Health and Sex Education modules. In the opinion of a number of contacts, far more staff are aware of sexism now, and it is the accepted norm among younger staff not to make sexist jokes, and to challenge them when they occur. But the formal structure remains unchanged. There are few women staff, and only one above allowance B. Teachers set things off on their own initiative, and do not get blocked, but there is no support. 'It's a way of keeping people happy, but not taking anything on board.' When a contact suggested 'gender' as a suitable issue for a Baker Day, it received the lowest number of votes from the senior staff to whom she made the proposal.

In another mixed comprehensive in a racially-mixed area of a Midlands city, the staff used funding derived from TVEI to teach Dance. It is not uncommon to find funding from one project diverted into another, but TVEI itself has provided opportunities for developing non-traditional skills, and especially for encouraging girls to enter new or male-dominated areas (Fawcett Society, 1986). In an attempt to challenge sex-stereotyped choices, the Expressive Arts faculty devised a rotating curriculum for the first three years, where all students sample Dance, PE, Photography and Drama, Despite this, very few boys continued to choose Dance in the later years. (In Harehills School, in Leeds, Dance has been part of the core curriculum for many years, and has produced notable successes, such as the professional group of male dancers, Phoenix Dance.) In the Midlands school, the influence of a female deputy head, and a group of committed teachers has meant that gender issues are given prominence within the curriculum. Assertiveness training is taught within the Health Education programme and within Communication. Women's Studies is offered as a separate option, and there is some 'boyswork', which includes Dealing with Violence.

Some LEAs have decided to make Equal Opportunities a priority issue. ILEA was the best known, but I am not going to deal with initiatives within ILEA for two reasons. Firstly, they have been very well documented and publicised through the Equal Opportunities Inspectorate, ILEA, and have received a lot of controversial publicity. Secondly, ILEA became such a focus for Equal Opportunities initiatives that it acquired an aura of 'otherness'. People from outside ILEA dismissed the practicality of such progressive policies – they think 'Yes, but we couldn't do that here'. Bradford sets an example of what a more *ordinary* LEA can do.

In 1986, Bradford Education Committee decided that Equal Opportunities was important enough to merit the creation of a new advisory post. (This is important; many LEAs have written policies and guidelines, and dumped the responsibility for Equal Opportunities onto an adviser with primary responsibility for a specific subject, so the Equal Opportunities takes a weak second place, and does not require the LEA to spend much money.) The woman appointed wanted to set up a base to draw together all the local initiatives on Equal Opportunities, and so 'Gender Project Base' was created (see Key Addresses). As the LEA had designated gender as a local priority area, the INSET adviser was able to allocate money from the local budget to offer a year's secondment (now extended to two years). The applicants were asked to write their own proposal for their activities. The present postholder's involvement came from doing assertiveness training with girls in special schools. The base also has other staff on one-term secondments looking at such things as gender in first and nursery schools, upper and special schools, getting girls into CDT and carrying out an evaluation using *Genderwatch* (see Resources). Base workers are invited to contribute to other policy formation and curriculum review.

The Gender Project Base will provide anything that schools want. They keep resources which staff can use, and will send out boxes of books to schools, to use with staff and students. They go into schools and work with staff in curriculum areas and year groups (an academic year), and run assertiveness training with staff. They do some work with students in pastoral year groups, alongside the course tutor. The base has also organised three groups of gender trainers, who carry out training throughout the authority. The staff in the two school-based teams are usually 'lent' by their institutions on an informal basis, although occasionally supply cover is arranged. Several schools have used Baker days for Equal Opportunities training, with the help of trainers from the base.

The Gender Project Base is currently exploring single sex groupings within mixed schools, particularly for Maths, and gender bias in recording achievement. They have booklets for sale describing their activities, and are willing to discuss initiatives with people from other LEAs.

Equal Opportunities in the National Curriculum

Many feminist educationists have long argued for the establishment of a core curriculum as the only way to deal with the problem of boys and girls making sex-stereotyped subject choices (Byrne, 1978; Whyld, 1983; Headlam Wells and Holt, 1986). In the UK, relatively few girls choose to study Sciences, and relatively few boys choose to study Languages. In the USA, where Maths is not a compulsory subject, there is a similar problem of girls opting out. Although the 'liberal' argument for freedom of choice to develop personal interests is very persuasive, the evidence suggests that the majority of young people choose their subjects less on a realistic assessment of their own personal capabilities and future needs than on culturally determined expectations, according to sex and social class or other factors such as the amount of homework a subject is likely to generate, and whether they like the teacher. These choices will to a large extent determine their ability to follow certain career paths later on. So will the new National Curriculum be the feminist dream come true?

The response of the Fawcett Society (1987) to the National Curriculum consultation document (DES, 1987) criticises the proposals mainly for what is omitted. Although section A, 8(iii) states the intention of ensuring that all students 'regardless of sex' should have 'access' to 'broadly the same good and relevant curriculum and programmes of study', there is no reference to any special measures that may be necessary to remove practices that perpetuate sex-stereotyping. Even with a core Science curriculum, girls may be able to opt out of the Physical Sciences if a modular approach is adopted. No attention is paid to the research that girls and boys may have different styles of learning and may be motivated in different ways, and that current practice tends to use the style of learning preferred by boys. Unless more Science and Technology teachers are trained, there will be a shortage, which will mean that some students, probably those classified as less-able, including a high proportion of girls, will be taught by less qualified staff. With the emphasis on Maths, Science and Technology, less attention will be paid to the Humanities, where girls excel.

Opinions from other sources range from 'it won't make much difference' to 'it will be an absolute disaster'. Although the National Curriculum prescribes that a certain proportion of time should be spent on core and foundation subjects, it probably will have less effect on the way subjects are taught than the new GCSE syllabi and the persuasion of the individual teacher. For example, teachers of History have long been able to take a feminist perspective by looking at primary sources and considering the issues affecting the lifestyle of ordinary women and men in the past. The GCSE syllabi now require students to examine primary sources, detect bias, and show empathy, in a more people-centred approach to History. Several of the topics, such as 'Trade Unions', and 'The Old Poor Law', and themes such as 'People in Society' require a study of women's lives. But it will still be possible for teachers to choose more traditional topics if they wish, and to preserve the subject primarily as the study of the acts of important men.

The fact that what is prescribed within the National Curriculum is not alterable by other bodies, may have unexpected, progressive effects. The report (DES, 1988) from the Science working group, recommended that the programmes of study from 14 to 16 years (Years 10 and 11) should contain the recommendation that all pupils 'consider the technology of various methods of birth control and contraception'. Governors, if opposed to Sex Education, will have no power to veto it.

With the National Curriculum, there will be less opportunity for girls to opt out of Science, and for boys to avoid completely Languages and Humanities, but the core curriculum envisaged by feminists would include a 'Skills for Living' element (such as that at the Hackney Downs School, ILEA) (Askew and Ross, 1988a and b; BBC2, 1987, see Key Classroom Resources) in which both boys and girls would gain practical skills, such as survival cookery and home maintenance; emotional development, such as interpersonal skills, challenging prejudice and discrimination; and preparing for parenthood. The core curriculum of English, Maths and Science, is much more traditionally academic than this, and what feminists have considered as appropriate for a core curriculum, is what the National Curriculum allows as a matter of choice for schools. There will still be some time for work outside the foundation subjects (paras. 16–18), but will this be in terms of cross-curricular themes? It seems likely that schools which have already developed a PSE programme promoting Equal Opportunities, will continue to follow it, but that the limited time available for curricular activities other than the foundation subjects may deter uncommitted schools.

Conclusion

Gender can be dealt with in a variety of ways. Ideally, it is integrated throughout the curriculum, as a theme, which influences the organisation of the curriculum, occurs regularly in all subjects, and is given special prominence at certain times. In practice, in a few areas of the country, where there is political will and established practice among a core of committed teachers, the treatment of sex discrimination and the effects of gender typing has assumed prominence amongst a large proportion of the staff. However, in the majority of schools in the country, Equal Opportunities is still a peripheral issue, and an awareness of gender and a challenge to sexism is raised intermittently, by a few isolated teachers, or occasionally a small departmental group working together.

Fortunately, there are signs that things are improving. Although there are few schools which have given Equal Opportunities prime importance, in most schools there is now some awareness and concern. Young teachers entering the profession tend to be more aware, and willing and more able to encourage students to explore their own attitudes. At the top, funding bodies such as the Training Commission (now the Training Agency) and the EEC (through the European Social Fund), campaigning groups such as the Fawcett Society who make positive action awards (Fawcett, 1986, 1988), some LEAs, the FEU and the National Curriculum Council, and even the press, will all support good practice.

References and Further Resources

D. Agnew, *Breaking the Mould* (EOC, 1985)

S. Askew and C. Ross, *Boys Don't Cry* (Open Univeristy, 1988a)

S. Askew and C. Ross, *Equal Opportunities: What is in it for Boys?* (Moorland House Publishing, 1988b)

Beauchamp Community School, *Equal Opportunities Today and Tomorrow* (Beauchamp Community School, Oadby, Leicester, 1987)

Bradford Gender Project Base, *Gender Issues Training* (Gender Project Base, see Key Addresses, 1987)

E. Byrne, *Women and Education* (Tavistock, 1978)

A. Chisholm and J. Holland, 'Anti-sexist Research in School' in G. Weiner and M. Arnot (eds.), *Gender Under Scrutiny (New Enquiries in Education)* (Hutchinson/ Open University, 1987)

K. Clarricoates, *Dinosaurs in the Classroom* (1978)

DES, *The National Curriculum 5–16: A Consultation Document* (HMSO, 1987)

DES, *Science for Ages 5 to 16* (HMSO, 1988)

EOC, *Equal Opportunities in Craft, Design and Technology* (EOC, 1983)

EPC and EOC, *Guidelines for Avoiding Sex-stereotyping in Children's and Educational Books* (EOC, 1981)

Fawcett Society, *Opening Doors* (Fawcett Society, 1986)

Fawcett Society, *Exams for the Boys* (Fawcett Society, 1987)

Fawcett Society, *Getting Started* (Fawcett Society, 1988)

FEU, *Curriculum Development for a Multicultural Society* (Further Education Unit, 1985)

GIST, *Girls into Science and Technology, Final Report* (Manchester University Press, 1984)

M. Grant, 'Craft, Design and Technology' in Whyld (ed.), *Sexism in the Secondary Curriculum* (Paul Chapman Publishing, 1983)

J. Headlam Wells and A. Holt, *Opting for Different Worlds* (Professional Centre Publications, Humberside College of Higher Education, Hull, 1986)

E. Hendry, *The Discount Matrix applied to Gender Awareness* (Heron Publishing, 152 Park Street Lane, Park Street, St Albans, Herts AL2 2AU, 1988)

A. Kelly, *The Missing Half – Girls and Science Education* (Manchester University Press, 1981)

A. Kelly *et al.* in Weiner and Arnot (1987) (see below)

T. Lloyd, *Working with Boys* (National Youth Bureau, 1986)

V. Millman, *Teacher as Researcher*, in Weiner and Arnot (1987) (see below)

V. Millman and G. Weiner, *Sex Differentiation in Schooling: is there really a problem?* (Longman, 1985)

Northam, in Weiner and Arnot (1987) (see below)

B. Smail, *Girl-friendly Science: Avoiding Sex Bias in the Curriculum* (Longman, 1984)

D. Spender, *Invisible Women* (Writers and Readers Publishing Co-operative, 1982)

M. Stanworth, *Gender and Schooling* (Hutchinson, 1983)

G. Weiner and M. Arnot (eds.), *Gender Under Scrutiny: New Enquiries in Education* (Hutchinson/Open University, 1987)

J. Whyld, *Sexism in the Secondary Curriculum* (Paul Chapman Publishing, 1983)

J. Whyld, *Anti-sexist Teaching Strategies with Boys* (Moorland House Publishing, Caistor, Lincs LN7 6SF, 1986)

J. Whyte, *Girls into Science and Technology* (Routledge and Kegan Paul, 1986)

Writers and Readers Publishing Collective, *Sexism in Children's Books* (1976)

Key Teacher Resources

Cassoe, newsletter (7 Pickwick Court, London SE9 4SA)
Small, cheap, bi-monthly, with details of new initiatives and publications. The easiest way of keeping up-to-date.

ILEA Learning Resources Branch, *Anti-sexist Resources Guide* (ILEA Learning Resources Branch, Television and Publishing Centre, Thackeray Road, SW8 3TB)
Gives details of hundreds of organisations, AVA and books, most still in existence.

SCDE Publications, *Genderwatch* (SCDC Publications, Newcombe House, Notting Hill Gate, London W11 3JB)
A resource pack for monitoring sexism in the school, and particularly useful for in-service training, with ideas for subject by subject analysis and resources.

J. Whyld (ed.), *Sexism in the Secondary Curriculum* (Paul Chapman Publishing, 1983)
A subject by subject analysis, with teaching ideas.

Women and Training Group, *Women, Work and Training Manual* (Women and Training Group, Gloscat, Oxtalls Lane, Gloucester GL2 9HW)
A compilation of participative exercises designed for helping women return to work, but adaptable for use in the classroom and for in-service training.

Key Classroom Resources

C. Adams, P. Bartley and C. Loxton (eds.), *From Workshop to Warfare: The Lives of Mediaeval Women* (Cambridge University Press, 1988)
One of the *Women in History* series of books, which present a fascinating compilation of primary sources and contemporary illustrations.

ATSS, 'Gender and Education Notes', *Social Science Teacher* (Association for the Teaching of the Social Sciences, P.O. Box 461, Sheffield S1 3BF)
Journal of the ATSS, gives details of new initiatives and publications, and teaching ideas.

BBC2, *Men and – Masculinity / Intimacy / Work*, 1987
Series of half-hour programmes.

Careersoft, *Encounters* (Careersoft, OP14, Deansclough Industrial Park, Halifax, HX3 5AX)
An interactive computer game for 14- to 19-year olds, on boy–girl relationships, with student and resource material.

G. Crampton Smith and S. Curtis, *Sex roles* (One of the *It's Your Life* series from Longman Resources Unit)
Student booklet with cartoon strip story of girl pressured not to get qualified for a good career, points for discussion, and a quiz.

Equal Opportunities Conference, *Equal Opportunities – What's in it for boys?* (Moorland House Publishing, Caistor, Lincs LN7 6SF)
A pack of exercises prepared by a group of teachers who attended the conference of the same name. All the exercises can be adapted for work in mixed groups, and also provide ideas for consciousness raising with teachers.

Institute of Physics, *Women and Physics* (Institute of Physics, 47 Belgrave Square, London SW1X 8QX)
A set of 28 sheets of women talking about their physics-based jobs, for use in Careers. Particularly good for the descriptions of little known occupations such as a 'Real-Time Computing Scientist'. Unfortunately, no black women are depicted.

C. Meade, *The Him Book*, (Central Library, Sheffield, S1 1XZ)
A resource book of ideas for anti-sexist work with boys and young men, but many adaptable for work with mixed groups.

New Internationalist magazine, *The New Internationalist* (Subscriptions Office, 120–126 Lavender Avenue, Mitcham, Surrey, CR4 3HP)
Each issue of this monthly magazine deals with an aspect of world poverty and inequality. Many of the articles are easily accessible for less-able students, and statistics are imaginatively presented. It is written from a femininist, ecological perspective, but of particular relevance to gender issues are: 'Sex' no. 158; 'Masculinity', no. 175; 'The Politics of Housework', no. 181.

Spencer Park Teachers' Centre, *Sex Equality and the Pastoral Curriculum* (Spencer Park Teachers' Centre, Trinity Road, London SW18)
A pack of activities to use in Tutor Time, particularly suitable for lower school students.

J. Thomson, *All Right for Some! The Problem of Sexism* (Hutchinson, 1986)
A student workbook, for 14- to 18-year olds, with sections on sex roles, sexuality, work, law, media, power and harassment. Full of information, activities and points for discussion.

WEA Girls' Talk Project, *Girls' Talk* ('Connexion', 4th floor, 18–20 Dean Street, Newcastle NE1 11DG)
Video snips of conversations between teenage girls, with notes. Imaginative discussion starter.

Key Addresses

Equal Opportunities Commission (EOC),
Education Section,
Overseas House,
Quay Street,
Manchester M3 3HN
  Produces free reports, booklets on various aspects of sexism in education, e.g. Home
  Economics, PE, CDT, Careers – and posters, e.g. *Women Scientists.*

Fawcett Society,
46 Harleyford Road,
London SE11 5AY
  A prestigious pressure group, whose education committee responds to government
  initiatives, co-ordinates and publishes some research and makes awards for positive
  action.

Gender Project Base,
Room 40,
Fairfax Community School,
Flockton Road,
Bradford BD4 7 RJ

• 8 •

MULTICULTURAL AND ANTI-RACIST EDUCATION:

EDUCATION FOR A JUST SOCIETY

Barry Dufour

Origins

The origins of Multicultural and Anti-racist Education in the UK, while dating from the 1950s, are really located deeper in history with Britain's involvement in the Slave Trade and with its colonial relationship with major parts of the globe. These historical encounters have had a key influence both on certain aspects of persisting racist ideas today and on patterns of immigration which have contributed to the multi-ethnic nature of present-day Britain.

As a result of these imperial and Commonwealth links, numbers of people from the New Commonwealth have settled in the UK: people from ex-colonies in Asia (especially from the Indian Subcontinent) and from the Caribbean and Africa. People from the Old Commonwealth, mainly the white dominions of Australia, New Zealand and Canada, have also settled. Groups such as the Irish have had particular historical links with the UK. But there are many other groups who have contributed to a multi-ethnic and culturally diverse nation, including Jewish refugee groups who have made their homes here during this century and earlier (Walvin, 1984; Fryer, 1984).

But it has been the black presence, resulting from settlement of people from the New Commonwealth, in the post-war period, that has been the prime focus of racist and discriminatory attitudes and practices in most spheres of society, including education. Most of the movement to the UK, especially after the Second World War, was in response to Britain's severe labour shortage. Appeals went out from Britain to Commonwealth citizens, in the Caribbean, for example, inviting them to come and work in Britain – in the factories, the hospitals and the transport services. The British Nationality Act, 1948, allowed dual citizenship, therefore facilitating the free flow of labour.

Traditionally, Multicultural Education has been largely a response to the black presence but it has not always been a response to racism; indeed, although often well-intentioned, Multicultural Education itself has been infused with racist and ethnocentric assumptions at various stages of its development, as the following brief history will indicate.

From Assimilation to Cultural Pluralism

A standard analytical model for the history of Multicultural Education in Britain relates theory and practice in race and education to three stages of development: the 'assimilationist phase' (1950s to 1965): the 'integrationist phase' (1965 to the early 1970s); and the 'cultural pluralist phase' (early 1970s to early 1980s). There is only space here for a brief summary but reference can be made to Mullard (Mullard, 1982) for a detailed critical exposition. Other authorities have also used a version of the model (Lynch, 1986).

The assimilationist phase

The period from the 1950s to 1965 was characterised by an assumption that the children of Commonwealth immigrants in the 1950s and onwards should be absorbed into British society and culture as soon as possible in order to enhance their future opportunities and to maintain a harmonious nation where differences were not accentuated. Cultural and linguistic assimilation into white 'host' society would achieve this and the central vehicle for it would be to teach the children English. This emphasis was given important official encouragement by the DES 'English for Immigrants' initiative in 1963.

Although apparently pragmatic, there were extremely negative features in these policies. The linguistic, social and cultural traditions of ethnic minority groups (still called 'immigrants' then – and now by some people) were seen as problematic. A 'deficit' view of immigrant children was apparent in the official practice of 'bussing' numbers of black children in various cities (Birmingham, for example) from one school to another (DES, 1965). The dispersal of black children was intended to protect white pupils from the undue influence of large concentrations of immigrant children with 'language difficulties'. Although the teaching of English to pupils whose first language is not English remains a priority today, good practice would also support and encourage bilingualism. Furthermore, advanced practice today, in several LEAs, supports the teaching of community languages at all age levels.

The integrationist phase

1965 to the early 1970s represented a move away from racist notions of superiority inherent in the assimilationist position to a view or policy which placed more emphasis on equality of opportunity and which adopted a more liberal stance on ethnic minority identity. Dispersal of immigrant children was officially abandoned, which suggested a greater acceptance of diversity. Some school courses, in English and Social Studies, began to incorporate material on ethnic minority backgrounds and race relations. By the end of the period, a few inner-city schools had instituted 'Black Studies' courses – Tulse Hill School in south London, for example – but these separatist moves were opposed by a Select Committee (Select Committee, 1973).

Several positive funding initiatives were put in place. The Local Government Act, 1966, contained Section 11 which gave central government support for extra teachers in LEAs with a defined percentage of Commonwealth immigrants. The 'Plowden Report' (Plowden, 1967) called for redistribution of resources to the inner cities through EPAs (Educational Priority Areas) and the Burnham Committee in 1968 agreed special allowances for teachers in schools with special difficulties – again one of the criteria was the number of immigrant children on roll in the schools. An Urban Aid programme was set up in 1969. A key quotation for the period came from Roy Jenkins, then Home Secretary, when he said that what was needed was 'not a flattening process of assimilation but equal opportunity, accompanied by cultural diversity, in an atmosphere of mutual tolerance' (Jenkins, 1966). Community Relations Councils (CRC) had been set up in many inner-city areas and some LEAs had made advisory appointments for E2L (English as a Second Language) and community issues.

During this period, a strange dual policy was operated by government, combining increasingly stringent immigration controls which were racist in their conception, such as the Commonwealth Immigrants Act, 1968, with Race Relations Acts, in 1965 and 1968, which were designed to combat the effects of racism on ethnic minorities. There was now an official acceptance that prejudice had to be dealt with in schools, and various proposals were made for a multicultural curriculum: the Schools Council (SC) began working on Multicultural Education and the Humanities Curriculum Project directed by Lawrence Stenhouse included a resource pack on Race although, for various controversial reasons, this was never published. Schools were into the era of the New Social Studies, characterised by more critical and broadly-based investigations by pupils in the classroom (Lawton and Dufour, 1973). However, the extent of the changes in this period are difficult to assess. While there was an increasing understanding and tolerance of cultural diversity, there was little evidence of an increase in equality of opportunity in an economic and political sense.

The cultural pluralism phase

The early 1970s to the early 1980s involved a modification of attitudes and policies embedded in the previous two phases. There was a move away from a central assumption or preference for a culturally and politically unified society to an acceptance of distinct cultural or ethnic groups as a reality and as a positive feature of British society. But it can be interpreted in many different ways, suggesting varying degrees of commitment to or toleration of autonomy and diversity from the white majority towards ethnic minority communities, in school or outside. Cultural pluralists are often unclear about the degree of political power and influence minority groups do or should have in school and society, and while a strong position is taken against discrimination, policy often fails to acknowledge the extent of structural inequality and the persistence of racism which ethnic minority groups endure.

In practical terms, there were many developments. In 1973, the DES abandoned its use of the term 'immigrants' to refer to ethnic minority children. It was now inaccurate and inappropriate as many were second generation and had been born in Britain. In 1976, the Race Relations Act was passed, which set up the Commission for Racial Equality (CRE) and tightened the laws on direct and indirect discrimination. LEAs were given guidance on the educational implications of the Act. At the DES, policy was linking in ethnic minority needs to general problems of poverty through its 'Educational Disadvantage Initiatives' (1974–1980), and the Home Office was acknowledging the special problems of West Indians and other groups in terms of 'racial disadvantage'.

On the streets, from the mid-1970s into the 1980s, there was an increasing number of marches and clashes involving provocative demonstrations from the National Front, the extremist right-wing organisation, and counteraction from anti-racist groups including the Anti-Nazi League. For example, several serious clashes took place in Southall in 1976 and 1979. The beginning of the 1980s witnessed the inner-city riots in 1981 and the stringent British Nationality Act of the same year, which introduced further controls on rights of entry and residence in the UK.

The DES, at last, pronounced that the school curriculum must take account of multicultural Britain (DES, 1980) and many LEAs were developing statements and policies on Multicultural Education. Section 11 was further clarified in 1983. According to Craft, teacher education had still made no real response to a multi-ethnic Britain and to multi-ethnic schools (Craft, 1981), although a teacher education project was set up in 1983. A wide range of curriculum projects and books were now being published. General discourse was placing race and racism higher on the agenda, in school and society, and educational reform and development were apparent at all levels.

The Era of Anti-racist Education

It is not really clear where Anti-racist Education began but it certainly increased in the early 1980s. Elements of it were around in the late 1970s with the direct treatment, in some schools, of Race and Racism as a curriculum topic along with broader issues of disadvantage and inequality. One of the key features was the growing lobby of black educationists and parents who were focusing on racism as the major cause of disadvantage. Essentially, Anti-racist Education is about 'education for all', to draw on the title and philosophy of the 'Swann Report' (Swann, 1985). It is about inner-city schooling as well as education in the 'all-white' schools in the suburbs and counties of the UK.

There is an attempt to develop inter-cultural understanding and to reduce prejudice. This is within a framework of learning about and combating racism and discrimination, which involves structural changes in school and society as well as attitudinal changes. A comprehensive definition would be that an anti-racist approach to education comprises a range of aims and practices relating to professional, curriculum and institutional development which together celebrate and enhance cultural diversity in society while equally identifying and combating racism and discrimination. This definition incorporates often mutually exclusive standpoints on Multicultural Education and Anti-racist Education, by recognising cultural diversity and, at the same time, emphasising and supporting the struggle for justice and equality.

The major elements of good practice in Multicultural and Anti-racist Education would involve understanding and action on the following features on the part of policy-makers, teachers, pupils, parents and governors:

1 racism and discrimination in the UK
2 ethnic minority experience
3 language
4 the curriculum
5 education and schooling: a whole-school policy

Racism and Discrimination in Britain

In Multicultural and Anti-racist Education, perhaps more than in any other area of schooling, the attitudes and awareness of teachers are as crucial as those of the pupils. Many teachers, with the exception of those from an ethnic minority background, remain unconvinced about the extent of racism and discrimination at three important levels, and for any successful programme of development to work, teachers (and parents and governors) need to be aware of:

1   the evidence of racism in contemporary Britain in most spheres of social relations and the social structure
2   the evidence of widespread racist or ethnocentric attitudes and practice amongst staff in schools and colleges
3   the evidence of widespread racist attitudes and behaviour amongst young people in school, college or elsewhere

There is insufficient space here for presenting the extensive range of research and information available but a few recent and compelling sources can be cited.

In relation to racism in Britain today and how it affects the ethnic minority black population in particular, *Different Worlds* (Gordon and Newnham, 1986) provides a comprehensive summary of evidence from a wide range of areas – housing, employment, education, social services, the media and many more. More recent accounts of particular fields provide harrowing reading, such as *Living in Terror* (CRE, 1987) about racial harassment in housing and *Policing Against Black People* (IRR, 1987).

With regard to schooling, one of the most important research reports is *Education for Some* (Eggleston *et al.*, 1985) published in the same year as the Swann Report, *Education for All* (Swann, 1985) (see also Runnymede Trust, 1985) but certainly, and regrettably, less well-known. It describes the educational and vocational experiences of 15- to 18-year-old black youths, experiences which were far from auspicious and add up to an indictment of many schools, teachers and senior managements for their insensitivity, unfairness and racist practices.

The Swann Report itself, compendious and authoritative, contains significant evidence of racist practices in schools and explores the vital requirements for change. In doing so, it presents a comprehensive review of most of the key areas and issues: the link between education and society in relation to racism and cultural diversity; the history of Multicultural Education; key areas of concern defined by the communities, such as language issues and the role of religion in schools, especially the 'separate' schools debate; needs and issues relating to the West Indian and Asian communities, but with sections on smaller groups such as the Chinese, the Italians, and the Travellers (known as 'gypsies' in popular discourse). There is also a brief summary of the 1981 Rampton Report which was an Interim Report entitled *West Indian Children in Our Schools* (HMSO, 1981), a document which is important in its own right because of its analysis of institutional racism as a contributing factor in the underachievement of Afro-Caribbean children in schools. In spite of its high profile, or because of it, many critics believe that the Swann Report (being a government-commissioned report) did not sufficiently acknowledge the depth and extent of racism in school and society. Other educational commentators on race and education feel the necessity of sharper and more radical critiques, such as Barry Troyna's on-going contributions to the debate (Troyna and Williams, 1986; Troyna, 1987).

In terms of children and school pupils, it has long been known that even very young children develop attitudes to race (Milner, 1983), but there has been more interest in older pupils. While it is true that children of all groups can develop inter-ethnic rivalries and prejudices, a central concern has been with the racist attitudes and behaviour of white children as expressed in schools and public places such as football matches, concerts, and on the streets in everyday life, or at National Front marches during the 1970s and 1980s (CCS, 1981). In spite of the apparent decline of the Young National Front (YNF) as a regular feature on the streets and television screens during demonstrations or marches, there are no grounds for complacency – the rise and fall of the YNF should not be taken as a main indicator of the fortunes of racism: other forms of measurement and social reporting suggest that racist attitudes are fairly entrenched amongst large numbers of white British youths (Billig, 1984; Williams, 1986).

Ethnic Minority Experience

In society and school, blacks, Jews, the Irish and other groups have often been at the sharp end of racism. Firstly, it is important, therefore, for teachers and pupils to learn about this experience and to know something about the forms of resistance engaged in by the communities and by anti-racists in general. This would be a major component of any attempt to understand ethnic minority experience in the UK. Secondly, teachers, pupils, parents and governors need to develop an awareness of certain aspects of the background of various communities in terms of their cultures and beliefs. Thirdly, some understanding of their socio-economic and political location in Britain is also necessary for a better understanding. In the space available here, it is difficult to discuss ethnic minority experience in general or in relation to specific groups. It would be more appropriate to discuss the ways in which teachers and pupils might learn about ethnic minority experience.

The 'cultural background' approach has long been the traditional core of Multicultural Education, especially with teachers and pupils in the urban areas where most of the communities live. Although teachers and pupils in all-white schools have a similar need, because they live in a culturally-diverse society – even if they do not belong to a culturally-diverse school – it has been particularly incumbent upon inner-city teachers to possess, as part of their essential professional knowledge, some understanding of ethnic minority cultures and of key educational issues relevant to cultural diversity. This would include knowing something about customs and festivals, religious and cultural taboos and preferences associated with worship, food, dress codes and so forth.

It should also include a positive appreciation of language issues and awareness of the 'underachievement debate', that is, why do many ethnic minority children, especially Afro-Caribbeans, underachieve proportionately more than other children? They should also know the importance of involving parents and the community in the school. Useful discussions of ethnic minorities and education are to be found in Jeffcoate (1984), Tomlinson (1983 and 1984).

To support the 'traditional' multicultural approach, there is now a wide array of resources available for teachers and pupils, dealing with the cultural and religious background of the various communities – far too numerous to mention here (although some guides are cited in the Key Resources section of this chapter). In spite of this excellent range of resources, there is always an ever-present risk of stereotyping and of relying on inaccurate or insufficient information, leading to only superficial understanding. Critics of Multicultural Education have criticised the popularity of the 'festivals' or 'samosas, saris and steel bands' approach in primary and secondary education as unduly narrow and often superficial since it is often the *only* element of Multicultural Education in many schools. The socio-economic and political aspects of ethnic minority experience are also important, but teachers are often less acquainted with this than they are with the cultural aspects of minority groups; consequently, pupils have very little opportunity of learning about these important matters. A more comprehensive view of ethnic minorities can be found in 'Minority Experience' (Open University, 1985), a book suitable for teachers for background information.

Whatever interpretation is given and however comprehensive, the approach to be recommended is one of careful research and open-mindedness along the lines of the following checklist.

Ways of Finding Out about Ethnic Minority Experience

(For teachers and for their planning of work with pupils and students.)
    Teachers should ensure that they:

- draw upon the knowledge and experience of children and parents, especially if the school has a multi-ethnic composition
- contact local representatives/members of a culture/group
- consult information/resource/educational agencies associated with a particular culture/group
- consult community and political organisations associated with a particular culture/group
- consult the community press/media associated with a particular culture/group
- consult academic research/writing on a particular culture/group

● draw upon key 'authentic' books/resources – for adults or young learners ('authentic' here means preferably compiled by a member of the particular community or someone with established expertise); even here problems of stereotyping and bias may still be present.

Language

Multicultural Education began with a central focus on language – the English language. The teaching of English to immigrants, as a second language, was seen as the priority in the 1950s and there is little to suggest that mother-tongues were actively valued or encouraged. Today, the situation is more complex. While some sections of educational opinion still adopt a sceptical 'deficit' view of minority languages (that they are less worthy) and advocate the teaching of 'standard' English as the sole task of language teaching (apart from also teaching a modern European language), other educationists, based at certain LEAs and universities, adhere to a concept of linguistic diversity which has a commitment to encouraging the linguistic skills brought into school by all pupils, including those who are bilingual or bidialectical, with the latter including the varieties of speech of children with Caribbean links and of children from all parts of Britain.

Rosen and Burgess, in their survey of the language and dialects of London school children, found that only a small percentage were judged, by teachers, to be speakers of 'standard' English. There were 20 kinds of UK-based English, 42 overseas dialects of English and 58 world languages (Rosen and Burgess, 1980). A broad school policy on language will value all language and dialectic abilities in the school or college while also teaching English, 'standard' or otherwise. But a comprehensive language policy would still be incomplete without a consideration of the issue of community languages and community language teaching, especially in the context of the urban school.

Some community languages are taught in the UK in supplementary schools, outside normal school hours. These schools are primarily concerned with linguistic, religious and cultural maintenance for a wide range of minority communities including South Asian, Afro-Caribbean, Irish, Jewish and other communities. The degree of emphasis on language varies and, in some cases, developing literacy (as compared with fluency) in a community or heritage language may not be a prime objective. Nowadays, in response to ethnic minority demands and with the support of informed opinion from many language experts, some LEAs are exploring the teaching of particular community languages as an option in the mainstream school curriculum. In a multicultural Britain as well as a European Britain, some facility in a minority language such as Gujarati or Punjabi, for white and black children, has an equal claim to relevance as a facility in a modern European language. (See Spolsky, 1986, for a thorough discussion of bilingualism and community language issues).

The Curriculum

Throughout the 1980s, official reports from the DES and HMI, and curriculum guidelines from all sections of education, have advocated a multicultural dimension for the school and college curriculum:

> The curriculum ... should ... be of a kind which opens the minds of the pupils to other traditions and other ways of viewing the world, and which challenges and dispels the ignorance and distrust which breed racial prejudice and discrimination.   (DES, 1985)

This kind of statement from such an authoritative source is extremely important, but many LEAs, curriculum organisations and publishers had already adopted this view in the 1970s and especially during the 1980s. Consequently, there are now many curriculum strategies and a wide range of educational resources for teachers, pupils and students that support broad multicultural objectives across the entire curriculum. Only a brief reference can be made here to a few of these ideas and resources but further information can be obtained from the various professional subject organisations and from several comprehensive curriculum and resource guides such as those compiled by Alma Craft and others (Craft and Bardell, 1984; Craft and Klein, 1985).

The Arts and Humanities subjects have been developing multicultural and anti-racist approaches for a long time, but by the 1990s all areas of the curriculum could draw on good practice and resources – they are available, even if teachers in many schools and colleges do not always use them. The most significant recent growth areas are in the fields of Mathematics and Science. Key publications on resources and teaching ideas include *Anti-racist Science Teaching* (Gill and Levidow, 1987), *Mathematics in a Multicultural Society* (Mathematics Association, 1988) and *Mathematics for All* (Wiltshire LEA, 1988).

Furthermore, the National Curriculum Council reports from the various Subject Working Groups all contain references to ethnic and cultural diversity (along with Equal Opportunities and Special Needs). The first two to be published followed this pattern – *Mathematics for Ages 5 to 16* (DES, 1988a) and *Science for Ages 5 to 16* (DES, 1988b) – although it seems likely that there will be some variation in the quality of the proposals, given the reactionary stance in the Mathematics report and the contrastingly enlightened attitude to ethnic diversity in the Science report.

Education and Schooling: A Whole-School Policy

None of the initiatives in Multicultural and Anti-racist Education can be completely successful unless they form part of a whole-school policy. And whole-school policy development is unlikely to be encouraged in the many LEAs that do little more than produce a policy document. A whole-school policy, or whole-college policy in the case of the Further Education colleges, would include awareness and practice incorporating all of the issues and themes discussed above but it would specifically involve:

1   A formal policy statement on education for an ethnically diverse society which would include a discussion of all the key elements and how they should affect the total life and ethos of the school or college.
2   A code of practice for staff and pupils which sets out clear procedures on a number of issues including how to deal with racist remarks and behaviour (a useful model which also includes a checklist is the Leeds Council code, printed in the appendix of *Learning in Terror*, CRE, 1988).
3   Clear procedures for linking the school with the homes of the pupils and with the local community. This is especially important in ethnically diverse communities. Teachers need to liaise with parents, school governors and representatives of local ethnic minority groups.
4   A staffing policy which includes INSET provision on Multicultural Education and 'Racism Awareness' and also a non-discriminatory selection and promotion procedure.
5   A system for monitoring pupil/student progress which would include techniques for identifying underachievement and for promoting progress in learning. An awareness of the key issues in the debate about underachievement in relation to ethnic minority pupils and students should be part of the professional knowledge of all teachers.
6   A policy and awareness in the school which takes an informed and positive account of religious diversity in matters such as general religious commitments, religious festivals, school meals, assemblies and dress regulations.
7   A language policy which includes a general commitment to linguistic diversity and which, where appropriate, offers positive support for dialect variations, mother-tongue teaching and community languages, and English as a Second Language, while assisting all pupils to achieve a fluent level of written and oral standard English.
8   A developed system of pastoral care which takes a sensitive account of personal and social disadvantage especially where this is part of ethnic minority experience and which includes mechanisms for counselling and for educational and vocational guidance.
9   A policy on resources for learning (in classroom, library or elsewhere in the

school) which adopts a critical approach to ethnocentric material and which actively encourages the purchase and use of materials that reflect an ethnically diverse Britain and that incorporate a balanced and non-stereo-typical perspective on peoples and issues around the world.

10 A consideration of school ethos which would take account of all the elements featured above but would include a range of approaches and procedures signifying a sympathetic awareness of a multicultural Britain and a culturally diverse world and, at the same time, a commitment to anti-racism. For example, in visual terms, this might include multilingual and multicultural signs, posters and pictures in the school or college (especially near the entrance) and a display in the corridors and classrooms of a brief statement of the school's anti-racist code of practice. At the level of relationships, staff and pupils would interact in a respectful way which embodied many of the principles outlined above.

11 A built-in mechanism for continuous review.

Conclusion

It has been argued, in this brief analysis, that the sometimes mutually exclusive traditions of Multicultural, as opposed to Anti-racist Education, can be integrated and that, furthermore, they can be incorporated into every school. But, along with many other cross-cultural perspectives included in this book, a curricular approach alone is inadequate and even counter-productive to the successful achievement of the broad general aims of Multicultural Education. Positive images in the textbooks and classrooms are neutralised if institutional practices elsewhere in the school or college are racist. Whole-school policies are therefore essential. However, many contradictions remain which may slow the growth of Multicultural Education in the 1990s. At the central government level, the National Curriculum Council, the DES and HMI all appear commit-ted to encouraging schools to reflect cultural diversity in a positive manner and to combat racism in the school curriculum and in the general institutional procedures. Likewise, the Further Education Unit (FEU) at the DES has published a major project for staff development and curriculum development for a multicultural society (FEU, 1988). Yet, in 1988, the Secretary of State for Education announced the end of centrally earmarked INSET funds for Multicultural Education from 1989 onwards ('Baker Diverts Training Cash', *Guardian*, 16.8.88). At the LEA level, many local education authorities have yet to develop wide-ranging policies on Multicultural Education which are properly funded and monitored, especially LEAs in the so-called all-white areas.

It would therefore appear that even before Multicultural Education has fully established itself in many schools and areas it needs to protect itself from cuts in funding and opposition from some quarters (Palmer, 1987). Critics have observed that the Secretary of State for Education has made many policy commitments for education in the early 1990s yet the financial support for them is often woefully deficient or absent.

The post-Education Reform Act era is replete with uncertainties, and a clear path for the future of Multicultural Education is difficult to see. What can be said with certainty is that most sectors in society are now convinced of the importance of Multicultural and Anti-racist Education in our schools and colleges. The churches, ethnic minority organisations, HMI, many LEAs, the teachers' unions and professional subject associations, and many more have addressed themselves to the issue. But vital to all of this is the continued support of central government and one of the most important factors here which always concentrates the mind of government in matters of race and ethnicity – and which might ensure the continuation of Multicultural Education in some form – is the spectre of social disorder. 1981 and 1985 – years marked by major urban riots – may prove to be auspicious years for Multicultural Education in the 1990s.

References and Further Resources

M. Billig, 'I'm Not National Front Myself, But ...' in *New Society* (17 May 1984)

CCS, *Rock and the Right: Nazis on the Terraces; Nazis in the Playgrounds* (Centre for Contemporary Studies, 1981)

M. Craft, *Teaching in A Multicultural Society: The Task for Teacher Education* (Falmer Press, 1981)

A. Craft and G. Bardell (eds.), *Curriculum Opportunities in a Multicultural Society* (Harper and Row, 1984)

A. Craft and G. Klein, *Agenda for Multicultural Teaching* (Longman, 1985)

CRE, *Living in Terror* (Commission for Racial Equality, 1987)

CRE, *Learning in Terror: A Survey of Racial Harassment in Schools and Colleges* (Commission for Racial Equality, 1988)

DES, Department of Education and Science, Circular 7/65 (1965)

DES, *The School Curriculum* (HMSO, 1980)

DES, *The Curriculum from 5 to 16* (HMSO, 1985)

DES, *Mathematics for Ages 5 to 16* (HMSO, 1988a)

DES, *Science for Ages 5 to 16* (HMSO, 1988b)

J. Eggleston *et al.*, *Education for Some: The Educational and Vocational Experiences of 15–18 Year-old Members of Minority Ethnic Groups* (Trentham Books, 1985)

FEU, *Staff Development for a Multicultural Society* (The Further Education Unit, 1988)

P. Fryer, *Staying Power* (Pluto Press, 1984)

D. Gill and L. Levidow, *Anti-racist Science Teaching* (Free Association Books, 1987)

P. Gordon and A. Newnham, *Different Worlds (Racism and Discrimination in Britain)*, 2nd edition (Runnymede Trust, 1986)

HMSO, *West Indian Children in Our Schools (The Rampton Report)* (HMSO, 1981)

IRR, *Policing Against Black People* (Institute of Race Relations, 1987)

R. Jeffcoate, *Ethnic Minorities and Education* (Harper and Row, 1984)

R. Jenkins, *Address given by the Home Secretary to a meeting of voluntary liaison committees* (1966)

D. Lawton and B. Dufour, *The New Social Studies* (Heinemann Education Books, 1973)

J. Lynch, *Multicultural Education: Principles and Practice* (Routledge and Kegan Paul, 1986)

Mathematics Association, *Mathematics in a Multicultural Society* (Mathematics Association, 1988)

D. Milner, *Children and Race (Ten Years On)* (Ward Lock, 1983)

C. Mullard, in J. Tierney (ed.), *Race, Migration and Schooling* (Holt, Rinehart and Winston, 1982)

Open University, *Minority Experience* (reprinted edition) (Open University, 1985)

F. Palmer (ed.), *Anti-racism – An Assault on Education and Value* (Sherwood Press, 1987)

Lady Plowden, *Children and Their Primary Schools* (Central Advisory Council for Education, HMSO, 1967)

H. Rosen and T. Burgess, *Languages and Dialects of London School Children* (Ward Lock, 1980)

Runnymede Trust, *Education for All (A Summary)* (Runnymede Trust, 1985)

Select Committee, *Report on Education* (Hansard, 1973)

B. Spolsky (ed.), *Language and Education in Multilingual Settings* (Multilingual Matters, 1986)

Lord Swann, *Education for All* (the Report of the Committee of Inquiry into the Education of Children from Ethnic Minority Groups. Chairman: Lord Swann) (HMSO, 1985)

S. Tomlinson, *Ethnic Minorities in British Schools* (Heinemann Educational Books, 1983)

S. Tomlinson, *Home and School in Multicultural Britain* (Batsford, 1984)

B. Troyna (ed.), *Racial Inequality in Education* (Tavistock, 1987)

B. Troyna and J. Williams, *Racism, Education and the State* (Croom Helm, 1986)

J. Walvin, *Passage to Britain* (Penguin, 1984)

M. Williams, 'The Thatcher Generation' in *New Society* (21 February 1986)

Wiltshire LEA, *Mathematics for All* (Wiltshire LEA, 1988)

Key Teacher Resources

A. Craft and G. Klein, *Agenda for Multicultural Teaching* (Longman, 1985)
A popular and accessible handbook which offers guidance on whole-school policies and ideas for a multicultural dimension for all the main secondary school subjects.

CRE, *Learning in Terror (A Survey of Racial Harassment in Schools and Colleges)* (Commission for Racial Equality, 1988)
Deals with case-studies, research and ways of tackling the problem. The appendix section includes the well-known Leeds Metropolitan District Council code of practice,

'Combating Racist Behaviour in Educational Institutions', which has proved helpful to so many schools grappling with the problem for the first time (see also *Code of Practice*, CRE, 1989).

V. Edwards, *Language in Multicultural Classrooms* (Batsford, 1983)
There are more recent books on language issues but none that are both comprehensive and accessible. This is still one of the best.

C. Gaine, *No Problem Here (A Practical Approach to Education and 'Race' in White Schools)* (Hutchinson, 1987)
A useful and timely book which discusses the issues and principles of Anti-racist Education in all-white schools while providing practical strategies and ideas for teachers.

J. Lynch, *Prejudice Reduction and the Schools* (Cassell, 1987)
A complete guide to every possible teaching device for reducing prejudice, drawing on research and teaching strategies from both sides of the Atlantic.

Open University, *Minority Experience (E354 Block 3 – Ethnic Minorities and Community Relations)* (Open University, 1985)
One of the few comprehensive books which deals with the main communities in Britain and draws upon a wide range of perspectives – historical, economic, social, political and sociological.

B. Spolsky (ed.), *Language and Education in Multicultural Settings* (Multilingual Matters, 1986)
One of the best recent treatments of the issue of community languages, amongst other language themes, although it is not an easy read.

Swann/Eggleston, *Education for All* (Runnymede Trust, 1985), *Education for Some* (Runnymede Trust, 1986)
These two booklets are summaries of the two main reports, the report by Lord Swann and his committee (*Education for All*) and the report by Professor John Eggleston and his research team (*Education for Some*).

J. Twitchin and C. Demuth, *Multicultural Education (Views from the Classroom)* (BBC Publications, second edition, 1985)
A practical guide for teachers in primary and secondary schools to accompany the BBC programmes which many LEAs retain as videos. The book and the programmes are useful training materials for teachers.

Key Classroom Resources

BBC, *Getting to Grips with Racism*, (BBC, 1988 and 1989)
A series of television programmes for lower secondary school pupils, with teachers' notes and pupil material.

P. Gordon and A. Newnham, *Different Worlds (Racism and Discrimination in Britain)* (Runnymede Trust, second edition, 1986)
A best-selling information booklet for adults and school pupils. It deals with racism in most aspects of daily life and institutions and supports its analysis with pictures, statistics and quotes from key sources.

IRR, *Roots of Racism (Book One)*, *Patterns of Racism (Book Two)*, *How Racism Came to Britain (Book Three)*, *The Fight Against Racism (Book Four)* (The Institute of Race Relations, 1982, 1985 and 1986)
Four well-illustrated books for secondary schools dealing with the history of racism.

P. Page and H. Newman, *They Came to Britain (The History of a Multicultural Nation)* (Edward Arnold, 1985)
A 48-page illustrated book for a wide age and ability range which deals with the usual lists of invaders – Romans, Normans and so forth – but then continues with the story up to the 1980s, dealing with settlers and refugees, black and white, from all nations.

M. Raleigh, *The Languages Book* (ILEA, The English Centre, 1981)
A best-selling and attractive classroom book on all aspects of language. Lots of interesting exercises and activities.

Key Addresses

Commission for Racial Equality,
Elliot House,
10/12 Allington Street,
London SW1E 5EH
Tel: (01)828–7022
   Useful for information and publications

Commonwealth Institute,
Kensington High Street,
London W8 6NQ
Tel: (01)603–4535
   Worth a visit for children learning about different cultures but there is also an extensive bookshop, library and information service.

Institute of Race Relations,
2–6 Leeke Street,
London WC1X 9HS
Tel: (01)837–0041
   Useful for information and publications

Runnymede Trust,
178 North Gower Street,
London NW1 2NB
Tel: (01)387–8943
   Useful for information and publications

• 9 •

GLOBAL EDUCATION:

LEARNING IN A
WORLD OF CHANGE

Graham Pike

What is Global Education?

> 'I started a new project at school today', announced nine-year-old Jane proudly to her family at teatime. 'What's this one about?' asked her mother. 'The World,' declared Jane crisply and confidently, and then, noticing and recognising a look of slight anxiety and alarm in her mother's eyes, she hastened to reassure her: 'Oh don't worry that it may be too much for me, Mummy – there are two of us doing it.'
>
> (Richardson, 1985)

Robin Richardson's introduction to 'The World Studies Story' neatly encapsulates a likely response to the terminology and content of Global Education, or – to use a term more widely understood in England and Wales – World Studies. It also hints at the difficulties in summing up a philosophical and practical approach to education which – in common with others featured in this book – fails to fit squarely into the old paradigm, subject-bound and content-oriented school curriculum.

Global Education, in short, is a contemporary response to the urgent need to educate young people for a world of increasing interdependence and rapid change. Jane, even at the age of nine, already finds herself inextricably enmeshed in an interdependent world system which brings her food, clothes and toys from all parts of the world. Inevitably, the course of her life will be bound up in global economic, political and cultural systems in which she will act as an agent of change – as a worker, voter, consumer, parent, tourist. What are the implications for the global system of giving Jane an education which does *not* adequately equip her with the skills and understanding necessary to make informed and far-seeing decisions in all spheres of her life? Schools have a responsibility, global educators argue, to foster the development of such skills

133

and understanding to enable students to participate constructively in a world of rapid change and uncertainty.

Some Aims of Global Education

In their influential handbook, *World Studies 8–13*, Simon Fisher and David Hicks suggest that the broad aim of World Studies teaching is 'to help children develop the knowledge, attitudes and skills which are relevant to living in a multicultural society and an interdependent world' (Fisher and Hicks, 1985). Pierre Pradervand echoes these sentiments whilst offering a little more depth and precision in his three central goals of Global Education:

1   creating an understanding of the oneness of all things
2   creating a vision of a world that works for all – this, he suggests, is the most important goal in that the greatest challenge to humankind is not material poverty, but the poverty of our thinking
3   generating the individual commitment to translate vision into action

(Pradervand, 1987)

Graham Pike and David Selby provide a more detailed summary of aims modelled on the seminal work of Robert Hanvey, *An Attainable Global Perspective* (Hanvey, 1982). For many years, Hanvey's five aims had constituted the underpinning of much Global Education, particularly in the United States. Whilst recognising the pivotal influence of Hanvey's writing, Pike and Selby argue that it is insufficiently forceful in its promotion of the need for a global perspective and, thus, offer five aims which together make up the 'irreducible global perspective'.

Systems consciousness

Students should:

● acquire the ability to think in a systems mode (how systems, political, economic, etc. operate)
● acquire an understanding of the systemic nature of the world
● acquire an 'holistic' conception of their capacities and potential.

Perspective consciousness

Students should:

● recognise that they have a view of the world that is not universally shared
● develop receptivity to other perspectives

Health of planet awareness

Students should:

● acquire an awareness and understanding of the global condition and of global developments and trends
● develop an informed understanding of the concepts of justice, human rights and responsibilities and be able to apply that understanding to the global condition and to global developments and trends
● develop a future orientation in their refeclection upon the health of the planet

Involvement consciousness and preparedness

Students should:

● become aware that the choices they make and the actions they take individually and collectively have repercussions for the global present and the global future
● develop the social and political action skills necessary for becoming effective participants in democratic decision-making at a variety of levels, grassroots to global

Process mindedness

Students should

● learn that learning and personal development are continuous journeys with no fixed or final destination
● learn that new ways of seeing the world are revitalising but risky

(Pike and Selby, 1988)

In both Pradervand's and Pike and Selby's summaries of the aims of Global Education there is evidence of the influence by writers who have criticised the 'mechanistic paradigm' – the view of the world, originating in the scientific thinking of Descartes and Isaac Newton. This compartmentalises reality into building blocks, each of which can be taken out for analysis and repair without any change to the overall structure. Such a vision, argue the so-called 'new age' philosophers and scientists such as Fritjof Capra, Marilyn Ferguson and Jean Houston, has resulted in unparalleled advances in technology but an ever-deepening social, ecological and cultural crisis in most, particularly the industrialised, parts of the world. This is characterised by an alienation of humankind from the natural world, a deep division in all spheres of life between person and planet (Capra, 1983; Ferguson, 1980; Houston, 1982). It may be useful at this point to look briefly at the history of Global Education and World

Studies in order to fully understand the context in which such 'new age' thinking has flourished.

International Understanding and Person-Centred Learning

In an exploration of the evolution of Global Education it is possible to discern a number of strands of influence, some 'socio-political', some 'educational' – though it should be recognised that such categorisation oversimplifies the inter-relatedness of change processes.

The Socio-Political Background

Three major socio-political strands come to mind. Firstly, the dawning real-isation of the world's interdependence or 'systemic' nature. We can, suggests Lee Anderson, conceive of the world as having a global economic system, dominated by trans-national corporations and regulated, to some extent, by supra-national bodies such as the World Bank; a global political system, in which political power has been wrested from nation states by 'non-state actors', such as the United Nations; and lastly, a global cultural system, in which the differences between societies in terms of their popular values and patterns of social behaviour are becoming less marked (Anderson, 1979).

Secondly, the realisation of global interdependence has resulted in an urgent, if somewhat belated, call to understand and find solutions to the many global problems faced by humankind. An interdependent relationship is not neces-sarily an equitable one; inequalities and injustices worldwide have resulted in environmental and developmental catastrophes, gross violations of human rights and innumerable examples of life-wasting conflict. They have resulted, too, in a sheaf of global reports. Some, such as those written by the Club of Rome, are apocalyptic; others are more measured in tone but none the less definite in their demand for urgent action. Amongst the latter are the Brandt Report (Brandt, 1980), the World Conservation Strategy and the Brundtland Report (Brundtland, 1987).

The third major socio-political strand of influence is less tangible, less quantifiable or explicable but perhaps, ultimately, the most potent strand of all. It is characterised by grassroots movements and networks of people worldwide who demonstrate, through their actions, the rejection of 'old paradigm' ways of thinking and doing. Environmental and peace movements, community and women's groups, individuals pursuing 'holistic' health care or committed to ecological living – they all constitute what Marilyn Ferguson has called 'the aquarian conspiracy', people who, in all walks of life and unbeknown to each other, are inspired by the ideals and philosophies of the new age (Ferguson,

1980). A formidable *Zeitgeist* is beginning to influence conventional Western attitudes to science, to medicine, to industry, to religion and, belatedly, to education. Fritjof Capra suggests that we are experiencing a dramatic cultural transformation which will eventually involve a thorough change in the mentality of Western culture and will be accompanied by profound modifications of social relationships and forms of social organisation (Capra, 1983).

The Educational Background

All of the above strands have significant implications for education. Running parallel to these, however, are four major educational strands of influence on Global Education. The first is the post-1918 concern for education for international understanding, formalised in the magazine entitled *The New Era* and its associated network of educators from more than fifty countries (latterly known as the 'World Education Fellowship'). The vision of greater understanding between peoples and nations leading to increased tolerance, respect and peacefulness is engraved in the constitution of UNESCO and has been carried forward in the UK principally through the work of the Council for Education in World Citizenship (CEWC), founded in 1939. An academic at the London Institute of Education actively interested in education for world citizenship, James Henderson, began to work closely in the 1950s with an all-party group of MPs and peers at Westminster, the Parliamentary Group for World Government. In 1952 the Group founded an educational charity, the One World Trust which in turn, in 1973, set up a curriculum project known as the World Studies Project. Under the direction of Robin Richardson the Project produced a teachers' handbook – including the influential *Learning for Change in World Society* (Richardson, 1976) – and a series of students' booklets. In 1980 Simon Fisher, from the One World Trust, and David Hicks, from the newly-formed Centre for Peace Studies at St Martin's College, Lancaster, joined forces to launch the World Studies 8–13 Project, part-funded by the Schools Council (Richardson, 1985).

The origins of World Studies, however, are more diverse than the above potted history suggests. A second strand of influence comes from the US Global Education movement which was similarly concerned to foster understanding about other countries. But, as Steven Lamy notes, it was concerned for less altruistic reasons: 'Global Education emerged as an integral part of our national security arsenal, the purpose being to serve our national interest by enhancing political, economic and socio-cultural influence throughout the world' (Lamy, 1983). The Soviet launch of Sputnik in 1957 hastened the development of a worldview in which US citizens were encouraged to see themselves as defenders of the 'free world'. To some extent, Global Education in the United States has not shaken off its self-orientation, nor its preoccupation with 'area studies' –

studying countries or regions of the world in which the US has particular economic or political interests. However, the influence of writers such as Lee Anderson, James Becker and Robert Hanvey can be noted in the UK in terms of their exposition of the nature, and complexity, of contemporal global interdependence and the concomitant responsibility of schools to educate young people for global citizenship. The term 'Global Education' itself originates from across the Atlantic, though the definitions offered earlier in this chapter are somewhat broader than those found in most US writing on Global Education (Anderson, 1979; Hanvey, 1982).

A third major strand of influence stems from other areas of the new social curriculum featured in this book, particularly Environmental Education, Gender Education, Human Rights Education, Multicultural and Anti-racist Education, and Peace Education. Their overlapping aims and concerns will be clearly evident from other chapters, as will their differences in emphasis and perspective. A feature of the new social curriculum must surely be its preparedness to transgress rigid subject boundaries, and to positively encourage the cross-fertilisation of concepts, perspectives and practices to the point where 'ownership' of a particular idea or approach becomes far less important than the impact it has upon other areas or themes.

Another significant area in terms of the evolution of Global Education has been Development Education. From an emphasis on teaching about poverty in Third World countries in the 1960s, Development Education has itself evolved into an area whose objective is 'to enable us to comprehend and participate in the development of ourselves, our community, our nation and the world' (see Key Addresses, National Association of Development Education Centres). This latter view of world development, as a process in which all humans have a stake and a responsibility, underlies much World Studies teaching in the UK.

The fourth educational strand of influence is all-pervasive: it is reflected in Global Education's concern for the processes of teaching and learning, a consideration of *how* learning takes place in addition to (and in interaction with) *what* is learnt. The origins of such concern can be traced back to those visionary educators who were dissatisfied with the dominant authoritarian mode of education, personified by Mr Gradgrind in Charles Dickens' *Hard Times*, and who proposed an alternative, 'child-centred' approach. Amongst these were John Dewey in the USA, Rabindranath Tagore in India and Maria Montessori in Italy; their influence was paramount in the philosophy of the 'progressive' school movement that began in England at the end of the nineteenth century. The emphasis of these educators on the importance of individuality, self-realisation and learning through real experiences, was also fundamental to the ideals of the international group mentioned earlier who were associated with *The New Era*. Thus, the 'twin pillars' of World Studies and Global Education in the UK, child-centredness and worldmindedness, have a pedigree dating back to, at least, the last century (Richardson, 1985).

Over the past two decades the single most formative influence on the development of the 'process-oriented' and child-centred approach advocated by global educators has been that of the humanistic psychologist, Carl Rogers. In addition to the concerns of Dewey and Montessori for individuality and self-realisation, Rogers points to the crucial significance for learning of the quality of interpersonal relationships operative in a classroom. The teacher, he argues, should be 'a facilitator of change and learning', a role for which the principal qualifications are to be genuine in relationships with the students, to prize and to have empathy with the learner (Rogers, 1983). Rogers' ideas for a 'person-centred' mode of learning find expression in the World Studies class-room in the form of co-operative and experiential learning, an emphasis on raising students' levels of self-esteem, and a concern to actively involve students in the initiation, direction and evaluation of their learning. There are strong links too, between Rogers' ideals and the vision of education held by many new age writers. New age writers encourage us to view the world holistically, to see all phenomena and events as dynamically interconnected. 'This is what all of us bring into life and to school', writes Theodore Roszak, 'a wholly unexplored, radically unpredictable identity. To educate is to unfold that identity – to unfold it with the utmost delicacy, recognising that it is the most precious resource of our species, the true wealth of the human nation.' (Roszak, 1981).

New Initiatives

The 1980s saw a burgeoning of interest amongst primary and secondary teachers in World Studies, the creation of new projects, centres and networks, the development of syllabi and examinations and a move in some quarters towards a preference for the term Global Education. A measure of the degree of interest and practice in World Studies in England and Wales[1] may be registered, perhaps, by the fact that it has been criticised, from both left and right political perspectives (as well as from within its own ranks).

The 1980s witnessed, too, a downward trend in the phase of schooling primarily targetted by World Studies practitioners, from the 14–16 age range orientation of the original World Studies Project, through the middle-school emphasis of the World Studies 8–13 Project to the work currently being developed by and for teachers of the 3–7 age group. Implicit in this trend is the belief that Global Education aims are significant at all levels of schooling and that there is an important cumulative factor. Research evidence indicates that between the age of 8 and 13, a child's cognitive development is sufficiently advanced for the child to be curious about and accept a variety of viewpoints;

unless opportunities for raising a child's global awareness at this time are exploited, the child will show a tendency towards intolerance at other perspectives and inflexibility in attitudes. Early childhood teachers argue that the foundations of Global Education must be laid in the infant classroom, by strengthening each child's self-esteem and by developing the skills of effective communication and co-operation (Greig, Pike and Selby, 1987).

The World Studies 8–13 Project, through its national conferences, regional workshops and its major publication *World Studies 8–13: A Teacher's Handbook* (Fisher and Hicks, 1985) has been the main source of inspiration to middle school teachers. Some 47 Local Education Authorities (LEAs) are now involved in the Project. A crucial in-service education role for both primary and secondary teachers has been played by the Centre for Global Education at the University of York (formerly called the World Studies Teacher Training Centre), established by David Selby in 1982. The Centre runs advanced diploma and other courses in a range of LEAs; it also runs research and curriculum development projects, the principal outcomes of which to date have been two teacher's handbooks, *Earthrights: Education as if the Planet Really Mattered* (Greig, Pike and Selby, 1987) and *Global Teacher, Global Learner* (Pike and Selby, 1988). The Centre was also instrumental in drawing up, in collaboration with a group of teachers from Devon and Cornwall, the first GCSE syllabus in World Studies (for the Southern Examining Group). The syllabus is a response to the many secondary teachers who have argued that World Studies will be devalued as a curriculum area, by students, parents and staff, unless a public examination is provided. Others, however, have strongly resisted any attempt to subject World Studies aims and objectives to the kind of formal assessment required even under the more flexible GCSE system. As Richard Hedge has remarked, it is tempting to pose the question, 'Is World Studies assessable?' as 'Can we nail jelly to the ceiling?' (Hedge, 1988).

At the level of pre-service education for teachers, Global Education has made few inroads. Optional courses in World Studies have featured at East Anglia, Exeter, and York universities but in general it seems that the vast majority of teachers are leaving their training courses ill-equipped to prepare young people for the challenges of the twenty-first century. The advice given to one teacher about to embark upon her probationary year, 'Don't smile until Christmas', reflects an attitude to the profession which is in total opposition to the humane, empowering classroom of Carl Rogers.

Fortunately, opportunities for newly qualified teachers to become involved in Global Education are growing through networks, organisations and materials. The World Studies 8–13 Project has its own national network of committed teachers and advisers, as does the Centre for Global Education. The latter produces a quarterly newsletter and also houses the national journal for global educators, *World Studies Journal*. A national teachers' conference is staged biennially by the World Studies Network. Many local and regional networks and projects exist, often formed around teachers centres or development education centres, providing short in-service courses, curriculum advice and materials on global issues. Just as the concerns of Global Education overlap with other elements of the new social curriculum, so too do the various networks and support services which have grown up around them. Thus, conferences on World Studies and Anti-racist/Anti-sexist Education, Global Education courses featuring development, environment, peace and human rights themes, informal contacts and sharing between World Studies teachers and those involved in Personal and Social Education, Health Education and TVEI . . . all of these are commonplace occurrences.

At the classroom level, World Studies courses – or curricula with a global perspective – are on the increase. The first core World Studies course, at Groby Community College in Leicestershire (started in the late 1970s), has spawned many similar developments in secondary schools, notably in the South-West of England. Here, in largely rural and Conservative authorities, World Studies provides a politically acceptable vehicle for introducing concepts and perspectives which might otherwise be deemed too controversial. The World Studies 8–13 Project, too, is encouraging many middle-school teachers to explore with their students controversial and complex global issues. Through World Studies' emphasis on classroom process students have developed the skills of critical discussion, negotiation, consensus-seeking and decision-making, thereby enabling them to gain some insight into problems of peace, development, human rights and the environment.

Quality classroom materials and teachers' handbooks now abound, though few are yet available through mainstream educational publishers. Here the development and aid agencies, such as Christian Aid and Oxfam, make a vital contribution both in the production of low-cost teaching materials on global issues and in the setting up and funding of development education centres, many of which are themselves producing materials in collaboration with local teachers. *The Development Puzzle* (Fyson, 1984), now in its seventh edition, was for many years the principal sourcebook for teaching and learning about world development. More recently it has been joined by an extensive range of packs, kits and photo-sets, many of which seek to explore links between localities in the UK and the developing world (*The World in Birmingham*, Birmingham DEC, 1982; *From Dhaka to Dundee*, Leeds DEC / War on Want, 1987, see Classroom Resources). An increasingly common feature of these materials is the emphasis on active, participatory learning through role-play, group discussion activities and simulation games (good examples are the middle school packs produced at Carmarthen Development Education Centre, *A Rainforest Child* (1986), *Tomorrow's Woods* (1987) and *An Arctic Child* (1988)). Other publications of great value, particularly to the primary teacher, are the very practically oriented teachers' handbooks on co-operative learning and self-esteem building; many of these emanate from a US Quaker stable, though British publishers are beginning to respond to the growing market (see Resources section at the end of this chapter).

Key Debates and Controversies

Proponents of the new social curriculum are still debating whether it is better to be attacked by the forces of the political Right or ignored by them. In this regard, the 'coming of age' of World Studies might be dated at December 1985, on the publication of Roger Scruton's *World Studies: Education or Indoctrination?* (Scruton, 1985). In this pamphlet Scruton makes four principal allegations based on a mischieviously selective sample of World Studies materials and no direct classroom observation. The first allegation is that World Studies presents only radical interpetations of Third World inequality; the second concerns interactive learning styles which, he argues, manipulate feelings to the exclusion of rational thought; the third is that World Studies maintains a judicious silence about injustice in the communist world; and fourthly he alleges that World Studies is based on a Marxist analysis. In their full-page response to these criticisms in the *Times Educational Supplement*, Graham Pike and David Selby point to the hypocrisy in Scruton's writing: essentially his criticism of World Studies is that it lacks academic integrity and rigour, yet his own analysis, containing many factual errors as well as misinformation, displays an appalling disdain for such integrity and rigour (Pike and Selby, 1986).

Scruton's fourth allegation – that of Marxist underpinning – may well have amused both Richard Hatcher, who has attacked World Studies for excluding radical critiques of world capitalism (Hatcher, 1983), and Chris Mullard, who accuses World Studies of legitimising race, gender and class inequalities by ignoring them (Mullard, 1982). Gender blindness is a recurring allegation, too. In a recent issue of the *World Studies Journal* entitled 'Half the World Studies', Jean Garreau and Ruth Versfield take the publication *World Studies 8–13: A Teacher's Handbook* to task for not providing classroom exercises which actively confront gender, race and class inequalities (Garreau & Versfield, 1987), whilst Aileen McKenzie contends that 'despite the nature of the oppression we [as women] experience, those of us engaged in World Studies are very much aware that our contribution is likely to be of far greater significance than that made by all or most men involved in the same field of work' (McKenzie, 1987). Chris Brown, who incidently considers Mullard's accusations 'hardly fair', suggests that nationalism is the greatest obstacle in the path to global citizenship and admonishes World Studies for not having come to terms with this 'major force in modern Britain' (Brown, 1984).

There are criticisms, too, of World Studies' emphasis on the process of teaching and learning. There is a danger of being 'process rich and content poor' contends Ian Lister (Lister, 1987), whilst Maureen Stone from a black anti-racist perspective argues that any exploration of values, attitudes and feelings is a waste of time for black students whom, she suggests, need formal didactic instruction in the 'three Rs' if they are to attain positions of power and influence in our society (Stone, 1981). Interestingly, there are signs that others at the leading edge of the anti-racist movement are now attaching much importance to the process of learning in schools (see, for example, Troyna, 1988).

The continued emergence of such criticisms, from a broad range of political and philosophical viewpoints, indicates a healthy level of analysis and debate amongst those interested or involved in Global Education, from which the field itself should draw strength. It also serves to remind global educators of the controversial nature of their task, in two senses. Firstly, much of Global Education will be deemed controversial by many because it attempts to deal with complex political, social, economic and cultural issues about which young people are encouraged to make judgements by analysing available evidence and employing their framework of values. To Scruton, for whom education traditionally has 'no political programme' (Scruton, 1985), such a position is untenable. Yet teachers can find a wealth of governmental and international documents which regard this as a legitimate goal of formal education, including the UNESCO 'Recommendation concerning education for international understanding, co-operation and peace and education relating to human rights and fundamental freedoms' (Paris, 1974), and the Council of Europe recommendation on 'Teaching and Learning of Human Rights in Schools' (Strasbourg, 1985) – both of which the UK government has officially supported. There are supporting statements, too, in the Department of Education and Science publications of 1977 (*Education in Schools: a consultative document*) and 1980 (*A Framework for the School Curriculum*), in the major report on *Education for All* (The Swann Report, 1985) and in the various recommendations of the Commission for Racial Equality (CRE) and the Equal Opportunities Commission (EOC).

However, Global Education remains controversial in another, more profound sense. Just as the disciples of Dewey and Montessori challenged the accepted orthodoxy of education in the early part of this century, so have the global educators of the 1980s contested the established doctrines of today. The insights of 'systems theory' and of new age writers, the foresight of futurists and observers of global trends, the latest research into child development and the implications of learning style theories – all of these elements combine to construct an educational theory and practice which is deeply radical. Global educators with missionary zeal need to have no illusions about the enormity of challenging old paradigms, nor should they forget one of the basic tenets of the systems theory – that any new paradigm offers a single, coherent framework for present thought and action. It will, in turn, be challenged and overtaken.

The National Curriculum and the Future: Crisis or Opportunity?

A popular feature of contemporary Global Education literature is to use the Chinese character 'ji', which means both crisis and opportunity, as symbolic of the state of the world at the present time. It might be applied with equal validity to the state of education at the onset of the National Curriculum. Given everything I have written in this chapter about its philosophical base, fitting Global Education into the National Curriculum could well be likened to forcing a square peg into a round hole or, less 'mechanistically', a round whole into a square hole!

Many of the central aims of Global Education, however, are reflected in the DES consultation document; for example, the need to equip pupils 'for the responsibilites of citizenship and for the challenges of employment in the modern world' (para. 4); to help pupils 'to develop their capacity to adapt and respond flexibly to a changing world' (para. 3); and the development in young people of qualities such as 'self-reliance, self-discipline, an enterprising approach and the ability to solve real-world problems' (para. 68) (DES, 1987). Debates will no doubt continue as to whether Global Education should enter the gladitorial arena alongside other worthy claimants of the curriculum time that is left over by the 'core' and 'foundation' subjects, or whether 'the global perspective across the curriculum' angle might not be more productive. Much will depend on particular school contexts: teachers of curricula which at present include a World Studies syllabus may want to pursue a different line of argument to those who infuse their more traditional subject areas with a global perspective. The introduction of GCSE syllabuses and assessment procedures is at least giving the latter group a little more leeway.

Such debates, of course, centre on the *content* of Global Education. A fundamental flaw in the National Curriculum proposals as outlined in the consultative document is that it has little to say about the *process* of education, apart from stating that 'how teaching is organised and the teaching approaches used will be for schools to determine' (DES, 1987, para. 27). In failing to recognise the crucial importance of styles of teaching and learning to the attainment of curriculum goals, the ideal of a National Curriculum – for good or ill – may be seriously undermined. This inherent weakness, however, presents great opportunities for Global Education. Research into preferred learning styles (Dunn and Dunn, 1978; Gregorc, 1982; McCarthy, 1981) has produced overwhelming evidence indicating the need for a conscious diversity of teaching styles and learning approaches if the particular learning needs of all students are to be met and, hence, the potential of each individual is to be realised. Co-operative and experiential learning will motivate some students highly, lectures and individual research will be preferred by others. All learning style researchers agree that it is simply not good enough to leave decisions about teaching styles and classroom environment up to the individual teacher without that person first becoming aware of the various impediments to learning likely to be operative in any classroom. As Postman and Weingartner remark, the commonly held notion that something can be 'taught' by a teacher but not 'learnt' by students displays a similar degree of naivety to that of the salesperson who remarks 'I sold it to him but he didn't buy it' (Postman and Weingartner, 1971).

The experience of Global Education practitioners, gained through many years of trial and refinement of new and different teaching approaches, is badly needed by all those who are putting into practice the aims of a National Curriculum. In years to come, any evaluation of its effectiveness in producing 'better educated' young people will be at least as much an assessment of the processes employed as of the eventual content. With hindsight, too, it may be that the most valuable contribution of Global Education to the on-going 'Great Debate' will be seen to be its efforts to raise teachers' consciousness of the diverse learning needs of students for life in the twenty-first century and how these needs can be best satisfied in the classroom. This, in itself, would represent no more and no less than a continuation of the quest initiated in British education by the progressive educators of the early twentieth century, a desire to restore the child's right and freedom to develop his or her potential to the full.

Note

1   Cognisant of the impending wrath of global educators north of the border, I should hasten to add that Modern Studies in Scotland certainly pre-dates World Studies and shares many, but not all, of its aims. There have also been significant projects, at Jordanhill College and elsewhere, concerned to promote a global perspective in Scottish education.

References and Further Resources

L. Anderson, *Schooling and Citizenship in a Global Age: An Exploration of the Meaning and Significance of Global Education* (Mid America Program for Global Perspectives in Education, Bloomington, Indiana, 1976)

J. Becker, *Schooling for a Global Age* (McGraw–Hill, 1979)

Birmingham DEC, *The World in Birmingham* (Birmingham Development Education Centre, 1982)

W. Brandt, *North–South: A Programme for Survival* (Pan, 1980)

C. Brown, 'National Identity and World Studies' in *Educational Review*, vol. 36, no. 2, pp. 149–56 (1984)

Brundtland, *Our Common Future* (World Commission on Environment and Development, OUP, 1987)

F. Capra, *The Turning Point: Science, Society and the Rising Culture* (Flamingo, 1983)

Carmathen DEC publications, *A Rainforest Child* (1986), *Tomorrow's Woods* (1987), *An Arctic Child* (1988) (All Greenlight Publications, Ty Bryn, Coombe Gardens, Llangynog, Carmarthen, Dyfed)

DES, *The National Curriculum 5–16: a Consultation Document* (HMSO, 1987)

R. Dunn and K. Dunn, *Teaching Students through their Individual Learning Styles. A Practical Approach* (Reston Publishing Company, Reston, Virginia, 1978)

M. Ferguson, *The Aquarian Conspiracy. Personal and Social Transformation in the 1980s* (Granada, 1980)

S. Fisher and D. Hicks, *World Studies 8–13. A Teacher's Handbook* (Oliver and Boyd, 1985)

N. Fyson, *The Development Puzzle* (Hodder and Stoughton/CWDE, 1984)

J. Garreau and R. Versfield, 'World Studies 8–13. A Teacher's Handbook. A review' in *World Studies Journal*, vol. 6, no. 3, pp. 8–10 (1987)

A. F. Gregorc, *An Adult's Guide to Style* (Gabriel Systems Inc, Massachusetts, 1982)

S. Greig, G. Pike and D. Selby, *Earthrights: Education as if the Planet Really Mattered* (World Wildlife Fund/Kogan Page, 1987)

R. G. Hanvey, *An Attainable Global Perspective* (Global Perspectives in Education, New York, 1982)

R. Hatcher, 'The Construction of World Studies' in *Multiracial Education*, vol. 11, no. 1, pp. 23–6 (1983)

R. Hedge, 'World Studies and Assessment' in Pike and Selby (1988)

J. Houston, *The Possible Human: A Course in Enhancing your Physical, Mental and Creative Abilities* (J. P. Tarcher, Los Angeles, 1982)

S. L. Lamy, 'Defining Global Education' in *Educational Research Quarterly*, vol. 8, no. 1, pp. 9–20 (University of Southern California School of Education, 1983)

I. Lister, 'Global and International Approaches in Political Education' in C. Harber (ed.), *Political Education in Britain* (Falmer, 1987)

B. McCarthy, *The 4 Mat System. Teaching to Learning Styles with Right/Left Mode Techniques* (Excel Inc, Barrington, Illinois, 1981)

A. McKenzie, 'World Studies and Feminism – the Unhappy Marriage' in *World Studies Journal*, vol. 6, no. 3, pp. 2–5 (1987)

C. Mullard, 'The Problem of World Studies in a Multicultural Society' in *World Studies Journal*, vol. 4, no. 1, pp. 13–17 (1982)

G. Pike and D. Selby, 'Scrutinizing Scruton. An analysis of Roger Scruton's attack on World Studies' in *Times Educational Supplement* (11 April 1986)

G. Pike and D. Selby, *Global Teacher, Global Learner* (Hodder and Stoughton, 1988)

N. Postman and C. Weingartner, *Teaching as a Subversive Activity* (Penguin, 1971)

P. Pradervand, 'Global Education. Towards a world that works for all' in *Geographical Education*, vol. 5, no. 3, pp. 12–18 (Australian Geography Teachers Association, 1987)

R. Richardson, *Learning for Change in World Society. Reflections, Activities and Resources* (reviesed edition) (World Studies Project, 1976)

R. Richardson, 'The World Studies Story: projects, people, places' in *PEP Talk*, no. 8, pp. 4–16 (1985)

C. Rogers, *Freedom to Learn for the 80s* (Charles E. Merrill, Ohio, 1983)

T. Roszak, *Person/Planet* (Granada, 1981)

R. Scruton, *World Studies: Education or Indoctrination?* (Institute for European Defence and Strategic Studies, 1985)

M. Stone, *The Education of the Black Child in Britain* (Fontana, 1981)

B. Troyna, '"Selection" and "Learning": Frameworks for Anti-racist Initiatives in Education' in *Multicultural Teaching*, vol. 6, no. 3 (1988)

Key Teacher Resources

F. Capra, *The Turning Point: Science, Society and the Rising Culture* (Flamingo, 1983)
A brilliant book: a turning point for many who read it. Explores how the mechanistic worldview of Newton and Descartes has led to the current global crisis and identifies an ongoing shift towards a holistic/systemic worldview.

S. Fisher and D. Hicks, *World Studies 8–13. A Teacher's Handbook* (Oliver and Boyd, 1985)
Attractively presented and deservedly popular handbook of activities for top junior and lower secondary students. Contains a rationale for World Studies and a teacher education section.

N. Fyson, *The Development Puzzle* (Hodder and Stoughton/CWDE, 1984)
Now in its seventh edition, this is a popular and comprehensive source-book of information, resources, ideas and classroom strategies for teaching about world developments.

S. Greig, G. Pike and D. E. Selby, *Earthrights: Education as if the Planet Really Mattered* (Kogan Page/World Wildlife Fund UK, 1987)
Offers an overview of current global problems and trends and explores the implications of the person/planet relationship for schools.

G. Pike and D. Selby, *Global Teacher, Global Learner* (Hodder and Stoughton, 1988)
Explores and develops the theory and practice of Global Education through identifying the needs of the global learner, suggesting approaches to the global curriculum and giving a profile of the global teacher. Half the book is given over to 'the global classroom' – some 200 practical and stimulating activities for the primary and secondary classroom.

C. Rogers, *Freedom to Learn for the 80s* (Charles E. Merrill, Ohio, 1983)
A seminal book for the global teacher. Carl Rogers' writing continues to dominate person-centred education and to inspire its adherents. Contains an important chapter on research findings, including the monumental research programme of Aspy and Roebuck.

Key Classroom Resources

International Year of Shelter for the Homeless / Save the Children Fund, *Doorways* (1987)
A lavishly produced pack which looks at homelessness as a global issue through a series of 22 case-studies, 24 photosheets (mainly in colour) and 6 activity sheets. The case-studies provide a good balance between negative images of inadequate shelter and positive examples of individual and community action to improve housing conditions. A wealth of classroom material is provided, along with some suggestions for its use.

M. Kidron and R. Segal, *The New State of the World Atlas* (Pluto Press, 1984)
An invaluable source and reference book for the classroom. 57 statistical maps on issues ranging from 'Arms and the State' and 'Holds on the Mind' to 'Natural Resources' and 'Labour'. Because of the creativity and clarity of its presentation, this Atlas provides easy accessiblity for students to relevant data surrounding major world issues.

Leeds Development Education Centre/War on Want, *Dhaka to Dundee: Bangladesh and Britain in an Unequal World* (1987)
A good example of a resource which explores connections between UK communities and Bangladesh focusing on injustice within and between the two countries. The seven teaching units cover Family Life, Rural Life, History, Jute, International Trade, Aid and Development, Migration and Racism. Suggestions for active learning are given, as are background notes and instructions for teachers.

S. Lyle and M. Roberts, *A Rainforest Child* (Greenlight Publications, 1987)
Suitable for the lower secondary school, this pack explores the complex global issues surrounding the destruction of rainforests through eighteen classroom activities. It provides a good example of how such issues can be made more accessible to younger students through an active and participatory learning process.

Manchester Development Education Project, *Teaching Development Issues* (1985)
An excellent series of seven booklets under the following titles: *Perceptions, Colonisation, Food, Health, Population Changes, Work, Aid and Development*. Each is comprehensive in its scope, including key ideas, related activities for students and further resources for the teacher. A wealth of activities and ideas can be found in each booklet.

Trocaire, *Food Matters: A Question of Food in the World* (1987)
One of the clearest, yet most thorough books for students on the complex issues surrounding food, written in the wake of the Ethiopian crisis of 1984–5. It explores food as a basic need, perceptions of poverty and hunger, global inequalities in trade and resources and includes a case-study of Ethiopia. Students are encouraged to discuss and evaluate alternative solutions to the problem of hunger. Attractively produced, with good use of maps, photographs and cartoons.

Key Addresses

Centre for Global Education,
University of York,
Heslington,
York YO1 5DD

> For information and resources on Global Education. Runs in-service training courses, research and curriculum development projects. Publishes a quarterly newsletter, *Global Education News*, and the termly *World Studies Journal*.

Centre for World Development Education,
Regent's College,
Inner Circle,
Regent's Park,
London NW1 4NS

> Stocks an extensive range of student and teacher resources on global issues. Publishes a quarterly review of recent publications, *Checklist*.

Concord Films Council,
201 Felixstowe Road,
Ipswich,
Suffolk IP3 9BJ

> The largest UK distributor of films and videos on global issues, with a wide choice for both primary and secondary teachers.

Council for Education in World Citizenship,
Seymour House,
Seymour Mews,
London W1H 9PE

> For information and resources on education for international understanding. Runs a speakers' service for schools and conferences for secondary students. Publishes a bi-monthly *Newsletter* and *Broadsheet*.

National Association of Development Education Centres,
128 Buckingham Palace Road,
London SW1W 9SH

> For information on the growing network of Development Education Centres throughout the UK. Publishes a monthly newsletter, *Newsdec*.

Oxfam Youth and Education Department,
274 Banbury Road,
Oxford OX2 7DY

> One of the principal UK funding bodies for Development Education. Provides printed and audio-visual resources for schools on development and related issues, including a bi-monthly magazine, *Bother*. Regional offices throughout the UK.

• 10 •

ENVIRONMENTAL EDUCATION:

TEACHING FOR
A SUSTAINABLE FUTURE

John Huckle

The aims of Environmental Education are to develop an understanding of ecological systems and of the place of humankind within those systems; also to enable students to reflect upon how best individuals and human societies can live in harmony with the planet, and to develop the skills necessary for active and responsible participation.

(Greig, Pike and Selby, *Global Impact*, 1987b)

During the past decade a number of reports, most recently that of the World Commission on Environment and Development (WCED, 1987), have presented us with the same stark message: the future does not work. While prevailing forms of economic production and development are resulting in accumulating damage to the natural systems and processes on which all human societies depend, our social institutions appear powerless to prevent this damage and bring about a transition to more sustainable ways of life.

The nature and scale of environmental problems is truly alarming and the resulting costs fall most heavily on the poor, particularly in the developing world. In 1988, deforestation in the Himalayas triggered widespread flooding and human misery in Bangaladesh. 'Leper' ships such as the Karin B roamed the world in 1988 in search of a home for their toxic cargoes. In newspapers and on television these events capture our interest, and the steady and continuous deterioration of 'ecological systems' and processes often hits the headlines. Increased land degradation, water pollution, deforestation, climatic change, and species extinction, are among the trends which reduce the potential for development, and increase global insecurity.

Such events and trends result from the workings of the world's economic and political systems. The decisions taken by the owners and managers of industrial and finance capital, state planners and politicians, generally seek to increase their economic and political power. The danger is that this can result in forms of development and underdevelopment which exploit both people and nature.

Since much pollution and environmental degradation results from poverty, there is an urgent need for 'sustainable development' (in other words, development which meets the needs of the present, without compromising the ability of future generations to meet their own needs). The World Commission suggests that such development could revive economic growth throughout the world but insists that it can only take place if there is structural change, at both national and international levels, to increase the resources available to the poor. As well as this fundamental change, it calls for:

- a political system that secures effective citizen participation in decision-making
- an economic system that is able to generate surpluses and develop technical knowledge on a self-reliant and sustained basis
- a social system that provides solutions for the tensions arising from disharmonious development
- a production system that respects the obligation to preserve the ecological basis for development
- a technological system that can search continuously for new solutions
- an international system that fosters sustainable patterns of trade and finance
- an administrative system that is flexible and has the capacity for self correction   (WCED, 1987, p. 65)

This concise prescription begs expansion and clarification, but for the moment it is sufficient to prompt the assertion that any attempt to educate for sustainability is inevitably an exercise in social education. That being the case, it is regrettable that Environmental Education in Britain has tended to develop at some distance from Social Education and that the dialogue between environmental and social educators has rarely been extensive. Some of the reasons for this are revealed by examining the growth of modern environmentalism and Environmental Education.

Environmentalism as a Social Movement

The modern environmental movement emerged in Britain in the late 1960s and early 1970s, underwent something of a decline in the late 1970s, and re-emerged in the 1980s. Over three million people in Britain now belong to environmental groups of some kind and the popularity of certain publications and television programmes, together with the evidence of public opinion polls, suggests that issues of environment and nature conservation continue to claim widespread public concern. The movement does however contain groups and individuals with widely differing beliefs and values. They support different political policies, have differing relations with government, and adopt different campaigning strategies (Lowe and Goyder, 1983).

Tim O'Riordan (O'Riordan, 1981) suggests that two systems of belief are dominant within modern environmentalism. 'Technocentrism' is based on a human-centred view of the earth, coupled with a managerial approach to resource development and environmental protection. It supports the status quo in structures of economic and political power. There are two subdivisions which he labels 'optimism' and 'accommodation'. 'Optimists' have a strong faith in science, market forces and managerial ingenuity to sustain growth and ensure survival. 'Accommodators' feel that some reforms of existing institutions and mechanisms to accommodate environmental demands are needed. Technocentrism finds widespread support amongst right-wing politicians, leaders of industry, commerce and trade unions, and amongst skilled workers. Collectively they are termed 'the productive classes'.

'Ecocentrism' represents an alternative environmental belief system suggesting that people–environment relations cannot be disconnected from social relations. More harmonious relations with nature can only result from more harmonious relations between people. Power should therefore be redistributed towards a decentralised, federal political economy based on the 'interlinkage' of environmental and social justice (Bookchin, 1986). Ecocentrics divide into 'communalists' and 'Gaianists'. Communalists stress the co-operative capabilities of societies to be collectively self-reliant, using appropriate technology (technology which enables people to meet their own needs using local resources and which is both non-polluting and non-alienating). Gaianists draw on James Lovelocks's Gaia hypothesis (Lovelock, 1979) which proposes that the earth's living envelope, or biosphere, operates as a self-regulating system with its own natural feedback mechanisms. They are much concerned with the rights of nature and the essential co-evolution of humans and the natural world. Both turn ecology to political ends. Ecocentric thinking tends to be found amongst those on the periphery of modern economies; the so-called 'non-productive classes' which include teachers (Cotgrove, 1982; Frankel, 1987).

The post-war boom which nurtured these ecocentric environmentalists came to an end in the mid 1970s. By then the world economy was moving into recession and economic stagnation, inflation and rising unemployment diverted attention away from environmental problems in the 'rich world'. At the same time increased poverty and international debts accentuated environmental degradation in the 'poor world' (Timberlake, 1985). The erosion of social democracy (with its commitments to full employment, the Welfare State and non-authoritarian government) and the rise of the New Right (market-oriented and authoritarian), within the core states of global capitalism, facilitated the conditions for a new cycle of capital accumulation. Economic restructuring resulted in the scrapping of much labour and productive capacity, the global redivision of labour, and the widespread introduction of computer technology. This new technology has the potential to liberate people from alienating work, while encouraging sustainable development and decentralisation, but is being used, as some would argue, as the basis for new forms of social control (Gorz, 1985).

It was in this climate that a convergence of thinking took place between some ecocentric environmentalists and others concerned with global development issues (Redclift, 1984 and 1987). The notion of sustainable development which emerged from their dialogue, was later reflected in the report of the World Commission on Environment and Development. It also attracted attention from those concerned with such issues as unemployment, peace, and human rights, and was an important factor in the emergence of 'green' politics (Porritt, 1984; Spretnak and Capra, 1985). 'Greens' sought to overcome the growing tensions between East and West, North and South, men and women, and nature and society, but their attack on industrialism and consumerism and their proposed social alternatives, revealed the utopianism associated with much ecocentric thought. The ensuing 'Red/Green Debate' (between Socialists and Greens) was an attempt to clarify the ideal nature of a sustainable society and the means whereby it might be established. In the debate, Greens reminded Socialists of the need to transform both the mode and relations of production and accommodate the concerns and strategies of new social movements. For their part, Socialists reminded Greens of the continuing relevance of class analysis, the potential advantage of socialist planning in the field of environmental management and protection, and the need for a more realistic attitude to state power (Weston, 1986). The debate helped to clarify the nature of a future 'eco-socialist society' in which socially useful and sustainable production would be made possible by the extension of self-management from below, together with an amount of planning and co-ordination from above (Roberts, 1979; Hodgson, 1984).

Environmental Education

'Education about the Environment'

Environmental Education developed alongside the wider environmental movement and takes several forms, reflecting similar ideological tensions (Huckle, 1983). The dominant form, 'education about the environment' grew out of a concern for countryside conservation and rural resource management, and represents a blend of technocentric environmentalism and 'liberal education'. It provided a new lease of life for Rural Studies and was welcomed by a minority of teachers of Geography and Science as providing a more relevant curriculum –

particularly for less-able pupils. As Environmental Science, it often provides an initial education in applied ecology and environmental management which many would consider suitable for the environmental professionals of the future. Its advocates have, however, had limited success in winning it academic recognition and status as a new school subject. Established subjects have successfully fought off the new contender and gradually adapted their curricula to cover more environmental content (Goodson, 1983). In the past twenty years 'education about the environment' has seen much curriculum development, some of it funded by such companies as British Petroleum and Coca Cola.

The main weakness of much 'education about the environment' is that it adopts a technocentric perspective which, as we have seen, accepts existing social relations. Teachers and pupils rarely examine the structural causes of environmental problems and social alternatives which could enable sustainable development. In many lessons, environmental issues are presented as asocial or universal problems. They are attributed to such causes as overpopulation, resource scarcity, inappropriate technology, overproduction, and exploitative values, but these factors are not explored in a way which relates them to underlying social forces. The relationship between people and the environment is not taught in a context of economic, political, and cultural systems, with the result that pupils remain largely impotent as agents of social and environmental change.

'Education from the Environment'

A second form of environmental education, 'education from the environment' seeks to use the environment as a medium for education and reflects the utopianism associated with much ecocentric environmentalism. As Environmental Studies, it provides a rationale for topic-based learning by discovery from the environment, but generally it reflects a rather naive view of both children and nature. Much promoted by the colleges of education in the 1960s and 1970s, it remains an important influence on schools, particularly in the primary sector. Earth Education (Van Matre, 1979) can be seen as a new variant which uses elements of Gaianism and 'humanistic', non-didactic education to justify experiential encounters with nature. Education from the environment can do much to raise environmental awareness and sensitivity, but like education about the environment it generally gives too little attention to the way in which the environment is socially constructed.

'Education for the Environment'

The third and least common form of Environmental Education in schools, 'education for the environment', regards environmental well-being as its goal. It uses issue-based studies in the local community to develop pupils' 'social literacy' so that they can begin to 'read' and 'write' their own environment. Developing out of a long tradition of Urban–Community Education, associated with libertarian socialists and anarchists such as Paul Goodman and Colin Ward, it re-emerged in the late 1960s as part of a wider community movement. This attacked the bureaucracy of local government and sought to improve services by opening environmental management and planning to wider public participation. Urban Studies Centres developed new ways of involving school pupils and citizens in such issues as housing and transport, and these gradually filtered into schools. While the focus is often local and it rarely deals directly with the wider social use and abuse of nature, education for the environment represents a continuing tradition of socially critical Environmental Education which can be adapted to meet new aims. As we will see, this was essentially the challenge of the 1980s.

Anyone wishing to develop further insights into the development and nature of Environmental Education in Britain prior to the early 1980s could start by reading the papers prepared for the Tbilisi Conference in 1977 (DES, 1977), the collections edited by Martin and Wheeler (1975) and Carson (1978), and the report on education in *The Conservation and Development Programme for the UK* (Baines, 1983). The Council for Environmental Education's *Review of Environmental Education Developments* (now replaced by the *Annual Review of Environmental Education*) is also a useful source. Samples of the literature associated with 'education about the environment' and 'education from the environment' are not difficult to find in most schools. A taste for 'education for the environment' can be obtained from *Streetwork: The Exploding School* (Ward and Fyson, 1973), *The Child in the City* (Ward, 1979), *Counterweight: The Neighbourhood Option* (Gibson, 1984), and back issues of the *Bulletin of Environmental Education*. See also the sections on References and Key Teacher/Classroom Resources.

Environmental Education: A Recent Revival

At a time when public attention was increasingly being focused on global issues of environment and development, it was Development Education which challenged Environmental Education to take on a more socially critical role. The Labour Government and development agencies of the 1970s were concerned about the public's lack of understanding and support for overseas aid and development programmes. They therefore funded Development Education as a means of changing attitudes and increasing understanding of development and underdevelopment in an interdependent world. The World Studies Project for secondary schools (Richardson, 1979) was one early influential product and Robin Richardson's textbook, *Caring for the Planet* (Richardson, 1977), pointed in the direction which other teaching materials on environment and development issues were to follow. Agencies such as Oxfam, Christian Aid and the World Wildlife Fund (now the World Wide Fund for Nature), began to produce their own materials and by the mid 1980s, these were challenging the parochialism and conservatism of much that was produced by commercial publishers and environmental organisations. Such materials put sustainable development firmly on the Environmental Education agenda and became more widely known and used in schools as the staff of a growing network of Development Education Centres worked alongside teachers.

The media attention surrounding the environmental crisis in Africa during the 1980s, the European Year of the Environment (EYE 1987 to 1988) and the publication of *Our Common Future* (WCED, 1987) provided a stimulus for yet more teachers to become involved. The Council for Environmental Education circulated an education pack (CEE/EYE, 1987) to all schools to mark EYE. Rex Beddis and a team of teachers produced curriculum materials to accompany the BBC television series, *Only One Earth* (Beddis, 1988), while Thames Television broadcast a new World Studies series dealing with environment and development issues (1988).

Two strengths of Development Education are its holistic approach to global issues and its commitment to experiential learning. Development and under-development are processes which occur at all scales from the local to the global, affecting people, communities, nation states and the international order. Shaped by political economy, they have a major impact on people's health, the exploitation of women, race relations, the use and abuse of nature, the global division of labour and human rights. Development Education could claim to be the new social curriculum for there is much evidence that its supporters have not only recognised these links but reflected them in their teaching. The book *Earthrights: Education as if the Planet Really Mattered* (Greig, Pike and Selby, 1987a), for example, is based on the premises that:

> Those working at the broad (global) focus have come to recognise that their respective principal concepts – development, environment, human rights and peace – are complementary, interdependent and mutually illuminating . . .
> The thinking of those at the broad focus of each field (Environment, Development, Peace and Human Rights Education) is increasingly marked by a shift away from a compartmentalised view of reality to an acceptance of the interconnectedness of all things and what has been called the 'permeability of boundaries'.   (Greig, Pike and Selby, 1987)

The book outlines and expands on the links between Environmental, Development, Peace and Human Rights Education, and offers teachers not only a curriculum rationale for exploring environmental issues in a wider context, but pointers to teaching techniques and advice for working either within or across subjects.

Among the local authorities which adopted Development Education enthusiastically, were several that were experimenting with new forms of municipal socialism. Faced with economic restructuring which removed thousands of jobs in the manufacturing sector, and central government policies which cut public spending and had the effect of eroding local democracy, local authorities such as Greater London, Sheffield, and Manchester, fought back (Blunkett and Jackson, 1987). In the early and mid 1980s, they developed their own economic strategies and employment initiatives. They expanded local services and encouraged a new relationship between people and the local state. Their policies reflected some of the new 'eco-socialist' thinking with enterprise boards and workers' co-operatives developing socially useful products, cheap fares ensuring a cleaner and safer environment, and recycling centres reducing waste. Technology networks gave people greater control over new technology and popular planning sought greater participation in environmental decision making (Collective Design Products, 1985; Bodington, George and Michaelson, 1986). Municipal socialism was a popular and practical alternative to central government policy and for a while it did sustain forms of Community Education which further developed 'education for the environment' (Alexander, 1986).

The fact that few environmental and development educators identified with municipal socialism and recognised its experiments in sustainable development, is evidence of the hold of Conservative politics in the 1980s. A dialogue with social educators who had long been aware of the politics of school knowledge, was long overdue. It was therefore a potentially exciting event when Colin Lacey decided to get together environmental, development and social educators for a conference in 1986. The resulting book (Lacey and Williams, 1988), while not without its weaknesses, begins to explore the political economy of their related concerns. The Education Network Project, based at Sussex University, now seeks to bring together those in the environment and development agencies, education, and the media, to promote new initiatives.

By the late 1980s, 'education for the environment' had then widened its focus. To a long established concern with local development issues affecting the built environment, were added new concerns for more distant issues, the social use of nature, and links with other areas of the emerging new social curriculum. Environmental Education was now ready to make a greater contribution to this curriculum and Figure 10.1 is an attempt to outline what the components of that contribution should be. Readers might like to evaluate a school's social curriculum against these components and consider how they might best be incorporated into teaching programmes.

Figure 10.1 The Components of Environmental Education in the New Social Curriculum

Knowledge of the Natural Environment and its Potential for Human Use
Environmental Education should be based on a knowledge of major ecological systems, the processes which sustain them and their vulnerability to human modification. Scientists and geographers should develop appropriate knowledge and cultivate a sense of wonder and respect for nature.

A Theoretical and a Practical Grasp of Appropriate Technology
Lessons in Science and Craft, Design and Technology, should consider the environmental and social impacts of technology and develop pupils' theoretical *and* practical understanding of appropriate technology.

A Sense of History and a Knowledge of the Impact of Changing Social Formations on the Environment
Pupils should understand the impact of changing economies and societies on the natural world. They should understand how environments are socially constructed, how social relations shape environmental relations, and how landscapes and environments reflect technology and social organisation. Additionally, they should appreciate the potential benefits of sustainable development in the contemporary world.

An Awareness of Class Conflict
Pupils should be aware that rich and poor share unequally in the gains from our past and present use of nature, in control over economic development, and in the social costs of ecological disruption and the extent of environmental protection. People have frequently challenged the logic and costs of unbridled development and these issues deserve a place in our curriculum.

Political Literacy
The state is generally the arbitrator in disputes over the social use of nature and the environment. Pupils should develop 'political literacy' so that they are able to understand and participate in environmental politics. Appropriate knowledge, skills and attitudes should be developed through real or simulated involvement with environmental issues at all scales, from the local to the global. Due attention should be given to the social use of nature and environmental politics in societies organised on different principles than our own.

An Awareness of Alternative Social and Environmental Futures and the Political Strategies whereby they are Likely to be Realised
Pupils should consider alternative forecasts about society and the environment,

the desirability of a range of environmental possibilities, and the feasibility of bringing them about.

An Understanding of Environmental Ideology and Consumer Lifestyles
Pupils should study the environmental movement and relate its beliefs and strategies to wider political philosophies and programmes. They should recognise the consequences of consumer lifestyles on the environment.

Involvement in Real Issues
Pupils should be encouraged to identify for themselves practical ways in which they can work for a more sustainable relationship with the natural world. This is likely to involve changes in lifestyle, involvement in community projects, and possible political action.

Balance
Environmental Education should be balanced and avoid indoctrination, at the same time introducing pupils to a wide range of topics and ideas. While we should be committed to justice, rationality and democracy, rather than to a form of neutrality which leaves existing patterns of power and privilege undisturbed, we should protect students from our own powers of persuasion and cultivate tentativeness and constructive scepticism.

Optimism
If we are not to overwhelm pupils with the world's problems, we should teach in a spirit of optimism. We should build environmental success stories into our curriculum and develop awareness of sources of hope in a world where new and appropriate technologies now offer liberation for all.

Current Practice and Possibilities

A survey by the Conservation Trust in 1987 (Berry, 1987) suggested that the vast majority of schools claim to undertake Environmental Education. Most do this through Geography, Biology, Science, History, Social Studies, and Rural Studies, and in 28% of secondary schools it can be taken as a subject leading to an examination (generally GCSE). Teachers remain concerned about the low status of Environmental Education, and despite the efforts of non-governmental organisations, many still regard the lack of information and resources as a constraint. A 1986/7 survey by the Global Impact Project (Greig, Pike and Selby, 1987b) into both Environmental and Development Education, showed that:

- A narrowness and lack of diversity characterised both teaching content and methodology, especially amongst Science teachers. Only a small percentage of teachers who responded dealt with certain important themes. For example: land reform 12%; political development 17%; gender issues 25%; the arms trade 7%; alternative technology 24%.
- Many teachers' perceptions of Environmental and Development Education as being political and controversial, acted as a constraint.
- Development Education was poorly understood and Environmental Education narrowly interpreted. In both cases, active involvement and understanding of political, social and economic situations were regarded as of less importance than understanding interdependence and developing personal concern and responsibility.
- 69% of teachers considered that Environmental and Development Education were relevant to their subject areas. 67% thought that the political aspects of development were not too controversial to be dealt with.

There is clearly a need for more in-service education with teachers to alert them to the possibilities which 'education for the environment' now affords. Many over-estimate the constraints on innovation and fail to recognise the potential within such developments as GCSE.

The extracts in Figure 10.2, from the national criteria for Science, Craft, Design and Technology, and Social Science, suggest that GCSE allows much scope for promoting the components of Environmental Education listed in Figure 10.1. The Council for Environmental Education has compiled a data base of all the syllabi, and regards GCSE as 'generally good news' (Baines, 1987). While Environmental Studies and Rural Studies syllabi, taken by only small numbers of candidates, still have the most 'environmental content', Geography remains the pace-setter in tackling issues of environment and development. Its most progressive form is seen in such syllabuses as the Southern Examining Group's (SEG) Geography Syllabus B, and in new textbook series such as *Geography Today* (Clammer *et al.*, 1987) and *Issues in Geography* (Hopkin and Morris, 1987). The SEG's Environment syllabus deserves widespread support too for, like innovations in modular forms of Humanities, it allows new ways of exploring environmental issues together with other aspects of the new social curriculum (Whitty, 1988).

Figure 10.2 GCSE – Some National Criteria: Environmental Education

Listed within the aims of Science are the need to:
- stimulate interest in and care for the environment
- promote an awareness that the applications of Science may be both beneficial and detrimental to the individual, the community and the environment

Included within the objectives of Science are:
- knowledge and understanding of scientific and technological applications with their social, economic and environmental implications
- the skills and abilities to explain technological applications of Science and evaluate associated social, economic and environmental implications

Listed within the aims of Craft, Design and Technology is the need to:
- encourage technological awareness, foster attitudes of co-operation and social responsibility, and develop abilities to enhance the quality of the environment
- Candidates should also be able to describe the interrelationship between design/technology and the needs of society

Listed within the aims of Social Science is the need to:
- encourage a critical awareness of social, economic, and political arrangements and their effects

Content includes:
- the social development of human beings and the changing contexts (environments) within which that development takes place
- the process of income and wealth generation and distribution, the problems of scarcity and choice, and alternative means of allocating resources
- the ways in which ideas and values are generated in social life; the nature and role of these ideas and values in their changing social, economic and political context   (*GCSE: The National Criteria*, DES, 1985)

Alongside GCSE, Pre-vocational Education also offers new opportunities for Environmental Education. The TVEI and the CPVE mainly served to revive 'education about and from the environment' in forms which pay greater attention to economics and technology, but they have also opened some space for the consideration of social and environmental alternatives.

Despite its revival, Environmental Education was not mentioned in the consultative document on the National Curriculum which the government published in July, 1987. Subsequent statements by the Secretary of State, other ministers and the NCC (National Curriculum Council) have confirmed it as a cross-curricular theme, to be integrated with core and foundation subjects. As such it will require careful planning and co-ordination across the emerging National Curriculum and integration with other aspects of the new social curriculum.

Towards a Sustainable Future

As the environmental problems resulting from prevailing forms of development and underdevelopment worsen, the pressure for technocentric environmental management is likely to intensify along with calls for more 'education about the environment'. Environmental and social educators can use the resulting opportunities to introduce elements of 'education for the environment' which consider the real roots of environmental issues, and allow reflection and action on genuine social and environmental alternatives. The struggle for such education in schools resembles that for more socially useful and sustainable production and development in the wider world. Both are ultimately struggles for democracy, justice, and well-being, on which our future relationships with one another and with planet earth depend.

References and Further Resources

T. Alexander, *Value for People: Adult Education and Popular Planning* (Clapham–Battersea Adult Education Institute, 1986)

J. Baines, 'Part 7 Education' in *The Conservation and Development Programme for the UK* (WWF/Kogan Page, 1983)

J. Baines, 'GCSE and Environmental Education' in *Annual Review of Environmental Education*, pp. 17–18 (1987)

R. Beddis, *Only One Earth: An Introduction to the Education Pack* (WWF and North South Productions, 1988)

P. Berry, *Environmental Education Enquiries – UK* (Conservation Trust, 1987)

D. Blunkett and K. Jackson, *Democracy in Crisis: The Town Halls Respond* (Hogarth Press, 1987)

S. Bodington, M. George and J. Michaelson, *Developing the Socially Useful Economy* (Macmillan, 1986)

M. Bookchin, *The Modern Crisis* (New Society Publishers, 1986)

S. Carson (ed.), *Environmental Education: principles and practice* (Edward Arnold, 1978)

CEE, *Review of Environmental Education Developments* (now *Annual Review of Environmental Education*)

CEE, *Education for Life* (Council for Environmental Education, 1987)

CEE/EYE, *EYE on the Environment* (Council for Environmental Education/European Year of the Environment, 1987)

R. Clammer, B. Greasley, P. McLeod, R. Nichools, *Geography Today* (Collins Educational, 1987)

Collective Design Products (eds.), *Very Nice Work If You Can Get It: The socially useful production debate* (Spokesman, 1985)

S. Cotgrove, *Catastrophe and Cornucopia: The Environment, Politics and the Future* (John Wiley, 1982)

DES/Central Office of Information, *Environmental Education in the UK* (HMSO, 1977)

B. Frankel, *The Post-Industrial Utopians* (Polity Press, 1987)

T. Gibson, *Counterweight: The Neighbourhood Option* (Town and Country Planning Association/Education for Neighbourhood Change, 1984)

I. Goodson, *School Subjects and Curriculum Change: Case Studies in Curriculum History* (Croom Helm, 1983)

A. Gorz, *Paths to Paradise: On the Liberation from Work* (Pluto, 1985)

S. Greig, G. Pike and D. Selby, *Earthrights: Education as if the Planet Really Mattered* (WWF/Kogan Page, 1987a)

S. Greig, G. Pike, and D. Selby, *Global Impact: First Year Report* (Centre for Global Education, 1987b)

S. Greig, G. Pike and D. Selby, *Greenprints: for Changing Schools* (The World Wide Fund for Nature/Kogan Page, 1989)

G. Hodgson, *The Democratic Economy* (Penguin, 1984)

J. Hopkin and J. Morris, *Issues in Geography* (Heinemann Educational Books, 1987)

J. Huckle, 'Environmental Education' in J. Huckle (ed.), *Geographical Education: reflection and action* (Oxford University Press, 1983)

C. Lacey and R. Williams (eds.), *Education, Ecology and Development: The Case for an Education Network* (WWF/Kogan Page, 1988)

J. Lovelock, *Gaia: A New Look at Life on Earth* (Oxford University Press, 1979)

P. Lowe and J. Goyder, *Environmental Groups and Politics* (Allen and Unwin, 1983)

G. Martin and K. Wheeler (eds.), *Insights into Environmental Education* (Oliver and Boyd, 1975)

T. O'Riordan, *Environmentalism* (Pion, 1981)

J. Porritt, *Seeing Green: The politics of ecology explained* (Basil Blackwell, 1984)

M. Redclift, *Development and the Environmental Crisis: Red or Green Alternatives* (Methuen, 1984)

M. Redclift, *Sustainable Development: Exploring the Contradictions* (Methuen, 1987)

R. Richardson, *Caring for the Planet* (Nelson, 1977)

R. Richardson, *Learning for Change in World Society* (World Studies Project/One World Trust, 1979)

A. Roberts, *The Self Managing Environment* (Allison and Busby, 1979)

J. Seabrook, *The Race for Riches: the Human Cost of Wealth* (Marshall Pickering, 1988)

C. Spretnak and F. Capra, *Green Politics* (Paladin, 1985)

Thames TV, *World Studies Again* (Thames Television, 1988)

L. Timberlake, *Africa in Crisis: The Causes, the Cures of Environmental Bankruptcy* (Earthscan, 1985)

S. Van Matre, *Sunship Earth: An Acclimatization Program for Outdoor Learning* (American Camping Association, 1979)

C. Ward, *The Child in the City* (Penguin, 1979)

C. Ward and A. Fyson, *Streetwork: the Exploding School* (Routledge and Kegan Paul, 1973)

WCED, *Our Common Future* (Oxford University Press, 1987)

J. Weston (ed.), *Red and Green: The New Politics of the Environment* (Pluto, 1986)

G. Whitty, 'Integrated Humanities: A Curriculum Context for Ecology and Development Education' in C. Lacey and R. Williams (eds.), 1988

Key Teacher Resources

IIED/Earthscan, *Our Common Future: A Reader's Guide* (IIED/Earthscan, 1987)
A well illustrated synopsis of the 'Brundtland Report'. Guaranteed to get you interested and concerned about global issues of environment and development.

E. Goldsmith and N. Hilyard, (eds.), *Green Britain or Industrial Wasteland?* (Polity Press, 1986)
A comprehensive, if sometimes alarmist, introduction to Britain's environmental crisis.

S. Greig, G. Pike and D. Selby, *Earthrights: Education as if the Planet Really Mattered* (WWF/Kogan Page, 1987)
A theoretical and practical guide to the new Environmental Education from the Centre for Global Education in York.

R. North, *The Real Cost* (Chatto and Windus, 1986)
An examination of the real social and environmental costs of our coffee, cotton, computers, hamburgers, jobs, etc. A vivid introduction to the global division of labour and inequalities in environmental well-being.

I. Robottom (ed.), *Environmental Education: Practice and Possibility* (Deakin University, 1987)
An Australian collection which raises some fundamental issues about the nature of Environmental Education in schools. There are many parallels with the UK situation.

J. Weston (ed.), *Red and Green; The New Politics of the Environment* (Pluto, 1986)
A good introduction to the red/green debate from a socialist perspective.

Key Classroom Resources

MSC, *Geography for Young School Leavers* (MSC PP2, Freepost, PO Box 161, Bradford, BD9 4BR).
Seven curriculum modules for GCSE, TVEI and other pre-vocational initiatives. Strong environmental content.

N. Myers (ed.), *The Gaia Atlas of Planet Management* (Pan Books, 1985)
An acclaimed summary of our environmental predicament with excellent illustrations. Suitable for older pupils.

Oxfam, *Disasters in the Classroom: Teaching about disasters in the Third World* (Oxfam Youth and Education Department, 1985)
The activities in this pack enable teachers and pupils to study disasters without reinforcing the negative images of the 'Third World' presented in the media.

J. Seymour and H. Girardet, *Blueprint for a Green Planet* (Dorling Kendersley, 1987)
A valuable resource book for convincing older pupils that there are things they can do to change their world.

WWF, *What We Consume* (WWF/Richmond Publishing, 1988)
This module of the World Wide Fund for Nature's *Global Environmental Education Programme* explores the environment and development issues linked to the everyday products we consume. One hundred classroom activities in ten units.

WWF, *Only One Earth: a multi-media project for schools* (WWF/North South Productions, 1988)
A video and six booklets of classroom activities linked to a series of films first shown on BBC television in 1987.

Key Addresses

Conservation Trust,
George Palmer Site,
Northumberland Avenue,
Reading,
Berks RG2 7PW
Produces and catalogues a large amount of Environmental Education material.

Council for Environmental Education,
School of Education,
University of Reading,
London Road,
Reading RG1 5AQ
Provides information and advice on all aspects of Environmental Education and produces resource lists on available teaching materials.

Education for Neighbourhood Change,
School of Education,
University of Nottingham,
Nottingham NG7 2RD
Promotes active participation by people in changing and improving their neighbourhood. Produces materials, project ideas, and information of local community projects.

Global Impact,
Centre for Global Education,
University of York,
Heslington,
York YO1 5DD
A project which seeks to promote the inclusion of issues of development and environment across the curriculum in primary and secondary schools.

Green Teacher,
Llys Awel,
22 Heol Pentrehedyn,
Machynlleth,
Powys,
Wales SY20 8DN

A bi-monthly magazine relating the latest green movement debates to ideas and practices in education for the environment.

WWF United Kingdom,
Panda House,
Weyside Park,
Godalming,
Surrey GU7 1XR

Education department has an extensive range of curriculum materials on environment and development issues. Its termly newsletter *Lifelines* is mailed to schools.

• 11 •

TRADE UNION EDUCATION

IN SCHOOLS:

A PARTNERSHIP FOR
CURRICULUM CHANGE

Duncan Smith

Trade Union Education in the Context of the Education–Industry Debate

The growing interest on the part of teachers to introduce Trade Union Education into the curriculum has to be seen within the wider context of the substantial development over the last decade of the whole education–industry debate. Since the Ruskin speech of Prime Minister, Mr Callaghan, there appears to be no apparent decline in the number of initiatives designed to help students achieve a better understanding of the economic and industrial world in which they are growing up. Two examples serve to illustrate the point. The School Curriculum Industry Partnership (SCIP) began in 1978 with 5 LEAs, each with one schools–industry co-ordinator and a total of 25 secondary schools. Currently, it is working with over 80 LEAs and a network of over 100 co-ordinators. The government-sponsored Technical and Vocational Education Initiative (TVEI) began with 14 LEAs; in 1984 that figure had risen to 64 and by 1988 every single LEA in the country was involved in one or other phases of the scheme.

It is worth reflecting briefly on the pressures and influences exerted on both schools and industry to encourage them to work more closely together. Jamieson and Lightfoot (1982) identified three pressures: 'industrial society', technology and employment. The term 'industrial society' was used to represent the view in some quarters of both education and industry, that schools were not adequately preparing students for the economic and industrial world in which they were growing up. There was a need to help all students, not just those interested in and capable of gaining formal qualifications, to an understanding of the process of wealth creation, both in this country and abroad. From the trade union perspective, the concept of wealth distribution was something which they felt students particularly needed to appreciate (Jackson, 1979).

167

The pressure to introduce a technical perspective into the curriculum was equally powerful. Schools were left in no doubt that they had to respond to the need to equip students with the knowledge and skills of this increasingly important area of industrial activity, if Britain was to compete with the technological developments of its industrial competitors. For trade unionists, the debate in this area brought its own pressures, the introduction of 'new technology' had devastating effects on the jobs of many of its members. Nevertheless, they had to be seen to be making a positive response and indicate to students the ways in which they were accepting the need for technological change, while at the same time, trying to protect the rights and interests of their members.

The issue of employment, and in particular, youth and unemployment, was a constant reminder to schools of the difficulty of equating the importance of work in school, and the gaining of qualifications, to what would be the harsh reality for many students, of life without work. Jamieson and Lightfoot (1982) referred to this particular issue from one viewpoint of industry: 'many employers were concerned not so much about the formal qualifications and knowledge of young people entering employment, but about their attitudes to work and the workplace'. Trade unionists were concerned that students should be helped to appreciate the underlying causes of unemployment, particularly among young people. The government's economic policies were clearly the target of trade union criticism, especially the lack of investment in industry coupled with its failure or unwillingness to prevent substantial sums of money leaving the country for investment abroad. Linked to this was its apparent willingness to allow the products of countries, which enjoyed substantial subsidies, into the home market, with the consequent disastrous effect on some companies and their products in this country. For trade unions, these were some of the key issues with which they felt students needed to be acquainted.

It has to be said that some people, both within education and industry, found the situation somewhat paradoxical, that at a time when a number of industrial sectors seemed to be spiralling into decline and unemployment was heading for an all-time high, the government was openly promoting and financing closer co-operation and collaboration between education and industry. Resentment, particularly amongst those in education who had for many years been pleading for extra resources to be made available to schools, was fuelled by the implied criticism of schools that their curriculum did not adequately meet the vocational and technological needs of young people. When the Manpower Services Commission (MSC) intervened in the process of curriculum development (and set up the TVEI, supported by substantial funding), the suspicions of educationists were confirmed.

The plea for greater collaboration between education and industry was viewed with some misgivings by educationalists, industrialists and trade unionists. The educationalists questioned industry's motives for wishing to get involved with schools; was there an implied criticism of what schools were doing; was it an attempt to take over the curriculum? Industrialists questioned schools' motives for wanting to collaborate; were they genuinely interested in making their curriculum more meaningful and relevant by involving those with experience of the industrial world? Teachers' apparent unwillingness to spend some time in industry acquainting themselves with current practice only reinforced the prejudices of some industrialists. Teachers, of course, were levelling the same form of criticism at the industrialists! These worries were, in part, highlighted on occasions by the attempts of both education and industry to 'go it alone' with initiatives of their own, initiatives which occasionally displayed contradictions in their aims and philosophy.

Others, educationalists, industrialists and trade unionists saw the opportunity for collaboration as a challenge and a chance to share expertise for the benefit of the students. Many were becoming disillusioned by certain features of the world which all three of these groups inhabited. The concept of a partnership lay at the heart of the philosophy of the School Curriculum Industry Project. It encouraged the need for educationalists, industrialists and trade unionists to work together to design and implement experiences for students which would contribute to their greater understanding of the industrial and economic world.

The Challenge to the Trade Unions

While the stage was set, therefore, in the mid 1970s, for a substantial amount of progress to be made towards greater collaboration between education and industry, the problem for the trade unions was how to establish a centre-stage position in the debate alongside the industrialists and educationalists. There were a number of factors which would make that goal difficult to achieve.

The first of these was related to the tendency for the 'management' perspective to be predominant when discussions about industry, the world of work and related social and economic issues were introduced into schools. It did not go unnoticed in some quarters, for instance, that the so-called 'Great Debate' which followed Mr Callaghan's speech rarely referred to trade unions as contributors to the debate on the need for greater collaboration between education and industry. The frequency with which the viewpoint of the workforce, represented by trade unions, was introduced into the curriculum was extremely small. Schools seemed naturally to turn to representatives of management, when any industry-related topics were selected for investigation. Schools' use of industry in this period also tended to be narrowly confined to such people as personnel and training officers, financial and production managers (most of whom were male), for a perspective on industry. Schools claimed that trade unionists had difficulty finding the time to visit schools, and, of course, there was an element of truth in this. Trade unionists who did take the opportunity to work with schools often did it at their own expense, some even lost pay. Some schools said that they could not find 'the right person'. One recognised an element of truth in this statement, though often the same care to find the 'right person' was not applied in the search for an industrialist.

An interrelated factor was that while some teachers clearly believed that trade unionists were able to help students explore the role of trade unions in the workplace and examine issues specifically associated with industrial relations, they appeared to see no place for trade unionists in discussions on issues of industrial management or on the wider socio-economic and political issues in society. This situation was borne out by research carried out by SCIP and reported in Jamieson and Lightfoot (1982) which revealed that representatives of industrial management were frequently invited by schools to contribute to a range of curricula areas, Science, Economics, the Humanities, while trade unionists rarely, if ever, were given the opportunity to present a union perspective.

The dilemma facing trade unionists, therefore, was how to encourage teachers to adopt a broader appreciation of the role of trade unions from the one which just saw them as concerned merely with negotiating pay and conditions. Both the Trade Union Congress (TUC) and the individual unions had to set about redressing this balance through the literature which they produced, through the training of trade unionists who went into schools and by using the schools–industry organisations as a means of promoting this perspective.

A second factor which created difficulties for the trade unions was the unfavourable attitudes which many students and a considerable number of teachers seemed to hold towards them. Jamieson and Lightfoot (1982) wrote the following, based on SCIP research:

> Like the teachers, the pupils agreed with statements relating to the economic power of the trade union ... On practically every other statement, however, they took an unfavourable view of trade unions, and their attitudes were also more certain and clear cut than their views about industry in general. (Jamieson and Lightfoot, 1982)

The research also identified a relationship between the social class of parents and pupils' attitudes; 'the higher the socio-economic position of the father, the less favourable were the pupil attitudes towards unions.'

A further task for the trade unions was to try to offset some of the blatant anti-union material which some sections of the media regularly featured, material which, in the opinion of the unions, clearly contributed to the antagonistic attitudes of some sections of the community. Norman Willis, in his foreword to *Understanding Trade Unions: Curriculum Principles and Practice*, wrote:

> for some branches of the media, trade unions are normally only considered to be newsworthy when there is an industrial dispute, and industrial relations is presented as a series of head-on confrontations between management and unions about pay. All too often unions are portrayed as organisations which are, almost by definition, out to cause maximum disruption in industrial relations. (Smith and Wootton, 1988)

It was the TUC's concern with the negative attitudes of young people to trade unions which prompted its representatives to approach the Schools Council in 1976 with a proposal for a project on trade unions. The partners in those discussions about the project were eventually widened to include the Confederation of British Industry (CBI), and it was from those discussions that the Industry Project was to emerge in 1978.

There was a third factor related to the 'grass roots' problem of finding sufficient numbers of well-informed and capable trade unionists to debate the issues with industrialists and educationalists. While at the national level, the TUC could articulate its priorities with the CBI and representatives of education, at the local level that was simply not the case, a dilemma which the TUC clearly recognised.

Key Perspectives in Trade Union Education

Two basic perspectives appear to dominate the thinking of those concerned with the promotion of Trade Union Education in schools. One might be termed the 'consensus perspective', the other the 'conflict perspective'.

In the case of the former, the fundamental belief is that, in general, management and trade unions broadly share the same aims and objectives, the difference lies in their strategies for achieving those aims. Both are seen as concerned with achieving such goals as safe working practices, a good standard of rewards for employees and the creation of a quality product or service. Both are dependent upon one another for the long term security of jobs and the organisation. Teachers who adopt this perspective stress the need to emphasise the areas of collaboration and co-operation and strive on all occasions to create a balanced perspective in any debate on industrial practice (usually by making sure that a trade unionist and a representative of management always appear together). Occasionally, this consensus model is reinforced by the management representative and the trade unionist being invited from the same company. In fact, on some occasions, schools have been known to ask the industrialists if they would bring 'their own trade unionist', thus heightening the apparent consensus towards shared aims and objectives.

The second perspective is based on the assumption that there is an inevitable conflict of interests between the owners of capital and those who sell their labour. As Smith and Wootton (1988) explain, 'trade unions exist in order to protect the worker from the exploitation which some people see as inherent in a capitalist economy'. Attempts to portray consensus, therefore, are seen as a distortion of the essential principles which each side would claim to be the reality. Teachers who operate within this perspective would not only regard any attempt to bring management and trade unions together to portray the nature of industrial relations as contrived, but also fundamentally misleading. The question of balance is seen as achievable by each group putting their point of view independently of the other and certainly there would be no question of management bringing 'their trade unionist' along to reinforce the notion of consensus. The conflict of interest between capital and labour can be explored through such concepts as power, freedom, profit and exploitation.

Within one or other of these perspectives, trade unionists and teachers need to explore opportunities for students to examine the two key contexts of trade union activity, namely, the workplace and the wider socio-economic community.

Both the teachers and the trade unionists involved in developing Trade Union Education see the need to extend students' awareness of the workplace issues in which unions are involved. In the past, classroom work has centred almost exclusively on an examination of union involvement in industrial action in the form of strikes and claims for improved wages and conditions, in other words the stereotyped images of trade unions' concerns. New developments in Trade Union Education, however, endeavour to focus on other issues such as equal opportunities, the impact of new technology, health and safety in the workplace, as well as the broader questions concerning union structure and democracy both in the workplace and beyond. Smith and Wootton (1988) refer to this latter point; 'the issues of knowledge, accountability, representation, loyalty and individual freedom are, of course, central to any discussion of democracy in any organisation or in society as a whole.' They also quote a trade union official who emphasises the need to educate members; 'unless we can equip people with the basis on which to decide, we are wasting our time. Communication is essential to democracy, we need to talk to people in order to educate them about issues.'

The other concern of teachers and trade unionists is to help students to understand the role of unions in the local, national and international community. Apart from the work of the local trade councils and union representation on a whole range of local social and welfare committees, there is a need to point out to students the involvement which many unions have in issues such as human rights and political freedom. The support which NALGO (National Association of Local Government Officers), for instance, gives to organisations such as Amnesty International and to the anti-apartheid movement is illustrated by this quotation from one of the union's officials:

> for many years NALGO persisted in the view that trade unions were just about what happened in the workplace and that there was no place in politics for trade unionists. Over the last 15 years views have changed and there is a belief that political issues and trade unionism are interwoven, the political issues ultimately affect union members and their families.
>
> (Smith and Wootton, 1988)

Helping to change the purchasing policy of one West Midland's local authority from its previous one of buying from companies who supported apartheid is just one example of how a union such as NALGO demonstrates its social responsibility, not only for its own members in the workplace, but for the wider membership of the union.

It is these and other key issues which trade unionists feel strongly should feature in the presentation of their organisation to students. Inevitably, the question will be asked as to whether the classroom is being used as a platform to encourage students to become actively involved in trade union activity. In fact, the instances of teachers reporting such attempts on the part of the trade unionists are extremely rare. Almost all trade unionists are only too aware of the harm that canvassing openly for membership would do to their main aim of winning the support of teachers in their attempts to increase students' awareness of unions' role in a modern industrial society.

Trade Union Education in Practice

Three key principles underpin the development of Trade Union Education within the curriculum. The first of these is that it should be located within a definite curriculum context. One of the criticisms of schools–industry work in the past has been that it lacked a direct link into specific subjects or courses within which students were working. All too often in the past, the picture has been of industrialists and trade unionists, ('adults other than teachers' [AOT's] as these people have been called) appearing on the appointed day, often without any prior information from the school about the students they were to meet, the size of the group, how what they were to do fitted in (if at all) with previous work. They made their presentation, sometimes without the involvement of the teachers, and left. Little or no feed-back was given of the students' responses and no indication of how what they had done would be followed up. Little wonder that in many cases the AOT's did not return. Not all the fault, of course, should be laid at the door of the schools. Often, attempts by schools to contact the visitors beforehand do not prove successful and occasionally AOT's have not appeared at the last minute or their presentation has proved to be totally inappropriate to the age and ability of the students.

The lessons to be learnt from these situations are that schools, if they are going to involve trade unionists in the curriculum, should clearly identify the context within which Trade Union Education is to feature. It also requires a commitment from both groups to pre-planning; including the identification of objectives and teaching approaches and to a post-session evaluation. Details about the school, the students with whom they will be working, the style of working, where the topic fits into what has gone before and what will follow it, should all be part of the briefing for trade unionists before they face the students.

Conversely, if students are going out of school to work in organisations and, in particular, look at the role and function of trade unionists, there should be adequate preparation for them within a particular subject or course prior to the experience. There should be an opportunity for them to acquire some basic knowledge of the situtation in which they will be working and equally important, a chance to use some of the intellectual and social skills which will be of value to them in making sense of the experience.

The second key principle has already been referred to briefly, namely the involvement of the trade unionists in the planning of the curricular experiences. It is critically important that they have the opportunity to identify what they believe to be the key issues of trade unionism with which students should be acquainted, together with those which the teachers will have identified. Equally, it is necessary for this planning stage to include a discussion of how the trade unionist would prefer to work with the students, e.g., with the whole group, with small groups or pairs, whether they are happy making a formal presentation or whether they prefer to work exclusively through such things as 'role-play' and 'case-study'.

The involvement of trade unionists at this state is not only important in the planning of appropriate curricular experiences, but in giving both teacher and the trade unionist some understanding of each other's strengths, weaknesses, priorities and, equally important, personal values and attitudes. The trade unionists can, of course, not only provide very valuable first-hand experience of trade union practice, they can provide useful material which will support the classroom-based work. For example, Smith and Wootton (1988) describe, in two case-studies, how trade unionists were involved in the development of some work on trade unions with the 4th-Year students (Year 10), in particular helping to plan a simulation exercise on the privatisation of domestic services at a hospital.

The third principle relates to the direct involvement of trade unionists in the work with the students, and again some of the teaching approaches have already been identified. The School Curriculum Industry Partnership has long been identified with the philosophy of 'experiential learning', such as the direct involvement of students in shaping the nature and direction of their own learning experiences. The unsuitablity of the formal talk and didactic-style presentation, either by industrialists or trade unionists, has been realised for some considerable time. It is of some significance that these direct-involvement approaches have now begun to find acceptance even with examination-orientated courses, the obvious example being GCSE. The use of role-play, simulation, case-study, problem-solving, group discussion, negotiation and decision-making exercises allow the trade unionists to operate in a context with which they are generally more comfortable, namely the small group, acting as adviser, consultant and facilitator.

The Curriculum Context

The Subject Disciplines

Much of the curriculum work in which trade unionists have become involved has been directly related to specific curricular areas or courses. Although specific references to trade unions in the syllabi of subjects are quite rare, nevertheless teachers have found opportunities to involve trade unionists in areas such as Humanities, Science and Technology and English. The contribution of trade unionists to these areas can be regarded as all the more valuable in the context of the development of the National Curriculum, though it has to be recognised that involving 'adults other than teachers' in the classroom and the use of experiential-based learning approaches are demanding on time.

In Humanities, trade unionists have contributed to a number of areas such as History, Business Studies, Economics and Religious Education, exploring with students a range of issues including import controls and tariffs, the 'closed' shop, secret ballots, links between the trade unions and the Labour Party, the ethical issues of industrial action, and trade unionists' attitudes to political and humanitarian issues. In the areas of Science and Technology, trade unionists have worked with students on issues of health and safety, the impact of new technology, the role of trade unions in the training of apprentices, and the equally sensitive areas of nuclear energy and conservation.

Trade unionists have also contributed to a number of cross-curricular courses such as Personal and Social Education, General Studies and, in an examination context, CPVE and City and Guilds. Increasingly, trade unionists are also becoming involved in the various courses developed by schools for the Technical and Vocational Education Initiative (TVEI). It is also significant that trade unionists are being invited to work with younger students, as illustrated in the 'Trade Union Week' case-study (Smith and Wootton, 1988), where they were involved with 2nd Year students exploring the theme of a 'Campaign'. This project was also significant because it brought together a team of teachers from subjects such as English, Art, Drama and Music to work with trade unionists.

The involvement of trade unionists in the curriculum is also being extended to the primary age range as Smith (1988) illustrates through a variety of case-studies of industry–education practice.

Work Experience

An increasing amount of emphasis has been placed in recent years on the need to develop well-structured and educationally sound programmes of work experience. In the past it has been the subject of a substantial amount of criticism, from educationists, industrialists and trade unionists. The government-sponsored schemes designed to encourage industry to develop better links with education through the promotion of work-experience place-ments is one indication of the increased importance placed on this form of experience.

The trade unions have long emphasised the valuable learning which students can acquire from a well-planned and co-ordinated programme of work experience:

> it [work experience] should be planned to assist young people's personal development by involving them in working situtations where they will have an identifiable role and where they will come into contact for the first time with patterns of work and social relationships which differ funda-mentally from those they have encountered in school.   (TUC, 1979)

Work experience can provide students with the opportunity to examine the organisation and structure of a union within a specific context. They can, for instance, investigate the overall role and function of the different unions within one organisation as well as the individual functions performed by the union workplace representative, the convener, and the full-time official. Hopefully, in the larger organisations they may have the opportunity to see something of the way in which unions and management negotiate and how the former play a role in the wider policy-making of the organisation.

At another level, the student may be able to ascertain the views and opinions of individual members of the union to various aspects of industrial practice. It may be possible to talk to members about their commitment to the union and to particular elements of industrial relations such as the 'closed shop', pay and conditions, health and safety, and equal opportunities.

Inevitably, some students will find themselves in organisations in which the trade union representation is very small or even non-existent. The question of whether schools should use organisations which do not recognise trade unions is an extremely contentious one. Clearly there are some people who are of the opinion that such considerations should not colour the selection of an organisation. Equally, there are those who would argue that it is a highly desirable aim that students do have an opportunity, in the context of work experience, to appreciate the role of management and unions in an industrial setting. To put students, therefore, into an organisation which refuses to recognise one sector of that partnership, may be seen as establishing a bias which those who demand balance in the curriculum and in education generally, might find hard to justify.

If, however, students do find themselves in situations where union representation is low or even non-existent, there may still be an opportunity to examine the reasons and motives for such a situation. One would hope that those in management positions would be prepared to discuss the organisation's policy with regard to trade unions, without seeing the enquiry as some form of veiled criticism.

Enterprise Education

The growth in interest among schools in the idea of enterprise has been considerable over the last few years. The Mini-Enterprise in Schools Project based at the University of Warwick and the Young Enterprise scheme are just two of the agencies committed to developing this aspect of students' understanding of the concept. Inevitably, both the idea and the practice have received a variety of responses from teachers, industrialists and trade unionists ranging from the openly hostile to the wildly enthusiastic! Those openly hostile to the idea see it as an overtly political strategy to encourage students to 'get on their bikes', with the underlying assumption that the responsibility for 'getting on' lies firmly with the individual. Some interpret this as a deliberate ploy on the part of the Conservative government to shift some of its responsibility for the economic and social well-being of society. Naturally, say the opponents, such schemes are promoted in language which stresses individual collaboration and co-operation, all part of good educational philosophy. Underpinning the rhetoric, however, they would point to some of the fundamental capitalist principles, reinforced for many of them, by the preponderance of schools who claim success in these ventures on the basis of the profit made and products sold.

On the other hand, there are those firmly committed to a wider concept of enterprise than just the mini-company, who see the process as a genuine opportunity for students to develop some of the intellectual and social skills which most people would believe to be critically important. For these people, it is the 'processes' of learning which are important, rather than the more formal outcomes. Equally, they would argue that students' awareness of enterprise does not have to develop solely through the traditional models of capitalism and hierarchical managerial structures. There are numerous examples of school-based enterprises which are run on purely voluntary non-profit making lines and which operate within a co-operative structure.

For trade unions, the area of enterprise education has not to-date been one in which they have readily become involved. They would point to some of the inherent pitfalls in the area of small businesses for both the individual and the organisation as a whole. Some small businesses, anxious to survive and remain competitive, have to operate on the basis of long hours, small rewards and often poor, unsafe working practices. Trade unions, therefore, express concern for the rights of the individual workers involved in such an operation.

For schools, the challenge has been to examine ways in which Enterprise Education can include a trade union perspective. Sadly, in the vast majority of instances, this aspect of industrial practice rarely features in the school-based operations. Those schools which have invited trade unionists to become involved, have seen the opportunities to help students explore a range of issues related to business practice. These include the structure of the operation, whether on hierarchical lines or in the form of a co-operative, the protection of the 'workers' rights, the question of equal opportunities in the allocation of job roles, the issue of health and safety, and the handling of disagreements and disputes between individuals or groups. All these questions and many more are ones which enterprises do encounter. The role for the trade unionist in helping students to examine these questions is a vital one.

Work Shadowing

Watts (1986) describes work shadowing as a process 'in which an observer follows a worker around for a period of time, observing the various tasks in which he or she engages and doing so within the context of his or her total role'. Work shadowing in this country is a relatively recent concept; its origins lay largely in the USA and the idea of 'mentoring'. Work shadowing emphasises the opportunity which the 'shadow' has for observing the person performing a specific role or function in a variety of contexts, as well as monitoring the skills and qualities which that person possesses and demonstrates in the process. Work shadowing was seen by teachers and industrialists to have certain advantages over work experience in that it was possible to focus specifically on certain people, certain functions and specific contexts, thus controlling the nature of the experience more easily and allowing clearer monitoring and evaluation. A number of work shadowing schemes have developed, some of which have been extensively evaluated (Watts, 1988).

The instances of trade unionists being shadowed are to-date very small. In fact, there appears to be domination of this approach by the management sector of industry, and the very senior management sector at that. However, Smith and

Wootton (1988) include one case-study of a student shadowing a branch secretary of NALGO. In spite of the current lack of trade union involvement in this process, the potential learning for students through such a process is considerable. Apart from gaining a better understanding of the specific role of a union workplace representative, a convener or full-time union official, the opportunity is there to monitor the skills, qualities and judgement of the individual trade unionists within a range of contexts. Inevitably, students and the person being shadowed have reported a slight uneasiness in observing and being observed at such close quarters over a period of two or three days. Nevertheless, many students also reported the valuable insights into the role which they acquired through the experience (Peffers, 1988).

Conclusions

The principle of trade unionists' involvement in the development of the curriculum in order to help students acquire a greater understanding of their role within an industrial society must be maintained and developed within the context of the new National Curriculum. The momentum which has been created by the various education–industry organisations cannot be allowed to diminish. The government constantly refers to the need for a partnership between education and all sectors of the community it serves; one very vital sector of that community is the trade union movement.

There is clearly a need to broaden the base of trade union involvement in schools. Currently, much of this work is carried out by part-time or full-time officials who somehow manage to find the time within their busy workload, to support schools. As the case-study on the development of a trade union module in Smith and Wootton (1988) indicates, a much greater effort needs to be made to involve lay officials in this work. The responsibility for this must lie with the management representatives of industry who need to be encouraged to be more flexible in allowing trade unionists the opportunity to work with schools, and with the government who could encourage and perhaps provide a tangible support for those companies who do adopt this approach.

The area of in-service provision is also one which needs tackling urgently. The opportunity for teachers and trade unionists to work together to develop their own professional skills in order to deliver Trade Union Education in the curriculum must be created within the government's INSET funding. In this way, not only could both groups gain a greater understanding and awareness of their respective organisations, but also their ability to use such approaches as role-play, case-study and simulation would be enhanced.

With the Education Reform Act, 1988, giving more power and responsibility to the governing bodies of schools, there may also be an opportunity for the trade unions, through their individual members, to encourage schools to develop this area of the curriculum and for individual trade unionists to offer their support in making that goal a reality. While there is clearly a long way to go before it can be confidently demonstrated that Trade Union Education is a central part of the curriculum of all young people, there are sufficient examples of good practice in our schools to illustrate and support this vitally important principle.

References and Further Resources

R. Jackson, 'Schools and Industry: A view from the TUC' in *Trends in Education* (1979)

I. M. Jamieson and M. Lightfoot, *Schools and Industry: Schools Council Working Paper 73* (Methuen Educational, 1982)

J. Peffers, 'Work Patterns' in D. Smith (ed.), *Partners in Change* (Longman for SCDC, 1988)

D. Smith (ed.), *Industry in the Primary School Curriculum: Principles and Practice* (Falmer Press, 1988)

D. Smith and R. Wootton, *Understanding Trade Unions: Curriculum Principles and Practice* (Longman for SCDC, 1988)

TUC, *Learning about Trade Unions: Activities and Case Studies* (TUC, new edition, 1988)

TUC, *TUC Guidelines on Work Experience for School Children* (TUC, 1979)

A. G. Watts, *Work Shadowing* (Longman for SCDC, 1986)

A. G. Watts, *Executive Shadows* (Longman for SCDC, 1988)

Key Teacher and Classroom Resources

I. M. Jamieson, *Industry in Education: Developments and Case Studies* (Longman, 1985)
A book of case-studies of schools–industry practice which includes examples of work with trade unionists in SCIP schools.

I. M. Jamieson and M. Lightfoot, *Schools and Industry; Schools Council Working Paper 73* (Methuen Education, 1982)
The report of the first phase of the Schools Council Industry Project, outlining the background to the education–industry debate. It outlines the contributions to the Project by each of the partners, and documents examples of interesting practice.

I. M. Jamieson, A. Miller and A. G. Watts, *Mirrors of Work: Work Simulations in Schools* (Falmer Press, 1988)
The book documents a range of ways in which schools can introduce students to experiences of work. It includes specific references to the use of trade unionists in various work simulations.

D. Smith (ed.), *Partners in Change* (Longman for SCDC, 1988)
The book is in two parts, the opening chapters deal with key issues in schools–industry practice, the use of 'adults other than teachers', cooperative education, assessment and

evaluation. The second part contains a series of case-studies, including a number involving the work of trade unionists in schools.

D. Smith and R. Wootton, *Understanding Trade Unions: Curriculum Principles and Practice* (Longman for SCDC, 1988)
The book opens with trade unionists talking about a range of issues in and beyond the workplace. The second section explores practical ways of introducing these issues into the classroom and the final section contains a selection of case-studies.

TUC, *Learning about Trade Unions: Activities and Case Studies* (TUC, 1988)
A useful book of practical activities designed to be used by teachers and trade unionists with students in the 14–18 age range.

Key Addresses

SCIP National Headquarters,
Newcombe House,
45 Notting Hill Gate,
London W11 3JB

SCIP/TUC Education Project,
SCIP Northern Office,
Woolley Hall,
Wakefield WF4 2JR

TUC,
Congress House,
Great Russell Street,
London WC1B 3LS

TUC National Education Centre,
77 Crouch End Hill,
London N8

There are 10 Regional Educational Officers; their names and addresses can be obtained from TUC at Congress House

12

HUMAN RIGHTS EDUCATION:

EDUCATION FOR
DEMOCRACY, FREEDOM AND JUSTICE

David Selby

High Rhetoric, Belated Action

How many teachers are aware that as a signatory to the United Nations (UN), *Universal Declaration of Human Rights*, 1948, the United Kingdom pledged its schools and colleges to promote 'respect for human rights and fundamental freedoms'? Or that, immediately following the adoption of the Declaration by the UN General Assembly, the United Kingdom joined with other member states in calling for the Declaration's contents to be 'disseminated, displayed, read and expounded principally in schools and other educational institutions'? The number is probably very small; about as insignificant numerically as those who can discern any widespread, conscious, sustained and systematic effort within the education system to fulfil the commitments entered into in 1948.

The *Universal Declaration* arose from the ashes of the Second World War. Described by one writer as 'humanity's response to the Nazi death camps, the fleeing refugees, and tortured prisoners of war', the *Declaration* was the first internationally-agreed statement to list human rights in a systematic manner. As such, it set a standard of conduct for nations and peoples around the world. It also provided a potentially powerful statement of legitimisation for Human Rights Education. Until recently, however, Human Rights Education in the United Kingdom has remained a relatively under-developed area. It has continued to enjoy high-level support at international gatherings (at which the UK has been represented) and through a series of international declarations and resolutions (to which UK governments have been party) but it has received low-level support at national and local authority level and in the classroom. There have been 'many meetings of experts, and many resolutions for action, but little action by real teachers with real students in real schools' (Lister, 1983). Only recently has the situation changed, principally through the work of non-government organisations and networks of teachers and other educators. These have begun to fill the gaps in the provision of classroom materials and activities and, under the umbrella of legitimisation provided by international documents, to promote a grassroots awareness of the need for teaching and learning about human rights in schools.

From what international agencies and instruments have proponents of Human Rights Education principally found succour? Firstly, they have continued to look to the United Nations. Since 1948 a succession of important documents on human rights have come from the UN and its agencies, the most important of which (for teachers) has been the November 1974 UNESCO *Recommendation concerning education for international understanding, co-operation and peace and education relating to human rights and fundamental freedoms.* Amongst other things, the signatories (which included the United Kingdom) agreed to:

- formulate and apply national policies aimed at strengthening the ways in which education can contribute to developing respect for human rights
- provide the financial, administrative, material and moral support necessary to implement such policies
- ensure that the principles of the *Universal Declaration* become 'an integral part of the developing personality of each child, adolescent, young person or adult applying these principles in the daily conduct of education at each level'
- encourage the teaching of issues connected with 'the exercise and observance of human rights'   (UNESCO, 1974, Sections IV–V)

Between 1974 and 1985 the *Recommendation* was adroitly used to promote Human Rights Education, World Studies and related fields (see, for instance, Hicks and Townley, 1982; Fisher and Hicks, 1985) and in this period some interesting syllabi were drawn up (Cox and Selby, 1978) and classroom materials published (Richardson, 1978; Dunlop, 1980). For its part, the government of 1974/5 chose to follow the usual custom of circulating international agreements concerning education to local education authorities (DES, 1976) and delegating decisions as to implementation of them. Specific mention of Education for Human Rights in documents emanating from the Department of Education and Science after 1974 are absent although indirect reference can be found; for instance, *A Framework for the School Curriculum*, 1980, suggested that one aim of schooling was 'to instil respect for religious and moral values, and tolerance of other races, religions and ways of life'. The potency of the *Recommendation* as a means of influencing teachers and schools inevitably waned with the United Kingdom's decision to withdraw from UNESCO in 1985. Before that happened, however, the UK government had appended its signature to a recommendation document of the Committee of Ministers of the Council of Europe on *Teaching and Learning about Human Rights in Schools* (Council of Europe, 1985). The Council of Europe is the second major international agency to which British human rights educators have looked for inspiration and support. Founded in 1949, one of the responsibilities of the Council is to maintain and develop human rights across and within 21 member states. One of the first achievements of the Council was to draft and adopt the *European Convention on Human Rights* (1950), a treaty guaranteeing civil and political rights in member states and establishing a machinery – a Commission and a Court – to which parties seeking redress for human rights violations might have recourse. Picking up the Convention's exhortation to members to promote 'a common understanding and observance' of human rights, the Council has sought as energetically as possible within the constraints of its budget to promote Human Rights Education through recommendations, meetings of experts, teacher seminars, bursaries, research scholarships and publications.

The Committee of Ministers' *Recommendation* of 1985 is the latest in an important line of Council of Europe statements on Human Rights Education (for others, see Starkey, 1986). It is qualitatively different from its predecessors in its frank recognition that human rights are increasingly under challenge in the Western democracies. The *Recommendation* pinpoints effective Human Rights Education as a necessary pre-condition for a healthy democratic society (especially in times of crisis and threat). Democratic values such as respect for the dignity and freedom of the individual, responsibility, tolerance, equality of opportunity and justice, it maintains, need constantly reaffirming in the face of challenges locally, nationally and globally. Challenges singled out for particular mention include rising levels of violence and terrorism, the re-emergence of racist and xenophobic attitudes, and disillusionment amongst the young over unemployment, poverty and inequality in the world (Council of Europe, 1985).

The *Recommendation* calls for teaching and learning about human rights; vertically through all age groups and horizontally across a range of subject areas:

> Concepts associated with human rights can, and should, be acquired from an early stage. For example, the non-violent resolution of conflict and respect for other people can already be experienced within the life of a pre-school or primary class. Opportunities to introduce young people to more abstract notions of human rights . . . will occur in the secondary school, in particular in such subjects as History, Geography, Social Studies, Moral and Religious Education, Language and Literature, Current Affairs and Economics.   (Council of Europe, 1985)

Governmental dissemination of the Council of Europe's *Recommendation* has followed the discreet tradition described earlier. The recommendations have been made known to local education authorities and to national bodies that represent the authorities (such as the Society of Education Officers). Somewhat strangely, and perhaps inadvisedly, LEAs have not seen fit to incorporate reference to such an up-to-date internationally-agreed statement of legitimisation into policy documents on rights-related areas such as gender, race and equal opportunities. Perhaps the principal beneficiaries of the recommendations have been non-governmental organisations, teacher networks and Human Rights Education/interest groups. These became more numerous and more active in the 1980s, partly in response to the same challenges to human rights identified by the Council of Europe. Notwithstanding the democratic values listed in the Council of Europe recommendations, these organisations, groups and networks (singly or collectively) were also concerned with the continued presence of serious gender inequalities, the threat to privacy presented by increasingly sophisticated data-storage and retrieval systems, the ever-present danger of state encroachments on people's rights in times of international tension, the polarisation of politics, the decline in world resources and the environmental crisis. Some of the interest groups also identified with the movement to enact a Bill of Rights by incorporating the European Convention into British law. The 1980s witnessed a continued upward trend in the number of rights-violation complaints against the United Kingdom government that were put before the European Commission and Court of Human Rights (Ewing, 1986; Selby, 1987; Young, 1987).

The Development of Teaching Materials

Two non-governmental organisations that came to the fore in the 1980s were the British section of Amnesty International and the Minority Rights Group. In 1984 Amnesty published an eleven-unit pack for secondary schools, *Teaching and Learning about Human Rights* (see Classroom Resources), covering topics such as prisoners of conscience, censorship, 'disappearances' and torture. In 1985 Amnesty joined with the Centre for Global Education (see Key Addresses) to organise the first national conference for primary and secondary teachers on Human Rights Education. Some two hundred attended. The conference was, perhaps, a turning point. 'For the first time human rights was placed at the centre of the agenda of people actively involved with curriculum development and processes of change in schools' (Starkey, 1985). The Minority Rights Group has also produced some very useful materials for schools including *Profile on Prejudice* (1985), a pack for secondary schools on human rights and minority groups. It also undertakes in-service training in Human Rights Education and offers schools up-to-date information on the treatment of minorities around the world.

In addition, there are area or topic-specific interest groups which have produced educational materials, and also an important and well-known cluster of organisations concerned with promoting social and economic rights through education. Amongst the former are the Anti-Apartheid Movement, the Anti-

Slavery Society, the Central America Human Rights Committees and the Latin America Bureau. Amongst the latter are the Catholic Fund for Overseas Development, Christian Aid, Oxfam and UNICEF (United Nations International Children's Emergency Fund – now known as the United Nations Children's Fund).

The Centre for Global Education at York University has been involved in in-service education and curriculum development in Human Rights Education since 1982. It hosted the Amnesty conference referred to above and its publications include a book for upper secondary students on human rights, an activity file of human rights activities for the primary and secondary classroom and a teachers' guide to human rights organisations (see Pike and Selby, 1988a; Selby, 1987, see References and Resources sections). The Centre began a major three-year Human Rights Education project in September 1989 on behalf of Amnesty International.

Teacher networks include the Education in Human Rights Network and Right from the Start. The former holds regular meetings, publishes a bulletin and, in November 1988, held a large-scale Human Rights Education Forum and Fair in London to celebrate the fortieth anniversary of the *Universal Declaration*; the latter consists of early years and junior teachers working together to produce classroom activities and materials for 4- to 12-year-olds (for contact addresses see Key Addresses).

Key Concepts, Content and Process

Concepts

A framework for a human rights curriculum is provided by the major international documents. Human rights are often divided into two categories – 'civil and political rights' and 'economic, social and cultural rights'. Civil and political rights are concerned with giving individuals freedom of action and choice and freedom to participate in political life. They include the right to freedom of speech, the right to freedom of movement, the right to vote and the right to marry. They are listed in the *Universal Declaration* (Articles 12–21) and in the European Convention. Economic, social and cultural rights seek to protect people's physical, material, social and economic well-being. They include the right to work and the right to just and favourable conditions of employment, the right to rest and leisure, and the right to adequate food, clothing, housing and medical care. They are set out in the *Universal Declaration* (Articles 22–27) and in the European Social Charter of 1961. The abstract and legalistic tone of such documents makes them unsuitable for actual classroom use other than with senior secondary students. This problem can be circumvented in the case of junior and lower secondary students by using the simplified version of the *Universal Declaration* produced by the Geneva University Project on the Teaching of Human Rights (reproduced in Pike and Selby, 1988a).

However approached, the classroom explanation of human rights will bring into play a number of other key concepts and ideas. Are some rights more important than others? Are some rights so crucial to human dignity that they can never be curtailed or removed (the concept of *basic* human rights)? Or are all rights equal and interdependent so that the removal of one makes the defence and promotion of all others a more uphill task (the concept of *indivisibility* of rights)? How do we determine the right balance between our *freedom to* do what we want and people's *freedom from* having something harmful or distasteful done to them? How do we achieve a balance between the rights of the individual and the 'common good' or 'common interest'? Is the pursuit of *freedom* inevitably in conflict with the pursuit of *equality*? In what sense are rights and responsibilities in a reciprocal relationship? What are the economic, psychological, political and social consequences of denials of rights to minorities, marginal groups and those with little power (*discrimination*, *oppression*)? How do we set about achieving *justice* in such situations?

'Human rights need to be kept human' (Lister, 1984). In terms of content, Human Rights Education is at its most effective when students are presented with case-studies of real individuals or groups of individuals who have either effectively campaigned for human rights or who have suffered violations of their rights. Campaigns for human rights that have figured in Human Rights Education curricula include the Chipko women (India), Mahatma Gandhi (India), Martin Luther King (USA), Nelson and Winnie Mandela (South Africa), Archbishop Oscar Romero (El Salvador), Andrei Sakharov (USSR), Mother Theresa (India) and Archbishop Desmond Tutu (South Africa). Case-studies of individuals and groups suffering violations of their rights are readily available in reports published by Amnesty International, the Minority Rights Group, the Anti-Slavery Society and Survival International. Topics appearing in courses and class books on human rights include 'disappearances' and torture in Latin America, the treatment of dissidents and religious groups in the USSR, the condition of refugees such as the Palestinians and 'Boat People', apartheid in South Africa and the treatment of the aboriginal peoples of Australia. The best Human Rights Education courses, a point that will be returned to later, also bring human rights to the backdoor by examining rights infringements and denials in Britain and Western Europe.

Beyond the success stories of some well-known campaigners, Human Rights courses often include successes in the defence of human rights that have been achieved by international bodies, such as the United Nations and the European Commission and Court of Human Rights, and by pressure groups such as Amnesty International. Accounts of cases brought before the European Court of Human Rights are available free of charge from the Council of Europe and provide excellent case-study material on the defence of human rights. The cases can be used by teachers as a basis for project booklets, worksheets or role-play activities.

Content and Process

In Human Rights Education great store needs to be set upon learning which is experiential, interactive and participatory. It is not enough to exclusively focus upon knowledge objectives so that students learn *about* human rights, key concepts, international documents and case-studies of the violation and defence of human rights. It is just as, if not more, important that they are given the opportunity to develop and practise skills necessary for the defence and promotion of their own and other people's rights. Such skills undoubtedly include verbal and non-verbal communication skills, skills of co-operation and collaboration, the skills involved in establishing positive and non-oppressive personal relationships, problem-solving skills, non-violent conflict resolution skills (asserting, negotiation, consensus-seeking and decision-making), values clarification skills and non-violent action and campaigning skills. Skills-oriented Human Rights Education is often referred to as teaching/learning *for* human rights. Teaching/learning *in* or *through* human rights goes a stage further. The knowledge and skills objectives remain but, in addition, learning is reinforced through the very quality of the classroom climate and environment. The quality of interpersonal relationships and the methods of teaching and learning exhibit an intrinsic respect for the rights (whilst, of course, reaffirming the duties) of students and teachers.

If the teaching of human rights is not accompanied by dialogue between students, affirmation of individuals as valued and equal partners in the learning process, participation and negotiation, then message and medium are in potentially critical disharmony. Lister (1984) has characterised such a non-democratic teaching approach as creating a 'classroom of negation' whereas the goal should be a 'classroom of affirmation'. Some of the essential charactersitics of a 'classroom of affirmation' are open channels of communication, concern for the enhancement of self-esteem, emphasis on co-operation and negotiation, peer tutoring and learning (pupils helping each other), involvement in decision-making and regular opportunities for reflection and self/group evaluation. These characteristics necessitate a shift from vertical teacher–learner relationships principally consisting of one-way communication to horizontal relationships marked by high levels of interaction, flexibility and openness. The 1985 Council or Europe recommendation document recognised the pivotal importance of teaching/learning *in* or *through* rights for effective political education for democracy:

'Democracy' is best learned in a democratic setting where participation is encouraged, where views can be expressed openly and discussed, where there is freedom of expression for pupils and teachers, and where there is fairness and justice. An appropriate climate is, therefore, an essential complement to effective learning also about human rights.

(Council of Europe, 1985)

Available research points to the efficiency of the teaching/learning *for* and teaching/learning *in* or *through* approaches; it also suggests that knowledge *about* rights is better attained in the co-operative, interactive classroom. David and Roger Johnson (1983) have found that the greater the conceptual learning required to complete a task (and human rights embraces many difficult concepts), the greater will tend to be the effectiveness of co-operative learning over individualised or competitive learning. A monumental research project in the USA by David Aspy and Flora Roebuck into classrooms characterised by 'facilitative conditions' (for example, openness, trust, empathy) found that students learning under those conditions made greater gains in both the cognitive and affective domains (Rogers, 1983). From a survey of US research into the function of the school in political socialisation conducted by Lee Elman in 1977, it emerged that a democratic classroom climate correlated 'consistently and strongly' with 'positive political attitudes' (cited in Lister, 1984). Both US and UK research also suggests that regular immersion in collaborative and co-operative learning contexts tends to diminish prejudice and hostility based upon class, ethnicity, gender and handicap (Johnson and Johnson, 1985; Davey, 1983; Salmon and Claire, 1984).

In essence the kind of affirmative classroom climate outlined above provides a starting point and practice ground for education in human rights. One of the most difficult tasks facing the teacher is that of helping students grasp that human rights matter to *them*. This is not readily achieved by beginning a course by considering the *Universal Declaration* or by looking at human rights case-studies 'out there'. It is rather more easily achieved if the course begins with – and continually returns to – students' rights and responsibilities. Reference to two activities will help illustrate the point. In one upper primary/secondary activity, 'The Rights of the Child', students are briefly introduced to the idea of rights before undertaking group work involving 'brainstorming' the rights they consider children should have and jotting each one onto separate cards. All ideas are accepted. The students then arrange their cards in clusters offering similar or overlapping examples of children's rights. These are stuck on sugar paper with a circle around each cluster, together with an additional card summarising what each cluster is saying. Each group is then asked to get together with a second group and work out a ten point declaration of the rights of the child (using their collective summary cards as a starting point). This

189

process may involve omitting some rights considered to be less important, collapsing summary cards together or editing two or more closely approximating cards so they can stand as one statement. Following class presentations, groups reassemble and are given a copy of the UN *Declaration of the Rights of the Child* (1959). They discuss the differences between their declaration and the UN Declaration, the ways in which their document is better (for example, it may include reference to environmental rights which the UN Declaration, because of its vintage, does not) and the ways in which theirs is a less satisfactory document (the UN Declaration in all probability will contain fundamental rights that pupils had not thought of). The activity ends with plenary discussion and reflection (Pike and Selby, 1988a).

'Rights in the Classroom' begins with each student (and the teacher) writing down one right they feel should be observed in the classroom. Slips of paper are collected in and voted upon. Suggestions receiving the vote of more than half the class are written onto a large sheet of paper and prominently displayed as the 'Class Code of Rights'. Each right has to be observed by everybody in the class. Groups then take one right each and compile a list of responsibilities attendant upon the enjoyment of that right. Following class presentations and subsequent discussion, a class code of responsibilities is drawn up and displayed alongside the rights code. Subsequently, if any five members of the class feel that a right should be rephrased or removed or a new right added they can call a 'moot' to discuss and vote upon the matter (Pike and Selby, 1988a).

Co-operative and interactive classroom approaches not only include group and plenary discussion activities, such as the above, but also drama and role-play, experiential activities and simulations. Drama and role-play offer rich opportunities for the development of skills of communication, negotiation and imaginative and creative thinking, but also provide a vehicle enabling students to see a rights issue or problem from a variety of perspectives. Experiential activities (which provide a group-generated and, hence, original experience within an artificially constructed framework) and simulations (which seek to mirror or reconstruct actual events, issues or situations on a small scale) are excellent for helping students understand discrimination, oppression, inequality and injustice and their effects, and for helping foster feelings of empathy for and solidarity with the oppressed. Lists of such activities covering rights themes are available (Lister, 1984; Pike and Selby, 1988b).

An extension of active involvement in the classroom is active involvement in the school and wider community. Discussion and reflection upon human rights in class can generate a desire on the part of students (individually, or collectively) to campaign for human rights. There are a number of schools that have established Amnesty International groups in which students participate by writing letters (on behalf of prisoners of conscience) to the jailers, to the governments and embassies concerned and to newspapers. Many schools have mounted campaigns on behalf of the social and economic rights of the under-privileged by charitable fundraising for Oxfam, Save the Children Fund and similar organisations, and through promotional events to pinpoint the causes of poverty globally. Local exhibitions on human rights, action projects in support of the rights of the handicapped, letter-writing to commercial organi-sations about sexist advertising and street theatre to highlight human rights themes are other examples of student involvement spilling out of school. In school, students can seek to bring about reforms in what they conceive as rights denials. In a middle school in Oxford, nine- and ten-year-olds mounted a campaign, based on their right to a healthy environment, for the provision of drinking fountains and cleaner toilets equipped with soft toilet paper (Pike and Selby, 1988b). Through such involvement schools can further develop and refine the skills necessary for the defence and promotion of human rights, and help students appreciate that the task of supporting human rights requires sustained effort and vigilance. The development of 'involvement literacy' (i.e., developing the skills and exploring the avenues for participa-tion, accepting the frustration, limitations and pitfalls and enjoying the suc-cesses of action) is a crucial element in the empowerment of the individual. The risks notwithstanding (we shall return to these later), teachers need to recognise that school and community involvement is a perhaps ineluctable development from a thoroughgoing classroom programme in Human Rights Education.

Seven Questions for Human Rights Educators in the 1990s

Question One:
Can we establish systematic programmes of Human Rights Education across the statutory years of schooling?

It is often said that Human Rights Education is the province of the secondary school. Early years and junior school children, some hold, are too young to handle the concepts involved in the study of human rights. A growing body of research and writing is now suggesting that there should be a cumulative approach to Human Rights Education throughout the statutory years of schooling. Susan Fountain has argued that a solid basis for a future commit-ment to human rights can be laid in the first school through a systematic programme of esteem-building, communication and co-operative activities (Fountain, 1987). Judith Torney-Purta has suggested that the middle years are ones in which the 'plasticity principle' operates. Between about ages seven and twelve concepts and attitudes are not yet fixed, stereotypes still do not dominate the students' view of the world and cognitive development is sufficiently advanced to accept a diversity of viewpoints. This, together with a lively concern for 'fairness', a hallmark of the middle school child, mark out these years as crucial for Human Rights Education.

> At about the age of thirteen or fourteen there appears to be a lessening of attitudinal plasticity and increased stereotyping. Attitudes become rigid, and they are used more frequently as a way of confirming peer group solidarity and excluding those who are different. The equitable treatment of others, especially those who may be victims of injustice or lack of opportunity, seems to be less important then maintaining the superior position of the in-group during adolesence. (Torney-Purta, 1982)

A cumulative approach to Human Rights Education, the suggestion is, can prevent or, at least, restrain this tendency. An excellent insight into what a Human Rights Education primary programme – grounded in the immediate experience of children – can look like has been provided by Ross (1981).

Question Two:
Do we leave students believing that 'it couldn't happen here'?

In selecting content for a Human Rights Education programme, the tendency is for teachers to choose examples from distant times and distant places and so comfortably locate denials of rights away from contemporary times in our own country. This tendency is partly resource-led (the principal provider of resources and case-study materials – Amnesty International – has a constitution which does not permit it to target rights denials in the host country) and partly through fear of handling controversial topics that are too close to home. These are real dangers attendant upon avoidance of home country case-studies, not least of which is that of encouraging smugness and complacency with regard to the United Kingdom's human rights performance. Students need to learn to exercise a lively vigilance, for rights are hard won and easily lost.

Question Three:
Do we offer students a West-centric view of human rights?

Human Rights Education – under that name – has been promoted by non-governmental organisations that are primarily concerned with civil and political rights (e.g. Amnesty International) and under the umbrella of international documents that, taken together, give overall precedence to civil and political over social and economic rights (the latter take second place even in the *Universal Declaration* which was prepared and promulgated at a time when the Western democracies – which prioritise liberty-oriented rights – still held sway at the United Nations). Courses and resources tend to give less space to social, economic and cultural rights (the best materials on social and economic rights have been produced by Development Education agencies which, all too often, fail to conceive of their work in rights terms; the best materials on cultural rights come from multicultural and anti-racist educators who rarely set their thinking within a rights framework). Over-emphasis on individual civil and political rights offers a skewed picture of human rights perspectives and prioritisations globally. Whilst 'human rights collectively are probably the values system that will command the broadest consensus' (Starkey, 1986), are we sure that we are giving students an understanding of the wide range of rights perspectives to be found across religious and ideological divisions worldwide?

Question Four:
Why stop at human *rights?*

The 1990s will probably be the decade when animal liberation theorists drive home their attack on the species exclusivity of human rights doctrines. Animal liberationists maintain that the two principal pillars upon which the claim to human rights is built – that, as sensate creatures, we must be protected from pain and that, as reasoning beings with a conscience, a sense of history and progress, we are entitled to special protection – are deeply flawed. In the first place, they argue, there is ample evidence to show that non-human animals feel pain too. In the second place, we extend our rights protection to humans that clearly do not actually possess the special characteristics claimed for humans, for example, severely retarded people. This, writes Peter Singer (1985) is 'speciesism, pure and simple, and it is as indefensible as the most blatant racism'. A question for the human rights educator is, therefore: how do we respond at a theoretical and practical level to our animal rights critics?

Question Five:
How far should we go in helping students understand injustice?

Experiential learning and simulations, it was suggested earlier, can provide students with a powerful experience of what it is like to be unjustly treated. Generating a high level of emotional response, learning initially takes place primarily in the affective domain with later reinforcement chiefly in the cognitive domain through post-experience discussion and analysis. Some human rights educators argue that such artifical 'manipulation' of feelings is unnecessary for understanding human rights concepts in that everybody has experiences of human rights denials upon which to draw; such experiences, they also claim, are potentially destructive of levels of trust within the classroom. Advocates of the use of experiential and simulation activities respond by pointing to the powerful stimulus offered for learning, such activities creating an experience of discrimination going beyond what is encountered by most students. The efficacy of such activities, they add, depends upon a full and sensitive debriefing in which participants are encouraged to explore and analyse their feelings and to relate the experience to the wider world. Two rejoinders might be 'are the skills of most teachers sufficiently well-developed to debrief experiences of this kind effectively?' and 'what evidence do we have that students who have had a particularly vivid classroom experience of discrimination will show qualitatively stronger support for the oppressed or downtrodden than students that have learnt about unjustice in less startling ways?'

Question Six:
Can schools handle involvement?

Participation, it has been suggested, can and should spill out of the classroom and into the school and community. A problem for the school is in deciding what kind of involvement it can countenance. The examples given earlier would, for the most part, be supported by a bipartisan consensus; few feathers would be ruffled. What, however, if students picked up disarmament issues (in that money spent on arms could be spent on realising people's social and economic rights) or mounted a campaign against a local branch of a multinational, where many parents worked, because of the company's rights record in the 'Third World'? When would the point be reached when even a sympathetic executive would feel compelled to call a halt? What would such a decision do to the credibility of the school's Human Rights Education programme? As indicated earlier, another area of danger, for some schools, is that students coached in action skills may direct those skills against aspects of the institution in which they find themselves. This brings us to the question of what a whole-school policy on human rights might look like.

Question Seven:
What are the wider school implications of Human Rights Education?

Even though good Human Rights Education may take place in schools whose structures and general procedures do *not* affirm human rights (i.e., achieved by individual teachers in supportive classroom climates), an ideal of Human Rights Education is to develop a human rights school (Lister, 1984). What would such a school look like? A helpful approach in seeking answers to this question is to take documents such as the *Universal Declaration* and the *European Convention* and seek to translate them into rights'-respectful school practices and procedures. The Children's Legal Centre has done exactly that and has produced a draft bill of rights for schools, setting out a framework of rights and responsibilities for all members of the school community; systematic methods of consultation and participation by all members of the school community in decisions which affect them; and a grievance procedure for settling disputes and conflicts over rights. The bill has been reproduced in a special number of the *World Studies Journal* (Cunningham, 1986) devoted to the 'Human Rights School'. The number also includes articles on access to files, decision-making in democratic schools, school councils and rights' respectful disputes and punishment procedures. Other helpful contributions on the human rights school are by Lister (1984) and Starkey (1986). The question of the human rights school is a crucial one, for 'classrooms of affirmation' are clearly going to be at their most effective if set within 'schools of affirmation'.

Human Rights in the National Curriculum

On 12 May 1988 the present writer wrote to the Minister of State for Education enquiring about the place of Human Rights Education within the National Curriculum. In reply, the Schools Branch of the Department of Education and Science pointed to Clause 1 of the Education Reform Bill, 1988, which emphasises that the school's curriculum should promote 'the spiritual, moral, cultural, mental and physical development of pupils' and prepare pupils for 'the opportunities, responsibilities and experiences of adult life'. 'The Government', the letter went on (Lin to Selby, June, 1988), 'sees no need to add Human Rights to the list of proposed foundation subjects, or to single out an understanding of human rights from among the general aims mentioned in Clause 1. It is best dealt with in the context of the existing foundation subjects (for example through English, History and Geography) and through other non-foundation subjects such as Political Education and Law.' Working groups, the present writer was also informed, were being asked to have particular regard to the development of pupil's personal qualities ('including a sense of social responsibility') and to cross-curricular themes and issues ('education about human rights will no doubt be among these').

The letter gives grounds for cautious optimism, the stance adopted by the present government seeming to adhere to the style of discreet promotion of Human Rights Education practised by its predecessors. Human Rights Education can be seen as a cross-curricular theme. Whilst the Humanities foundation subjects are identified as perhaps the best vehicles for the delivery of Human Rights Education, some consideration of human rights issues could also occur in, say, foundation Mathematics and Science (for instance, statistical work on ethnic minority employment prospects and discussion of the rights implications of nuclear power). The possibility is there, too, for schools to continue with or adopt rights-oriented courses of an interdisciplinary nature such as the Southern Examining Group's GCSE in World Studies (Pike and

Selby, 1988a) within non-foundation time. It is also clearly the case that everything is still to be played for in terms of creating 'classrooms of affirmation'; the National Curriculum consultation document (DES, 1987) was extremely laissez-faire with respect to classroom climate and teaching/learning processes and styles. Human rights educators should not, however, forget the utilitarian 'UK Ltd' tone in which the consultation document was couched. The following quotation, discovered on the noticeboard of a headteacher's study in a Bradford secondary school, serves as a powerful reminder of the dangers of schooling which, however efficient, fails to foster our essential humanity:

> *Dear Teacher,*
> *I am a survivor of a concentration camp. My eyes*
> *saw what no man should witness:*
> *Gas chambers built by learned engineers.*
> *Children poisoned by educated physicians.*
> *Infants killed by trained nurses.*
> *Women and babies shot and burned by high*
> *school and college graduates.*
> *So I am suspicious of education.*
> *My request is:*
> *Help your students become human. Your*
> *efforts must never produce learned monsters,*
> *skilled psychopaths, educated Eichmanns.*
> *Reading, writing, arithmetic are important*
> *only if they serve to make our children more*
> *human.*

References and Further Resources

Council of Europe, *Recommendation no. R(85)7 of the Committee of Ministers to member states of teaching and learning about human rights in schools* (Strasbourg, 14 May 1985)

H. Cox and D. E. Selby, 'Living and learning in the global village' in *The new era*, vol. 59, no. 4, pp. 134–9 (1978)

J. Cunningham (ed.), 'The Human Rights School', *World Studies Journal*, vol. 6, no. 2 (1986)

A. Davey, *Learning to be prejudiced: Growing up in a multi-ethnic Britain* (Arnold, 1983)

DES, *Circular 9/76* (HMSO, 1976)

DES, *The National Curriculum 5–16: A Consultation Document* (HMSO, 1987)

J. Dunlop (ed.), *Human Rights* (Jordanhill Project in International Understanding, c/o Jordanhill College, Glasgow G13 1PP, 1980)

K. Ewing, 'Rights and wrongs', *The Guardian* (19 December 1986)

S. Fisher and D. W. Hicks, *World Studies 8–13. A Teacher's Handbook* (Oliver and Boyd, 1985)

S. Fountain, *Affirmation, communication and co-operation experiences in an early childhood programme* (1987) Diploma in Applied Education Studies thesis, University of York (to be published in 1989, in revised form, by the World Wide Fund for Nature as *Starting Points*)

D. W. Hicks and C. Townley, *Teaching World Studies. An introduction to global perspectives in the curriculum* (Longman, 1982)

D. W. Johnson and R. T. Johnson, 'The socialisation and achievement crisis: are co-operative learning experiences the solution?' in L. Bickman (ed.), *Applied Social Psychology Annual 4*, pp. 119–62 (Sage Publications, 1983)

D. W. Johnson and R. T. Johnson, *Learning together and alone: co-operation, competition and individualization* (Prentice Hall, 1985)

I. Lister, *Teaching and learning about human rights in the secondary school: some positive proposals*, talk given at the symposium on 'Human Rights Education in schools in Western Europe' (Vienna, 17–20 May 1983)

G. Pike and D. E. Selby, *Human Rights. An activity file* (Mary Glasgow Publications, 1988a)

G. Pike and D. E. Selby, *Global teacher, global learner* (Hodder and Stoughton, 1988b)

R. Richardson, *Fighting for freedom* (Nelson, 1978)

C. Rogers, *Freedom to learn for the 80s* (Charles E. Merrill, Ohio, 1983)

A. Ross, 'Human Rights Education: perspectives and problems in the primary school' in *World Studies Journal*, vol. 2, no. 3 pp. 13–16 (1981)

P. Salmon and H. Claire, *Classroom collaboration* (Routledge and Kegan Paul, 1984)

D. E. Selby, *Human rights* (Cambridge University Press, 1987)

P. Singer (ed.), *In defence of animals* (Basil Blackwell, 1985)

H. Starkey (ed.), *Teaching and learning about human rights. Report of a conference for primary and secondary teachers held at University of York* (11 May 1985)

H. Starkey, 'Human rights: the values for World Studies and Multicultural Education' in *Westminster studies in education*, vol. 9, pp. 57–66 (1986)

J. Torney-Purta, 'Socialization and human rights research: implications for teachers' in M. Stimmann Branson and J. Torney-Purta (eds.), *International human rights, society and the schools*, no. 68, pp. 35–47 (New York, National Council for the Social Studies Bulletin, 1982)

UNESCO, *Recommendation concerning education for international understanding, co-operation and peace and education relating to human rights and fundamental freedoms* (Paris, 19 November 1974)

H. Young, 'How to take the wrong attitude to citizen's rights' in *The Guardian* (15 February 1987)

Key Teacher Resources

J. Cunningham (ed.), 'The human rights school', *World Studies Journal*, vol. 6, no. 2 (1986)
Practically-oriented articles on the development of whole-school human rights policies. Available from the Centre for Global Education (see Key Addresses)

S. Greig, G. Pike and D. E. Selby, *Earthrights: Education as if the Planet Really Mattered* (Kogan Page/World Wildlife Fund, 1987)
Explores person-centred classroom approaches and the links between Human Rights Education and three related fields (Development Education, Environmental Education and Peace Education).

D. W. Hicks *Minorities. A teacher's resource book for the multi-ethnic curriculum* (Heinemann, 1981)
Offers guidance to teachers on thinking about majority/minority issues, plus teaching ideas/resources.

I. Lister, *Teaching and learning about human rights* (Strasbourg, Council of Europe, 1984) (see Key Addresses)
A succinct and readable 'state of art' account of Human Rights Education. Secondary-oriented.

G. Pike and D. E. Selby, *Human Rights. An Activity File* (Mary Glasgow Publications, 1988)
Contains twenty-eight top primary to upper secondary classroom activities (Years 3 to 11) and an introduction to human rights concepts and ideas for teachers. The activities include discussion and experiential activities, role-plays and simulations.

D. E. Selby, *A teacher's guide to human rights organisations* (Centre for Global Education, 1988)
Describes the services and resources offered to schools by fifty-eight UK based human rights organisations. All the organisations mentioned in this chapter are included. For the Centre see Key Addresses.

Key Classroom Resources

Amnesty International, *Teaching and learning about human rights* (Amnesty International, British Section, 1983)
Twelve-unit pack introducing human rights, giving case-study material, suggesting action projects and classroom activities.

J. Coussins, *Taking liberties: An introduction to equal rights* (Virage, 1979)
A lively pack on equality between the sexes.

J. Cunningham, *Human rights and wrongs* (Writers and Scholars Educational Trust, 1981)
Good introductory material for secondary students on civil and political rights.

D. E. Selby *Human Rights* (Cambridge University Press, 1987)
Comprehensive introduction to human rights concepts, issues and some case-studies for upper secondary students.

S. Woodhouse, *Your life, my life* (Writers and Scholars Education Trust, 1980)
An introduction to rights and responsibilities for 10- to 14-year-olds.

D. Wright, *Thinking about social and moral issues: rights*, (Pergamon, 1987)
The students' book which accompanies a similary titled teachers' book by Peter Brownjohn (Pergamon, 1987). Some interesting factual information and discussion topics.

Key Addresses

Amnesty International (British Section),
5 Roberts Place,
London EC1R 0EJ
Wide variety of reports on human rights in specific countries. Range of tape/slide and video material available, e.g. *Torture in the Eighties* (slide pack) and *Free at last* (video probing political persecution in seven countries). 'Young Amnesty International' brochure available on forming school Amnesty groups. Publications and audio/visual lists available on request.

Centre for Global Education,
University of York,
Heslington,
York YO1 5DD
Conducts in-service education and curriculum development projects in Human Rights Education. Catalogue of published materials available on request.

Council of Europe (School Education Division),
Council of Europe,
67006 Strasbourg Cedex,
France
Organises teacher seminars on Human Rights Education (bursaries offered); encourages research (grants given to teachers and academics); publishes booklets and reports on previous teacher seminars. Case-studies of European Court cases also available.

Education in Human Rights Network,
c/o Hugh Starkey,
Westminster College,
Oxford OX2 9AT
Publishes a bulletin; regular meetings; acts as a pressure group providing information for the media and the Department of Education and Science.

Minority Rights Group,
29 Craven Street,
London WC2N 5NT

MRG's Education Project offers advice to teachers, workshop sessions, curriculum support and in-service education. It also provides schools with up-to-date information on minorities and offers suggestions for practical classroom activities. Publications catalogue (primary and secondary titles) available on request.

Right From the Start,
c/o Sarah Woodhouse,
The Old Farmhouse,
Lancing College,
West Sussex BN15 0RN

An education project networking nursery, infant and primary teachers and preparing activities and materials for Human Rights Education with young children.

13

CURRICULUM CHANGE AND

ORGANISATION:

THE PLACE OF THE NEW SOCIAL CURRICULUM WITHIN THE NATIONAL CURRICULUM

Barry Dufour

Historical Background

The idea of a National Curriculum, although not in its present form, had its origins in the 1970s amongst educationists, DES officials and HMI when reference began to be made to a 'core curriculum' and a 'common curriculum'. The 1976 Ruskin College speech by the Labour Prime Minister Mr Callaghan and the subsequent 'Great Debate' acted as a watershed for policy on the curriculum. His mention of a 'core curriculum', along with other ideas about education, marked the official beginning of an increasingly interventionist and centralist era of government educational policy and the development of two different models for the common elements of the curriculum – one associated with the DES and the other with HMI.

In a short historical analysis, Clyde Chitty draws out features of the two approaches (Lawton and Chitty, 1988). The HMI model, the professional common-curriculum approach, was elaborated in the 'HMI Red Books' between 1977 to 1983 (DES, 1977, 1981, 1983). Although subjects might continue to be the main way of organising the timetable, their choice and form would not be dictated by HMI, which was not overly concerned with the rigid defence of subjects and boundaries, but with the way broad areas of experience could be used as a basis for curriculum planning. This would allow maximum flexibility in the teaching process and would suit the needs of individual children while also contributing to other aims. This common element would occupy two-thirds of the total timetable. By 1983, the idea of the 'entitlement curriculum' rounded off these ideas by suggesting that all pupils should be entitled to a broad curriculum that included vocational, technical and academic elements.

The DES model, characterised as the bureaucratic core-curriculum approach, is mainly concerned with efficiency and control of the system. The collection of information about pupil performance, based on a national standardised curriculum, would ensure that teachers were more accountable. Chitty contrasts the HMI 'professional' approach and the DES 'bureaucratic' approach in the following way:

> Whereas the professional approach focuses on the quality of input and the skills, knowledge and awareness of the teacher, the bureacuratic approach concentrates on output and testing. Whereas the professional approach is based on individual differences and the learning process, the bureaucratic approach is associated with norms or bench-marks, norm-related criteria and judgements based on the expectations of how a statistically-normal child should perform. Whereas the professional curriculum is concerned with areas of learning and experience, the bureaucratic curriculum is preoccupied with traditional subject boundaries.
>
> (Lawton and Chitty, 1988)

The National Curriculum: 1988 to the 1990s

In most respects, the National Curriculum, enshrined in the Education Reform Act, 1988 (DES, 1988a), reflects the DES model – a mechanistic, subject-specific curriculum with a central emphasis on testing and performance. To facilitate the closest possible link between the teaching of each subject and the assessment of it, detailed operational guidelines were suggested in the report of the Task group on Assessment and Testing, known as the TGAT Report (TGAT, 1987) and outlined in each of the Subject Working Group reports as they became available from 1988 onwards.

In each Subject Working Group report, aspects of knowledge (knowledge, skills, understanding) are linked to attainment targets. These targets are themselves amplified in a number of statements of attainment that are related to the ten levels of achievement (so that each attainment target can be assessed at a range of levels). The attainment targets are sometimes grouped into profile components, and specified programmes of study are outlined which will enable pupils to reach the attainment targets. Training courses have been mounted to help teachers to learn the system as it applies to their own subject areas. Hopefully, governors and parents will be given adequate opportunities to familiarise themselves with the complexities of the new education plan.

The National Curriculum is now mandatory and statutory. The ten defined subjects, the foundation subjects, occupy the majority of the timetable, leaving some space, but not much, for additional subjects to be chosen by schools and teachers, in consultation with governors. This optional element is especially relevant for the 14- to 16-year-old age range in Years 10 and 11. The 'core subjects' – English, Mathematics and Science – started with new arrangements in September 1989. The other 'foundation subjects' – History, Geography, Technology (with Design), Music, Art and Physical Education (PE) – have different schedules. Modern Languages is a foundation subject in all secondary schools, and special arrangements have been made for Welsh and other minority languages (such as Punjabi). Religious Education also features, although it is not counted as part of the National Curriculum. It was already a requirement under the Education Act 1944: a range of varieties and exemptions will continue to apply.

The relative status and importance of various subjects and themes may be indicated by the differential strategies employed in their planning and consultation. Music, Art and PE, for example, may not be accorded the status of a Subject Working Group – arrangements for their guidelines will be 'announced' in 1990 by the National Curriculum Council (NCC). Equally, the cross-curricular themes were not given a Working Group with a public system of deliberation and consultation: presumably, this is because the cross-curricular themes are non-statutory. However, the NCC has arranged for a system of consultation for the themes, through committees, so that issues relating to policy and implementation can be discussed by the wider educational community.

The question of consultation seems to be an important one. From the start, when the *National Curriculum Consultation Document* (DES, 1987) was published in July 1987, along with other consultation documents, public pressure ensured a slight extension of the consultation period. 20,000 submissions were eventually received in response to all of the consultation documents for the Education Reform Bill, 1988. No analysis by the government was made public, though, and the documents have never been published except in edited form by Julian Haviland (Haviland, 1988). In the case of the Subject Working Group reports, large numbers of teachers did not see them at the interim consultation stages, largely because of the restrictions on the numbers of each report sent out.

A problem in relation to implementing the National Curriculum in the 1990s is the availability of specialist staff to teach many of the subjects. DES figures show an alarming shortage of recruits to the teaching profession ('Alarm on Teachers', *Guardian*, 18.1.89). To deal with this, the Secretary of State for Education and the DES are introducing a scheme to allow people without the usual teacher qualifications to enter teaching and to train on the job. A similar scheme will allow student teachers from local training institutions to go straight into the classroom and be paid as they train ('Teacher Graduates to train in Schools', *Guardian*, 28.1.89). There was substantial resistance to both schemes from the teaching unions.

The timetable issue must also be resolved during the early 1990s. It is going to be extremely difficult to accommodate all of the foundation subjects in the timetable and leave space for additional subject options, not to mention cross-curricular themes. With reference to the enormous scramble for space on the timetable, Eric Bolton, a senior HMI, observed that if the often-repeated official phrase 'everything is still to play for' is true, it will resemble a battleground rather than a playground (*Times Educational Supplement*, 16.9.88). A period of intense lobbying and political activity in education will continue through the 1990s.

Permeation, Attachment and Integration

In the same way that discussion of the cross-curricular themes cannot be separated from the general issues and problems associated with the Education Reform Act and the National Curriculum, mentioned above, neither can they be examined in isolation from a number of possible models for their integration and delivery. The options include the following:

A   Complete Permeation

All cross-curricular themes in all foundation subjects. This is theoretically possible but perhaps difficult to implement.

B   Partial Permeation

1   All cross-curricular themes in some foundation subjects. This is theoretically possible but an unlikely alternative.
2   Some cross-curricular themes in all foundation subjects. This is a possibility with, for example, Multicultural Education and Gender Education.
    The important point about these two examples is that Multicultural Education and Gender Education are more than just themes: they represent fundamental issues which affect the entire school – they are or should exist as whole-school policies and not just curricular themes. The same may be said of PSE.
3   Some cross-curricular themes in some foundation subjects. This is a possibility. For example, Health Education could form part of Science and PE. It could also form part of another theme – PSE.

C   Attachment

A cross-curricular theme in a 'natural' foundation subject base. For example, Media Education in English.

D An Integrated Course – within the Foundation Curriculum

This could link History and Geography with some of the cross-curricular themes. This would be a Humanities approach. All children would have to follow this course, given that the foundation subjects are mandatory.

E An Integrated or Modular Course – outside the Foundation Curriculum

This could include many or most of the cross-curricular themes but there would be no guarantee that all children would participate because this non-statutory course would vary depending on teacher preferences, pupil needs and local circumstances.

These options and variations are not, of course, mutually exclusive. In the B2 option, for example, Multicultural Education and Gender Education could form a part of all foundation subjects. At the same time, Health Education, the example in B3, might become part of several foundation subjects, but not all. In addition, an integrated course could be created within the foundation curriculum *and/or* outside the foundation curriculum, drawing in various cross-curricular themes and a variety of subjects.

Provision of the Cross-curricular Areas before the Education Reform Act

The only impression of the place of cross-curricular themes in secondary schools in the 1980s, before the National Curriculum was implemented, was provided by the HMI report, *Secondary Schools: An Appraisal by HMI* (DES, 1988b) which was based on 'dipstick' inspections of 185 schools in England between 1982 and 1986. The observations suggested the very uneven provision in the schools. The systematic implementation of cross-curricular themes (or cross-curricular issues, as HMI call them) such as Multicultural Education and Equal Opportunities Education had proved a difficult matter. In the case of Equal Opportunities, very few schools showed evidence of systematic treatment. It was also found that there were major gaps in the schools in the promotion of Political and Economic Awareness.

Timetabled Careers Education and work experience were not available for the academically most able in many schools. In over half of the schools surveyed, all children were introduced to the world of industry and commerce. Nearly half of all schools included some element of Environmental Education: relevant material formed part of Geography, Science, History and Art, although much of the work was on the local environment rather than on the national and international environment. Nine out of ten schools included PSE in the curriculum, either as a special course or as part of tutorial programmes or as part of English, RE, Drama or History. With regard to Health Education most schools provided for it through a number of channels – as topics in Biology, PE, Home Economics, and in some schools, as a specialist course or as part of PSE.

HMI pointed out that many of the issues dealt with in the cross-curricular areas reflected recent concerns of society, and schools had attempted to respond through specially designed courses. However, 'only a small number have so far sought to analyse and implement the contributions which could be made by subjects (themes) across the curriculum' (DES, 1988b).

Having explored the range of possible models and the HMI account of provision before the implementation of the National Curriculum, the next task is to look at the themes more closely and to consider their place within the new curriculum structure.

Cross-Curricular Themes: The Unofficial List

During 1988 and the early part of 1989, an unofficial list of eleven cross-curricular themes was in the unofficial possession of a number of educationists. It was claimed to be a list of the themes that the DES, HMI and the National Curriculum Council had explored as an element in the education of all children between 5 and 16. The list included the following areas:

Health and Safety, including Sex Education
Economic Understanding
Consumer Education
Political Education
Social Education
Careers Education
Preparation for Adult Life and the World of Work
Information Technology
Media Education
The Understanding of Gender and Ethnic Issues
Design Education

If we survey the important themes featured in this book and compare them with the ones that appeared in government publications and the unofficial list above, an interesting picture of inclusion and exclusion emerges. The themes that were apparently endorsed by the government at another stage, by way of the DES and the NCC, include:

THE WORLD OF WORK AND COMMERCE
Pre-vocational Education, Work Experience, Economic and Industrial Awareness, Business Education, Consumer Education, Careers Education and Guidance, Technological Education and Information Technology, Design Education.

GENERAL SOCIAL EDUCATION
Personal and Social Education, Health Education and Safety, Sex Education, Media Education, Gender Education, Multicultural Education and Political Education.

Global Education: The Missing Link

A number of important themes are missing from the above lists. These include a range of themes that have been included in this book and which expanded in schools during the 1980s either as discrete courses, or as elements within traditional subjects or as part of a growing programme in World Studies or Global Education. These themes include: Development Education, Environmental and Ecological Education, Anti-racist Education, Peace Education, Trade Union Education (Education about Trade Unions) and Human Rights Education. These form an essential core of Global Education.

At the same time, it may not be too conspiratorial to observe that most, if not all, of these areas of focus have been unpopular with sections of the Conservative Party and with several academics, writers and theorists of the Right. They have produced a regular flow of articles and books critical of the nature and existence of these themes in school (see Scruton, 1985; O'Keefe, 1986).

Given the apparent opposition or lack of sympathy towards these themes from influential people in government, it will be interesting to see the extent to which the National Curriculum Council gives serious consideration to some of these important issues and themes in the 1990s. These major perspectives have an important contribution to make to the education of young people and there is no theoretical or curricular reason why this should not continue to be so. There are ways of integrating all of these themes into the curriculum through any of the models discussed above.

For example, all of these themes could be integrated with the foundation curriculum through History and Geography. Ecological and environmental issues already feature in many Geography courses, according to the HMI appraisal survey mentioned above, and in the light of Prime Minister Thatcher's new emphasis on 'green' issues (in speeches from September 1988 onwards), a positive view has been adopted towards the study of the environment – it has become an official cross-curricular theme. Furthermore, HMI, in early 1989, published a 'Curriculum Matters' report on Environmental Education for 5–16 which illustrated how this important theme could be integrated into all subject areas and linked with other cross-curricular themes. It admitted that 'environmental issues are of genuine personal concern to many pupils and can act as a useful means of exploring moral, social and political values'. It also pointed out that in May 1988 the Council of Education Ministers of the European Community agreed 'on the need to take concrete steps for the promotion of Environmental Education throughout the Community', while adopting a resolution on Environmental Education to that end (DES, 1989a).

Third World and development issues are already an integral part of Geography; Trade Unions, as a topic, often form a part of History, as do topics on Peace and Human Rights. Anti-racist themes easily integrate with History and Geography. It seems likely, therefore, that History and Geography will be the major curriculum areas where more detailed and systematic treatment of many of the cross-curricular themes can be located. History and Geography could be integrated and given a global interpretation.

However, a more challenging and coherent model, which fits with good modern practice and creates scope for the integration of several perspectives and subject contributions on an equal basis, is to adopt a Global or World Studies approach as the organising idea rather than taking History and Geography as the central subjects into which everything else has to fit. This would provide an opportunity for fundamental rethinking and real curriculum change. The fully-integrated global approach would draw upon a range of unifying concepts creating a curriculum which was both broad and balanced and could progress from 5 to 16.

Realistically, there is little possibility of this kind of approach being adopted for 5–16 unless a very liberal interpretation is made of the History and Geography Subject Working Group Reports and unless a substantial initial and in-service programme is mounted. But there seems to be no reason why an option in Global Education or World Studies should not continue to be offered as a GCSE course for the 14–16 age group in the non-statutory part of the school curriculum.

The Design of the Social Curriculum 14–16: The Real Battleground

The most severe pressure on the curriculum and timetable will be exerted at the 14–16 age level and it is here that a fair and rational programme will be the most difficult to achieve. The National Curriculum does not apply to this age group until 1992 for the core subjects and 1994 for History and Geography, but educationists at all levels of the system are grappling with the complex task of devising a formula for combining the various elements. Although there will be an opportunity for a choice of GCSE subjects and options in the non-statutory curriculum, there are three curricular strands or domains that have to be accommodated in the 14–16 curriculum:

1 The National Curriculum decrees that all pupils must study History and Geography from 5–16.
2 TVEI Extension curricular work must be part of the experience of all children which means it has to be integrated within the National Curriculum. In order to satisfy the TVEI requirements, the development of social, economic and environmental awareness must be an element in the curriculum.
3 The cross-curricular themes have to find a place in the curriculum, whether in the statutory or non-statutory sections.

Many schools may decide that a general course such as Humantities could be placed on the timetable for 14- to 16-year-olds, or indeed for 5- to 16-year-olds. This could link together the three strands listed above for the 14–16 range so that the curriculum would incorporate a wide range of issues and content including political, economic, social, global and personal dimensions. In terms of retaining and generating the interest of 14- to 16-year-olds – but also important for children of all ages – there would be an opportunity here for inquiry-based work, allowing and encouraging the exercise of pupil choice so that individualised resource-based investigations and projects could be conducted by pupils, choosing from a wide range of topics. Teachers would have to provide guidance and support to ensure that relevant criteria and assessment requirements were being met.

The GCSE system of courses and examinations must link with the three elements above in order to form a coherent structure for provision in Years 10 and 11 in the statutory and non-statutory curriculum. Revising the GCSE system may prove to be the most demanding task of all. However, the combined authority of the School Examinations and Assessment Council, (SEAC), which has oversight of all school assessment, and the DES, will prove formidable in persuading the GCSE examining groups and LEAs to begin immediately in planning for change. Already, the DES has been corresponding with the boards and the LEAs in order to lay the foundations for the operation of the new statutory provisions of the Education Reform Act, 1988, which will determine all qualifications and syllabi available to pupils of compulsory school age. The Secretary of State will approve the qualifications on the basis of advice from SEAC, and SEAC is responsible for approving syllabi and syllabus criteria.

It may be that another way to fit all of this together, in the social curriculum for 14- to 16-year-olds, is to devise a modular framework, as suggested in the

Table 13.1   A Model Timetable for the 1990s – Years 10 and 11* curriculum planning: TVEI extension and National Curriculum

	TVEI Extension	National Curriculum	Additional options	% of week
A	Maths	Maths		10
B	Balanced Science	Science	Technical subjects, Rural and Food Science	20
C	Communication and language	English	Drama	10
D	Communication language	Modern Language	Iron	10
E	Social Environmental Economic awareness	Geography, History	Economics Environmental Studies Politics and Social Studies	5 + 5
F	Design and technological capability	Technology (with Design)	Home Economics, Drama, Dance, Business Studies, Rural Science	10 (or 20)
G	Aesthetic Creative Expressive	Art, Music	Home Economics, Drama, Dance, Business Studies, Rural Science	10 (or 20)
H	Physical	Physical Education	Dance	5
I	Religious and Moral	Religious Education		5 (or 10)
J	Personal guidance and development			5 (or 10)
K	Possible uses for balance of time: More Modern Languages, Classical Languages. More RE, more PE, further options for rows E, F, G.			Max total 95

Assumptions for the purposes of this diagram: A single certificate GCSE course to be examined at 16 will normally require 10% of a students' school week in Years 10 and 11*.
A 5% proportion of the school week (approx 70 minutes) is assumed to be the smallest length of time worth using for curriculum planning calculations.
That all core and foundation subjects will be studied during – but not necessarily throughout – the two year period of Years 10 and 11*, irrespective of how time has been allocated to these subjects in earlier years.
(Source: A timetable devised by Peter Cornall, Senior Adviser for Cornwall, and discussed in the article by Maureen O'Connor in *The Guardian*, 31.1.89)

* Note: these are the 4th and 5th Years in the Pre-National Curriculum terminology.

timetable on page 210, whereby 'a modular Humanities option could lead to a GCSE and allow some specialisation in either History or Geography, and possibly Economics or Social Studies, with column K space for more modules if two GCSEs are preferred.' ('Pressure Beyond the Core', *The Guardian*, 31.1.89) The potential range of social subjects and themes for the GCSE 14–16 age range is, at present, fairly wide:

14–16 (GCSE Subjects/Courses)
Sociology
Social Science
Psychology
Economics
Commerce
Government and Politics
Integrated Humanities
History
Geography
Religious Studies
Business Studies
Media Studies
World Studies

These are the main ones. It is not an exhaustive list. PSE is a course in many secondary schools for 4th and 5th years (Years 10 and 11) but it is not usually examined.

The list includes National Curriculum foundation subjects (for example, History and Geography); social science single subjects (for example, Sociology); social science multi-disciplinary approaches (for example, Social Science); integrated approaches (for example, Integrated Humanities) and some elements of cross-curricular themes (for example, Media Studies). It is unlikely that all of these will survive in their present form in the 1990s. As mentioned above, the Secretary of State, Mr Kenneth Baker, threatened to abolish some courses unless faster progress was made by the GCSE examining boards towards rationalising the number of courses and towards standardising assessment in line with the National Curriculum requirements (*The Guardian*, 1.2.89). A subsequent Secretary of State, Mr John MacGregor, outlined a general policy on Key Stage 4 in the National Curriculum, indicating flexibility and the possibility of a number of options including combined GCSEs (TES, 2.2.90).

The Place of the Social Sciences and Humanities

Since the 1960s, a significant contribution to children's understanding of society and preparation for adult life has been provided through the teaching of the Social Sciences and through combined Humanities courses in schools (in single subject or integrated forms). Yet, these major disciplines and courses do not feature in the foundation subjects in the National Curriculum in spite of the fact that their popularity in the school curriculum has been continually expanding since the 1960s (Philip and Priest, 1965; Lawton and Dufour, 1973; Dufour, 1982; Holly, 1986). Combinations such as Social Science or Integrated Humanities and single subjects such as Sociology, Politics and Economics have become increasingly popular at the GCSE level. The recent HMI report on the secondary schools included evidence of this in the statistics for GCSE entries in these subjects (DES, 1988b). Their popularity as GCSE courses has also acted as a foundation and preparation for A-level study in the Social Sciences. There is also a large support network consisting of national subject organisations such as the Association for the Teaching of the Social Sciences (ATSS) and the Integrated Humanities Association (IHA) (see addresses in Resources) and initial teacher training centres in higher education to cover these areas. Furthermore, teachers trained in the Social Sciences and in integrated approaches to Humanities, have often provided special insights and expertise which have supported and developed the cross-curricular themes, whether taught as courses or topics. These subjects and approaches will, no doubt, continue to play a vital role in Key Stage 4, in some form, but specialist teachers in these areas will also have a major contribution to make to all of the cross-curricular issues throughout the 5–16 age range.

Initial and In-Service Education for Teachers

If the cross-curricular themes are to be viable in the schools, they will depend on an extensive training programme for teachers mounted both at the initial stage in the Education Departments in higher education and at the INSET stage with LEAs. There are implications here for increased staffing and funding at both levels. The amount of support needed may partly depend on the type of method chosen for the infusion and integration of the themes. Whatever approach is decided upon, credible training programmes will have to be established if the cross-curricular themes are to avoid the kind of criticism levelled at PSE (see Brown, Chapter 3; HMI, 1988d). LEAs have a key role to play in planning these programmes but also in offering guidelines to schools on implementation. Some guidance on this was provided in the major National Curriculum Publication, *National Curriculum: From Policy to Practice* (DES, 1989b) which clearly indicates that there will be flexibility and a variety of ways of organising the curriculum: 'The Education Reform Act does not require teaching to be provided under the foundation subject headings. Indeed, it deliberately allows flexibility for schools to provide their teaching in a variety of ways' (para. 3.7, DES, 1989b). Furthermore, 'The organisation of teaching and learning is a professional matter for the head teacher and his or her staff. The use of subjects to define the National Curriculum does not mean that teaching has to be organised and delivered within prescribed subject boundaries' (para. 4.3, DES, 1989b). It also reiterates the point that the foundation subjects do not constitute a complete curriculum and that the cross-curricular themes have a role to play in contributing to the whole curriculum and in securing 'the kind of curriculum required by section 1 of the ERA' (para. 3.8, DES, 1989b).

Senior management in schools must take responsibility for integrating the cross-curricular themes into a whole-school policy and LEA guidelines must make recommendations to this effect. In the final instance, it will fall upon governors, co-operating with teachers and headteachers, to satisfy themselves that the cross-curricular themes are being properly integrated into the whole curriculum.

The Role of Parents and Governors

One of the contradictory features of the Education Reform Act, 1988, was the extension of government centralised control over the curriculum and assessment while, at the same time, devolving power away from the LEAs and towards individual institutions. Many of the new structures, procedures and powers for governors, and for parents as governors, had been indicated and contained in the Education Act, 1986, which came into force, in stages, during 1987 and 1988.

The 1988 Act supersedes parts of the 1986 Act and makes it the duty of governors, along with the headteacher and the LEA, to ensure that the National Curriculum is implemented. The LEA is obliged to construct a policy statement on the curriculum and governors must also draw up a curriculum policy document in consultation with the headteacher. Governors must also 'have regard to' any representations made to them by the local community. It may be the case that heads will devise the draft statement, hopefully in consultation with staff, and that governors will adopt this or adapt it.

There are a number of other legally binding requirements, all of which broadly relate to the social curriculum, in the sense that they refer to ideas about society and to social behaviour. Both the 1986 Act and the 1988 Act gave governors certain powers over the policy on Sex Education. They can decide whether or not it should be included in the curriculum; if it is, they must have a written policy on how it is to be taught and, furthermore, it should (according to the 1986 Act) 'encourage pupils to have due regard to moral considerations and the value of family life'. Education circulars based on the 1986 Act require governors to ensure that teachers do not advocate homosexuality or present it as the norm.

The idea of asking governors to consult the local chief of police about the curriculum was to ensure that police had the opportunity to work with schools and that law and order issues played some part in the curriculum (for background, see Maclure, 1988). As regards wider Political Education in schools, the 1986 Act requires governors to ensure a balanced presentation of opposing views on controversial political topics in lessons or in the school's extra-curricular activities. The legislation on Sex Education, police consultation and political balance was part of the 1986 Act and all of these items were late additions to the Bill, inserted by the House of Lords (Maclure, 1988, offers more detail on this and on the general position of the legislation and interpretation of the curriculum aspects of the Acts).

Notwithstanding these statutory duties, there is scope for flexibility and variation in the school curriculum. Each LEA and every school may have their own particular perspectives on the total curriculum. There may indeed be differences in detail and emphasis. Within limits, governors can modify the LEA policy. It must also be noted that the National Curriculum is not intended to fill the whole timetable – there will be some choice within the additional subject time. In the early 1990s, it will be interesting to see just how much divergence and variation begins to develop as schools and LEAs attempt to reflect local needs and preferences. Hopefully, modifications will be agreed harmoniously after full consultation with interested parties. It is also likely, though, that a number of cases of disagreements between the parties, LEAs, governors, headteachers, teachers or parents may become classic examples of case law or *causes célèbres*. Only time will tell.

Taking an optimistic view, parents and governors are in a key position to ensure the extension and enrichment of the curriculum. There are well over 300,000 school governors. In his book for and about school governors, Mahoney offers guidance on the role they can exercise in supporting important aspects of the social curriculum, including Multicultural Education, Equal Opportunities and a wide range of the other cross-curricular areas (Mahoney, 1988).

It is to hoped that parents and governors will play a positive and collaborative role, working with teachers and headteachers to develop good practice and that, by interpreting the National Curriculum and the whole curriculum in the broadest terms (through incorporating additional subjects and cross-curricular themes) they will be defending the right of all pupils to a broad and balanced education which will contribute to their self-realisation and equip them for the challenges in tomorrow's world.

Notes

1 Since the introduction of the National Curriculum from September 1989, there has been a new description of school year groups.

Key Stage*	Description under National Curriculum	Abbreviation	Age of majority of pupils at the end of the academic year
	Reception	R	5
1	Year 1	Y1	6
	Year 2	Y2	7
2	Year 3	Y3	8
	Year 4	Y4	9
	Year 5	Y5	10
	Tear 6	Y6	11
3	Year 7	Y7	12
	Year 8	Y8	13
	Year 9	Y9	14
4	Year 10	Y10	15
	Year 11	Y11	16
–	Year 12	Y12	17
	Year 13	Y13	18

* The key stages of compulsory education are described in section 3 of the Education Reform Act. Assessment under the National Curriculum takes place at or near the end of each key stage.

References and Further Resources

DES, *Curriculum 11–16 ('HMI Red Book One')* (HMSO, 1977)

DES, *Curriculum 11–16: A Review of Progress ('HMI Red Book Two')* (HMSO, 1981)

DES, *Curriculum 11–16: Towards a Statement of Entitlement: Curricular Re-appraisal in Action ('HMI Red Book Three')* (HMSO, 1983)

DES, *Geography from 5 to 16 (Curriculum Matters 7 – an HMI Series)* (HMSO, 1986)

DES, *The National Curriculum: A Consultation Document* (HMSO, 1987)

DES, *The Education Reform Act* (HMSO, 1988a)

DES, *Secondary Schools: An Appraisal by HMI* (HMSO, 1988b)

DES, *History from 5 to 16 (Curriculum Matters 11 – an HMI Series)* (HMSO, 1988c)

DES, *A Survey of Personal and Social Education Courses in Some Secondary Schools (A Report by HMI)* (HMSO, 1988d)

DES, *Environmental Education from 5 to 16: Curriculum Matters 13 (an HMI Series)* (HMSO, 1989a)

DES, *National Curriculum: From Policy to Practice* (HMSO, 1989b)

B. Dufour (ed.), *New Movements in the Social Sciences and Humanities* (Maurice Temple Smith/Gower, 1982)

J. Haviland (ed.), *Take Care, Mr Baker* (Fourth Estate Ltd, 1988)

D. Holly (ed.), *Humanism in Adversity (Teachers' Experience of Integrated Humanities in the 1980s)* (Falmer Press, 1986)

D. Lawton and C. Chitty (eds.), *The National Curriculum, Bedford Way Papers 33* (Institute of Education, University of London, 1988)

D. Lawton and B. Dufour, *The New Social Studies* (Heinemann Educational Books, 1973)

S. Maclure, *Education Re-formed (A Guide to the 1988 Education Reform Act)* (Hodder and Stoughton, 1988)

T. Mahoney, *Governing Schools: Powers, Issues and Practice*, (Macmillan Education, 1988)

D. O'Keefe, *The Wayward Curriculum* (Short Run Press, 1986)

W. Philip and R. Priest, *Social Science and Social Studies in Secondary Schools* (Longman, 1965)

R. Scruton, *World Studies: Education or Indoctrination?* (Institute for European Defence and Strategic Studies, 1985)

TES (Times Educational Supplement), 'Timetable Solution that only Muddies the Waters', 2 February 1990. A report on the Secretary of State's speech to the Society of Education Officers' conference on 25 January 1990.

TGAT, *Task Group on Assessment and Testing* (DES, 1987)

Key Teacher Resources

DES, *Secondary Schools: An Appraisal by HMI* (HMSO, 1988)
An outstanding and very readable document which looks at all aspects of secondary schools, based on observations during inspections. It contains examination and subject statistics and includes discussion of some of the cross-curricular themes. HMI believe it could be used as a base for comparison in the mid-1990s to see how schools have fared after the full implementation of the Education Reform Act.

DES, *Geography from 5 to 16 (Curriculum Matters HMI series, no. 7* (HMSO, 1986)
In advance of the Subject Working Group report on Geography, promised for 1990, this important little document demonstrates how many of the cross-curricular themes are already part of a broad and balanced approach to Geography.

DES, *History from 5 to 16 (Curriculum Matters HMI series, No. 11)* (HMSO, 1988)
Emphasises the links between History and most of the cross-curricular themes but, even more, it cautiously suggests that one way to avoid overlap and overcrowding in the curriculum is to take a 'Humanities' approach by combining History and Geography, and drawing in Economics and Social Science.

DES, *Environmental Education from 5 to 16 (Curriculum Matters HMI series, no. 13)* (HMSO, 1989)
Stresses the importance of environmental issues in the interests and concerns of young people and illustrates how Environmental Education can form part of *all* subjects as well as integrating with other cross-curricular themes.

D. Lawton, and C. Chitty (eds.), *The National Curriculum* (Bedford Way Papers, no. 33, 1988)
Although prepared before the Education Reform Act became law, this is a wide-ranging and critical analysis of the idea of a National Curriculum and the implications for schools and children.

T. Mahoney, *Governing Schools: Powers, Issues and Practice* (Macmillan, 1988)
A readable and practical guide on all aspects of the role of the school governor. It has detailed chapters on Multicultural Education and Sexism in the Curriculum but deals with many other key areas of schooling. An informative book for teachers, parents and governors.

Key Addresses

ATSS (Association for the Teaching of the Social Sciences),
PO Box 461,
Sheffield S1 3BF
Information, conferences, local branches, expertise and a journal (*The Social Science Teacher*) on aspects of teaching the Social Sciences, for example, Sociology, and general social subjects in schools and colleges.

DES (Department of Education and Science),
Elizabeth House,
York Road,
London SE1 7PH
Tel: 01–934–9000
The headquarters of Her Majesty's Inspectors and education civil servants. Useful for information and details of publications.

FEU (Further Education Unit),
Grove House,
2–6 Orange Street,
London WC2H 7WE
Tel: 01–321–0433
The headquarters for major educational initiatives in Further Education. Useful for details of publications.

IHA, Integrated Humanities Association,
c/o D. Holly,
School of Education,
University of Leicester,
21 University Road,
Leicester LE1 7RF
Tel: 0533–522522
Contact address for information on the main initiatives in Humanities in the UK. The organisation holds conferences, produces a journal, amongst other activities.

National Association of Governors and Managers,
81 Rustlings Road,
Sheffield S11 7AB
Tel: 0742-662467
An increasingly important organisation given recent Education Acts. Provides information.

National Confederation of Parent Teacher Associations,
2 Ebbsfleet Industrial Estate,
Stonebridge Road,
Northfleet DA11 9DZ
Tel: 0474-560618
Another important organisation, given recent Education Acts. Provides information.

National Curriculum Council,
15–17 New Street,
York YO1 2RA
Tel; 0904-622533
The new organisation with oversight of curriculum and subject issues.

School Examinations and Assessment Council,
Newcombe House,
45 Notting Hill Gate,
London W11 3JB
Tel: 01–229–1234
The new organisation with oversight of assessment issues and examinations.

GLOSSARY

Active Learning Learning which actively involves the student in thinking, problem-solving and participation.

Baker Days Compulsory training and in-service days for teachers.

BFI British Film Institute

Black Papers A series of four papers produced by educationalists, academics and others of the Right.

BTEC Business and Technician Education Council

CBI Confederation of British Industries

CCDU Counselling and Career Development Unit

CDT Craft, Design and Technology

CEWC Council for Education in World Citizenship

CGLI City and Guilds of London Institute

Child Centred Education A form of education process or method that is sensitive and responsive to the needs and potential of the individual child.

COIC Careers and Occupational Information Centre

Core Curriculum In the Education Reform Act (1988), this refers to English, Mathematics and Science.

CPVE Certificate of Pre-Vocational Education

CRC Community Relations Council

CRE Commission for Racial Equality

CTC City Technology College

DES Department of Education and Science

ERA Education Reform Act 1988

EILO Education–Industry Liaison Officer

EOC Equal Opportunities Commission

EPA Educational Priority Area

E2L English as a Second Language

FEU Further Education Unit

Foundation Subjects The ten subjects which must be taught as required by the Education Reform Act (1988). These include English, Mathematics,

Science, Design and Technology, History, Geography, Music, Art, Physical Education and a modern foreign language.

GAOC   Girls and Occupational Choice

GIST   Girls Into Science and Technology

GRIST   Grant Related In-Service Training

HEA   Health Education Authority (formerly the Health Education Council)

HEC   Health Education Council

HMI   Her Majesty's Inspector

INSET   In-Service Training

ISDD   Institute for the Study of Drug Dependence

IT   Information Technology

JBPVE   Joint Board for Pre-Vocational Education

JUPVE   Joint Unit for Pre-Vocational Education

LAPP   Lower Achieving Pupils Project

LMS   Local Management of Schools

MSC   Manpower Services Commission (later Training Commission, now the Training Agency)

NALGO   National and Local Government Officers' Association

NATFHE   National Association of Teachers in Further and Higher Education

NCVQ   National Council for Vocational Qualifications

NAFE   Non Advanced Further Education

NEDO   National Economic Development Office

NRVQ   National Review of Vocational Qualifications

NUT   National Union of Teachers

PSE   Personal and Social Education

ROSLA   Raising of School Leaving Age

RSA   Royal Society of Arts

SCDC   Schools Curriculum Development Committee (now the National Curriculum Council)

SCIP   Schools Curriculum Industry Partnership

SEAC   School Examination and Assessment Council

SEFT   Society for Education in Film and Television

SILO   Schools Industry Liaison Officer

TACADE   Teachers' Advisory Council on Alcohol and Drug Education

Tracking   Streaming or setting

TA   Training Agency

TRIST   TVEI Related In-Service Training

TUC   Trades Union Congress

TVEI   Technical and Vocational Education Initiative (now the TVE or TVEX, Technical Vocational Extension)

UNESCO   United Nations Education, Scientific and Cultural Organisation

UNICEF   United Nations International Children's Emergency Fund (now the United Nations Children's Fund)

YTS   Youth Training Scheme

INDEX